MORE CURIOUS

MORE CURIOUS

SEAN WILSEY

MᴄSWEENEY'S
SAN FRANCISCO

McSWEENEY'S
SAN FRANCISCO

www.mcsweeneys.net

Copyright © 2014 Sean Wilsey

Cover design by Dan McKinley.

Some of this work appeared in different form in *McSweeney's Quarterly Concern*, the *Big Bend Sentinel*, the *London Review of Books*, *National Geographic*, the *New York Times*, *Time.com*, *GQ*, the *New York Times Magazine*, *Fast Company*, and *Vanity Fair*.

Illustrations by Sammy Harkham (p. 87, 131, 150, 153, 243, 249, 279), Pierre Dubois (p. 149, 157, 161, 172, 182, 198, 339), Sunra Thompson (p. 239), and Albrecht Dürer (p. 119, 145).

McSweeney's and colophon are registered trademarks of McSweeney's, a privately held company with wildly fluctuating resources.

Printer in Michigan by Thomson-Shore.

ISBN 978-1-940450-17-9

For Daphne

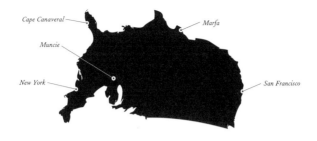

Cape Canaveral

Marfa

Muncie

New York

San Francisco

INTRODUCTION: INTRODUCTION

The notion that the species can be improved in some way, that everyone could live in harmony, is a really dangerous idea. Those who are afflicted with this notion are the first ones to give up their souls, their freedom. Your desire that it be that way will enslave you and make your life vacuous.

— *The New York Times Magazine*, April 19, 1992 (page 36)

Whereas the *Times* printed the statement above (which I'll discuss, along with the person who said it, later in this book) we were in our first full year post–Cold and Gulf wars. After remedying the cause of Los Angeles's race riots and knocking the unemployment rate from 7.5 percent down to 4.0 percent, the world's sole superpower was going to get down to the serious work: containing the global population explosion and reversing a full-on environmental crisis. Bill Clinton and Al Gore were elected for this reason. Or that's why I voted for them. In the absence of any credible enemies the opportunity to reverse our collective doom and evolve into an Edenic state had to get grabbed with both hands. It was also the only moment—post-wars, pre-Net—when the president and the press had the authority and the U.S. had the power to force the world to focus its attention on a single topic.

In the service of this goal Stanford University was funding a study on "optimum human population," published in 1994. There were 5.5 billion people in the world then—a number that included two Stanford scientists and an ecologist from UC Berkeley who thought this was more than double the ideal. If we didn't move fast, they said, we'd wind up "housed and nurtured by methods analogous to those used to raise battery chickens."

They wanted to see density, resource availability, and cultural diversity DJed into a harmonious global ambiance: "the population of the United States should be small enough to permit the availability of large tracts of wilderness for hikers and hermits, yet large enough to create vibrant cities that can support complex artistic, educational, and other cultural endeavors that lift the human spirit." A Stanford press release called for "national and international discussions of lifestyle preferences" so we could reach a consensus and get to work as soon as possible. The scientists held up 1930 as the exemplar: "many great cities, giant industrial operations, and thriving arts and letters. A great diversity of cultures existed, and members of many of them were not in contact with industrializing cultures. Large tracts of wilderness remained in many parts of the world." This in unattractive contrast to nowadays, or early-1990s thenadays, when, "Unfortunately, many cultures borne by small groups of people are in danger of being swamped by the dominant culture with its advanced technologies and seductive media."

To which I feel compelled to reply, from the current 7-plus-billion-people vantage point (and in the spirit of page 36 of the April 19, 1992, *NYT Mag*):

:(

* * *

Obviously none of this went anywhere. All America wanted to talk about was transparency. Not guilelessness, or anti-secrecy, but, *literally*, see-through-ness: colorless cola, clear beer, soap-that-was-not-milky. Coke, Microsoft, Miller, Pepsi, Procter & Gamble all launched "clear" or "crystal" products that were, as the Trends Research Institute put it: "an attempt by marketers to generate more sales of existing product lines... reformulating the products under the belief that clear means purity. It's a very shallow concept." The national media named this brief whim the "clear craze," lavishing a marketing campaign with the blanket coverage it was expected to devote to a news event. The *Los Angeles Times* dubbed it all a "search for clarity."

I noticed when Coors, for which I was the target demographic, took its weakest lager and filtered it through charcoal to remove color and taste, then added citrus flavor, creating a sort of nonlethal floor cleanser called Zima, which sold 1.3 million barrels (322,400,000 bottles) in its first year.

In one Zima ad a young woman asked a young man, manning a grill, "Are those *free-range* burgers?"

His reply, "Who cares? Have a Zima."

And then:

> Q: If Monica Lewinsky says that while you were in the Oval Office area you touched her breasts, would she be lying?
> A: That is not my recollection. My recollection is that I did not have sexual relations with Ms. Lewinsky and I'm staying on my former statement about that. ["I did not have sexual relations with that woman, Miss Lewinsky."] ...

Q: If she says that you kissed her breasts, would she be lying?
A: I'm going to revert to my former statement.

Q: OK. If Monica Lewinsky says that while you were in the Oval Office area you touched her genitalia, would she be lying? And that calls for a yes, no, or reverting to your former statement.
A: I will revert to my statement on that.

Q: If Monica Lewinsky says that you used a cigar as a sexual aid with her in the Oval Office area, would she be lying? Yes, no, or won't answer?
A: I will revert to my former statement.

Q: If Monica Lewinsky says that you had phone sex with her, would she be lying?
A: Well, that is, at least in general terms, I think, is covered by my statement. I addressed that in my statement, and that, I don't believe, is—

Q: Let me define phone sex for purposes of my question. Phone sex occurs when a party to a phone conversation masturbates while the other party is talking in a sexually explicit manner. And the question is, if Monica Lewinsky says that you had phone sex with her, would she be lying?
A: I think that is covered by my statement.

And that was the '90s—self-involved, prosperous, consumed on a mass level with things < trivial.

* * *

The essays that follow begin here, in 1998, in Marfa, Texas, a town so far from everywhere else that it created its own atmosphere. Marfa— unswamped; hermit rife—was the ideal place to go find something to notice for a writer with no experience. I sat in the town's darkest bar with a Lone Star and wrote the first draft of the first piece of serious writing I'd ever see published. It was accepted as a one-thousand-word (way too long) *New Yorker* Talk of the Town. When it got killed I mentioned it to a guy called Dave Eggers (we'd met in a bar), who, as the editor of a neophyte literary magazine (with an appealingly Irish name), said, "Make it longer." So I made it longer. Much, much longer. The version he published in *McSweeney's 2*, at the start of 1999, was 10,685 words. A second Marfa installment appeared in *McSweeney's 6*, in early 2001, and that one, in combination with another Marfa piece, written for *Vanity Fair* in 2012, revised and expanded here, ends this book and this arc.

Post-Clinton I was in a war with Time Warner. I spent the better part of a week attempting to get internet service, stuck in my Manhattan apartment "between the hours of ten a.m. and seven p.m.," awaiting technicians who never showed, or left after mumbling something about another sort of technician who would have to come, or drilling through my building's thick brick wall and hurling eighty feet of slack black cable off my roof, and then leaving me with a pile of orange dust, a plastic slash through my view, and, of course, no service.

I sent (by US mail) a scathing letter to Barry Rosenbloom, the president of Time Warner Cable, in which I complained that his company employed people who were "exceptionally cheerful but totally unhelpful" and "not interested in anything other than passing the buck." A few days later I went skateboarding and got caught in a downpour. Half an inch of water crashed into empty midtown Manhattan in a few seconds. When I got back home I stood dripping on my carpet and toweling my hair while my answering machine played back the voice of a woman who said, "The *president* would like to speak with you about your letter."

For a while I stood there confused. Then I put down the towel and listened to the message again. In a thick New York accent she said she was calling from Time Warner.

Time. Warner. President. Talk. These words ran through my mind as I fell asleep… and dreamed of the opportunity to reform a hated monopoly.

I was awakened by a group of women shouting: "Aaaaah! Aaaaah! *Aaaaaaaaaaaaaaaaaah!*"

I figured they were the first revelers of the Feast of San Gennaro, a drunken religious festival named for a fourth-century Roman martyr, Januarius, who got hurled into what sketchy reports suggest to have been a pizza oven, and emerged un-immolated, to the astonishment of his attackers, who then beheaded him. Every year, in his honor, the neighborhood outside my apartment would fill with pizza crusts, broken glass, urine, rats. Locals despised this invasion. As Robert De Niro put it in *Mean Streets* (1973): "I hate this feast with a passion."

But it was an enduring New York City tradition. From a 1939 *Catholic Worker*: "At two-thirty in the morning when the street was still full of celebrants, a street fight started. A dozen men started brawling, seizing empty pop bottles, breaking off the bottoms and slashing each other with them. Knives and guns were drawn and before the fray ended, two men were lying in the middle of the deserted street. One of them was taken to the hospital and the other lay there in the gutter until almost eight…"

It was eight forty-five a.m.

I said "Fucking San Gennaro," grabbed my skateboard, and got up to walk my dog, Charlie, who, as I rolled, liked to lope along behind. We headed three blocks east, to Chrystie Street, and then north along the perimeter of Sara Roosevelt Park. The weather was cool and clear. As Thomas Pynchon, master of foreboding, once wrote, it was "a Sunday-funnies" morning: "very blue sky with gaudy pink clouds in it." Though I didn't see any clouds. The city'd been washed so clean by the rain that it felt as though we'd been transported into another time. That Depression-era reporter on the San Gennaro beat for the *Catholic Worker* offered a glimpse: "the air was clear so that the stars shone brightly."

Then a motorcade—running red lights, at its heart a large blue-and-gold truck painted with the words MOBILE COMMAND CENTER and RUDOLPH W. GIULIANI—blew through the intersection of Houston and Chrystie streets and right past where I was standing.

With my eyes I followed the truck's trajectory down Chrystie Street until the World Trade Center came into view. Black smoke was oozing out of the north tower's tip like ink from a snapped pen. I skateboarded to Tompkins Square Park, and by the time I'd skated back, a smashed fire chief's car was sitting in the middle of Lafayette Street with people crowding around it taking photographs.

President Rosenbloom and I never did get a chance to have that talk.

* * *

These screaming women were an introduction. It was the end of those < trivial years.

My two favorite introductions are by Thomas Pynchon (to *Slow Learner*, a collection of the novelist's early short fiction) and Joseph Mitchell (to *Up in the Old Hotel*, a 716-page omnibus of the magazine writing that made him, in the words of one critic, "the great artist/ reporter of our century"). These are my heroes, two of my favorite writers, and I love them here because they say welcome-to-the-tone-and-aesthetic-of-my-stuff in a way that no third party could hope to say it. They also play against expectations, in that they're loose, lucid, conversational, and provide biographical material without making reference to the fact that one of them (Pynchon) lived in a self-imposed witness protection program, and the other (Mitchell) hadn't published in thirty years. And now—if to declare admiration and influence is to invite comparison—I've set myself up for failure.

Every word and punctuation mark in Mitchell is set there with finality. Much as the man (the gentleman) himself was fixed in place— not once straying in what he wrote from the environs of New York City and his birthplace in North Carolina. And every unbridled word and punctuation mark in Pynchon suggests that things are not as they seem. Much as Pynchon is restless, antic, unpredictable. Their two echt-American voices embody virtue and anti-virtue: precision (Mitchell) and paranoia (Pynchon)—each in a form so pure it seems to be the highest expression of these things.

Each writer's stuff is so refined it's like a controlled substance.

Writing *is* controlled substance. It acts with the least mediation and strongest effect. In the case of my introductory heroes: Pynchon =s drugs and Mitchell =s drink. The *best possible* drugs and drink. Pure stuff, their stuff. Narcotics that give you clarifying visions and spirits that are triple distilled, of the highest quality. Transportation to another place. Hangover—out of the question.

Subconsciously, as a young writer (and most of what I did as a young writer was subconscious), I was trying to bring these two men together. To take the always-controlled Mitchell on the road. Out into the wilds of America. Wake and shake and Pynch him...

Thomas Pynchon credits himself as a young writer with the good sense to give in to "temptation" and "go out and see what was happening" in the wider world. Equally good advice when what's happening in the wider world comes to see you. Desperate to push back against the powerlessness I felt in the immediate aftermath of the World Trade Center's destruction, I decided to volunteer at a "support center" run out of the Plaza Hotel by a bond trader who'd lost most of his employees from the uppermost floors of the north tower. The massive historical rupture of 9/11 left me baffled (along with everyone else in New York) by how to respond. An account of the experience is essay two in this book, published in the September 19, 2002, *London Review of Books*. On some level it barely begins to say anything; but I'm proud of it all the same.

From the introduction to *Slow Learner*:

> My first reaction, rereading these stories, was *oh my God*,
> accompanied by physical symptoms we shouldn't dwell upon.
> My second thought was about some kind of a wall-to-wall rewrite.
> These two impulses have given way to one of those episodes of
> middle-aged tranquility, in which I now pretend to have reached a
> level of clarity about the young writer I was back then.

Pynchon then ranges all over his personal history, making aslant remarks that knock sideways entire decades (JFK is "a congressional upstart with a strange haircut"). And he makes this confession:

"Somewhere I had come up with the notion that one's personal life had nothing to do with fiction, when the truth, as everyone knows, is nearly the direct opposite… for in fact the fiction both published and unpublished that moved and pleased me then as now was precisely that which had been made luminous, undeniably authentic by having been found and taken up, always at a cost, from deeper, more shared levels of the life we all really live." This from a man who sent a comedian to accept the National Book Award in his stead—not because he was afraid, or disdainful, but because, it seems to me, he wanted to remain free.

From the introduction to *Up in the Old Hotel*:

> In going over these stories—rereading some of them for the first time since they appeared in *The New Yorker*—I was surprised and pleased to see how often a kind of humor that I can only call graveyard humor turned up in them… I was pleased to discover this because graveyard humor is an exemplification of the way I look at the world. It typifies my cast of mind.

He offered two examples. On weekends, when Mitchell was a child, his family gathered at a cemetery to eat "rashers" of watermelon, "picked early that morning in our own gardens—long, heavy, green-striped Georgia Rattlesnakes and big, round, heavy Cuban Queens so green they were almost black." Then his seniormost aunt, who, as Mitchell's mother put it, was given to "coming out with" ribald pronouncements, led a procession through the graves:

> "This man buried here," she would say, "was a cousin of ours, and he was so *mean* I don't know how his family stood him."

And this man here, she would continue, moving along a few steps, "was so *good*, I don't know how his family stood him." And then she would become more specific. Some of the things she told us were horrifying and some were horrifyingly funny.

Mitchell's second cast-of-mind-forming incident came about in 1933 when, as a young reporter, he was sent by the *New York World-Telegram* to interview the "demonic surrealist" Frida Kahlo, while her husband, Diego Rivera, was "doing those Rockefeller Center murals." Kahlo showed Mitchell a series of engravings she'd hung on the walls of her hotel room: skeletons engaged in "many kinds of human activities, mimicking them and mocking them."

> I was astonished by these pictures, and what I found most astonishing about them was that all of them were humorous, even the most morbid of them... That is, they had a strong undercurrent of humor. It was the kind of humor that the old Dutch masters caught in those prints that show a miser locked in his room counting his money and Death is standing just outside the door.

Pynchon: "When we speak of 'seriousness' in fiction ultimately we are talking about an attitude toward death—how characters may act in its presence, for example, or how they handle it when it isn't so immediate. Everybody knows this, but the subject is hardly ever brought up with younger writers, possibly because given to anyone at the apprentice age, such advice is widely felt to be effort wasted." This essential point is where Pynchon and Mitchell meet. Death. Where we all meet, of course. And it's where they are each at their best. They destroy our self-importance, Pynchon by heading straight into the fear—making it terribly vivid—and then making wicked fun of it (writing, to paraphrase one reviewer, like an angel and clowning like the devil), Mitchell simply by digging right down and lying in the grave, while also, gently, teasing us.

That 9/11 essay made a passing reference to a skateboard. So Thomas Jones, my editor at the *LRB*, asked if I had anything to say about skateboarding: essay three of this book. Obviously an essay on skateboarding led to an essay on rats (which is really an essay on fatherhood, and Mitchell). Five. And at this point a Pynchon-emulating pattern of inappropriate juxtaposition, while writing about Mitchell-like subjects (rats, solitude, suffering), took up permanent residence in my writing. Now there was a certain amount of awareness about my efforts to fuse these dudes. Not just in prose, but in life. That's the struggle for me: living. Writing is simply an attempt to come to terms with things that are almost impossible for me to live with otherwise. On the rare occasions when life is perfect, when it makes sense, I am freed from the obligation to write. Or to write nonfiction. I suppose that if the world around me made sense I would become a novelist. But in the absence of such a world I can only give you what follows here. A lot of Pynchon-like roaming described with Mitchell-like ambitions. California, New York, Florida, Texas, Los Angeles, Alabama, Arkansas, Indiana, Wisconsin, Ohio, outer space—in these pages time gets spent in all these places.

Obviously the title *More Curious* is a play on that old saw that truth is stranger than fiction.

But there's more!

Literally.

More: excess, abundance; custom, convention.

Curious: a straightforward desire to know; strangeness.

And if you rip it up you get a dog (cur), a debt (IOU), and this writer's initial initial.

I suppose this is the sort of thing that reveals my own cast of mind.

I've always wanted to be good *and* free; a statement so true it makes me cringe (sort of the embarrassing bumper sticker on the car of my soul). So I drove—together with my wife and two small children—throughout the Midwest, canvassing in the 2008 Democratic primaries and general election.

It took all day to get from New York to Muncie, Indiana, where a local family offered my family a room in a big white house with a two-car garage and a basketball court. Our host, Mrs. Suneetha Kurra, barefoot, Indian, in her mid-thirties, newly moved to Indiana, was followed everywhere by a collie named Indy. The next morning our job was to go house to house in a run-down neighborhood, hanging door hangers stamped with specific polling-station information. They looked like Do Not Disturb signs.

"Shit," I said. "We drove all this way to be hotel housekeeping."

Walking around trying to interest strangers in a presidential candidate is a form of introduction, an endeavor to create a connection between the intrinsically remote—politician/voter—who, like writer/reader, need each other to survive. And it seemed like a concrete way to help end the historical period in which we'd all been stranded.

The neighborhood we walked was haunted by the living—both genders and all ages (if only two races: black and white) loitering in groups or wandering around solo on shattered sidewalks before half-collapsed houses. People stripped of purpose or belief by our seductive media! A tall, too-thin black man with a dangling earring in the shape of a handgun in his left ear opened a porch door, shot bloodshot eyes at my campaign button, then shook his head and said, "Never gonna happen."

An old black man told me he wasn't registered. So I asked him to tell his friends to vote. He said: "*Friends?* I don't have any *friends!*"

Not long after, a slender white woman with long, blonde hair gave me a wounded smile and said the same words: "Don't have any friends…"

And then the capper: a tiny old white woman with a halo of white hair (through which I could see the whole circumference of her skull), arm twinned with that of a younger woman, walked slowly toward me as I pushed my daughter in a stroller.

When we came abreast of each other the woman looked me in the eye and hollered out, with surprising force: "You're a *nigger lover!*"

In Wellston, Ohio, on Election Day, I entered a yard with my door hangers as a small blue Toyota pulled up and parked. A very old yet industrious-looking overall-clad man was at the wheel and a boy in a puffy red parka rode shotgun.

"Good morning," I said. "Is this your house?"

The man replied, "This is my son's house. He worked all night and now he's sleeping. Are you one of those?"

I was wearing a shirt that said APPALACHIANS FOR OBAMA. The boy threw open his door and shouted, "I like him! I like your guy!" Then he sat down again, shut the door, and gave me a double-fisted thumbs-up.

I said, "He likes him."

The man gave a single nod, gestured to the house where his son lay, drained of life, I imagined, after a night shift at the General Mills behemoth down the road, working, as that plant's description of employment opportunities put it, with "legendary brands," and said, "I'll make sure he votes." Pause. "But now he's asleep."

We shook hands. I thumbs-upped the grandson. He double thumbs-upped me back, fists in the air over his head, face framed by puffy red sleeves.

The last voter I spoke to before Jackson, Ohio's Democratic headquarters held a co-celebration with its Republican headquarters identified herself as Opal Crabtree and told me, "I always vote. I'm ninety years old. My mother was one of the first women to get the right to vote. And I voted for Obama."

Mitchell:

> I'm ninety-four years old and I never yet had any peace, to speak
> of. My mind is just a turmoil of regrets. It's not what I did I regret,
> it's what I didn't do. Except for the bottle, I always walked the
> straight and narrow; a family man, a good provider, never cut up,
> never did ugly, and I regret it. In the summer of 1902 I came real
> close to getting in serious trouble with a married woman, but I had
> a fight with my conscience and my conscience won, and what's the
> result? I had two wives, good, Christian women, and I can't hardly
> remember what either of them looked like, but I can remember
> the face on that woman so clear it hurts, and there's never a day
> passes I don't think about her, and there's never a day passes
> I don't curse myself. 'What kind of a timid, dried-up, weevily
> fellow were you?' I say to myself. 'You should've said to hell with
> what's right and what's wrong, the devil take the hindmost. You'd
> have something to remember, you'd be happier now.' She's out in
> Woodlawn, six feet under, and she's been there twenty-two years,
> God rest her, and here I am, just an old, old man with nothing left
> but a belly and a brain and a dollar or two.

The ur-Mitchell geriatric, the man of innumerable regrets quoted above, first appeared in the January 1, 1944, *New Yorker* under the rubric "Profiles," and—as drawn by the artist Abe Birnbaum—was a lean, cheerful, hairless, cleft-chinned, not-remotely-regretful-looking man in a bowler hat at the top right of a right-hand page opposite an article about volleyball, and above a caption that read "Hugh G. Flood." (Pynchon: *Nudge-nudge*.)

When Mitchell published three pieces about this character in his 111-page story collection *Old Mr. Flood*, he wrote a confession: "Mr. Flood is not one man; combined in him are aspects of several old men who work or hang out in Fulton Fish Market, or who did in the past." Then, forty-four years later, in the under-discussion intro to *Up in the Old Hotel*: "The three stories in the Flood book are fictional."

Flood was *him*. Mitchell even gave the man his own birthday: July 27. A bigger prank by far than sending a comedian to accept a literary award. Maybe P&M weren't so night and day in their virtues after all.

Mitchell was generally seen by his friends and colleagues less as Mr. Flood than Mr. Good. A sort of kindly specter, haunting his subjects, using his innate timidity as a force for precision. A process that eventually shut him down. As a close friend wrote about the last, silent thirty years of his life: "it was his congenital shyness and reticence about himself and his own depths of feeling that were getting in his way." He couldn't put himself into a story. And so "he was attempting 'Remembrance of Things Past' without the youthful Marcel to register it." He couldn't haunt himself. Never a problem for that devil, Pynchon.

Lies tell the truths we can't. As a society our central lie is velocity. That we can keep all this up. Perhaps that's why Mitchell stopped writing.

All those old people have probably died in the six years since I met them.

* * *

I didn't just canvas. I coughed up $28,500 (made co-editing a collection of essays) to the "Obama Victory Fund." The essay collection was called *State by State* and gathered together original writing by fifty writers on each of the fifty states, an idea based on the old American Guide series, published by the WPA during those broke-ass utopian 1930s as a way of employing out-of-work writers. This bought me a seat in the back of a room full of marble, mirrors, deep burgundy drapes (drawn for security), as far away as possible from a stand and microphone; the kids' table of a breakfast with Obama. The venue was the Metropolitan Club in midtown Manhattan. The other kids were either lawyers or in finance. Mark Gallogly, seated to my right, ran a private equity firm and would soon be eighth on the seventeen-member (alphabetical) list of the "President's Economic Recovery Advisory Board." When I said I was a writer everyone wanted to see the copy of *State by State* that I'd brought along.

The country's soon-to-be number-eight linguistically ranked economist said, "You've got to meet Reggie and make sure he keeps this for him."

Reggie was a former college athlete who'd become Obama's valet. The press called him a "body man." A bit of collective media strangeness as curious in its way as the coverage once devoted to the clear craze. Why employ a term that endorsed a level of vassalage straight out of ancient Rome? Gallogly waved him over. Reggie's last name was Love. He was 6'4", a college basketball star who'd also been recruited as a linebacker by the Dallas Cowboys. Obama described him to the *New York Times* as, "cooler than I am."

A bar-owning friend of mine knew and regularly drank tequila with Love. When I said so he laughed. "Yeah. I've seen the bottom of a lot of margaritas with that guy."

Then Obama and his Secret Service detail entered the room, through a small door built into one of the mirrors, a few feet behind our table.

* * *

I once met a Secret Service agent at a strip club (bachelor party) called Ten's [*sic*]. He told me that after a few tedious years on the vice presidential detail he left to work for the Service "full-time in Manhattan."

"Why Manhattan? Counterfeiting?"

"I'm guarding something."

"Not a person?"

"A device."

What inanimate object was so precious that it was being put on equal footing with the life of the president? An Iron Toad? Faithfully rendered, thousand-warted, and some say faintly smiling, a foot long at its longest, lurking at the bottom of a rank, shit-stained toilet, and hooked up to a rheostat rigged to deliver varying-though-not-lethal surges of electricity? Or a very large white Finger whose joints move with soft hydraulic sounds, its fingerprint an aerial view of the city of the future where every soul is known and there is no place to hide? Or an alembic dispensing chemical fertilizers so apples are big, red, shiny, beautiful, and absolutely tasteless, and vegetables have been improved until they're downright poisonous, and two thirds of the population has the stomach jumps? (Those being rejiggered quotations from *Gravity's Rainbow*, pages 604 and 566, and *Old Mr. Flood*, page 7.)

All I actually said was, "A *device*?"

A nod followed by a look that said this conversation was over.

As Obama's agents fanned out, this meeting came back to me, enhanced by the fact that both clubs—strip and Metropolitan—shared unusual features: mirrored walls, blacked-out windows, security. The only real difference was the female dress code. Metropolitan (house rules): "Appropriate attire for ladies is dresses, skirts, dressy pant suits and business pant suits. Jeans, shorts, stirrup pants, leggings, stretch pants, tight pants, sweats and T-shirts are absolutely not acceptable." Ten's' (customer observations and reviews): "C-section scars, bullet wounds, scrapes, cuts… A FAKE LEG."

One of the more attractive women present that night had looked a lot like a friend I'll call Lucy Stewart: ivory-skinned, Ivy-educated, a figure those of us in publishing—most everyone but the Secret Service agent—admired and desired. The agent and I were chatting about the constant golfing required of Gerald Ford's detail when the groom shouted: "*Sean, bring me Lucy Stewart!*"

I hurried off, found her, and said, "My friend wants to see you… Dance?"

She came over and pulled off her dress. As she went through her routine I told the Secret Service agent, "She looks just like a woman we know. Which adds a certain, you know, piquancy. But I wasn't expecting to feel so sad, too."

Obama went right to Mark Gallogly, my neighbor, embraced him, then addressed the economy from the podium: "I'll be looking for advice from all of you in this room."

I thought, *I'd tell you what I wanted to tell President Barry Rosenbloom. We have elevated money to the level of humanity. But money and humanity are enemies. Enemies who feed off, lie to, and use each other. There can be no freedom in this situation. Only fear. By elevating money you give it a vote. So what does money think is the ideal global condition? And what does humanity think is the ideal financial one? The disastrous answer to both these questions is: more.*

:)

Or, actually:

…

* * *

When his speech was over Obama made his way back to us. Mark Gallogly said, "Sean's a writer."

I nodded and said, "I brought you this book."

He took it and immediately started reading as I recited the history of the Federal Writers' Project. As Pynchon, in his *Slow Learner* intro, said, the American Guide series contained writing "so good, so rich in detail and deep in feeling, that even I was ashamed to steal from it."

Obama: "I know about it."

Then he turned to the chapter on Illinois, by Dave Eggers.

"Dave's a friend," he stated.

"Yeah, me, too," I replied.

It's thanks to Dave that *this* book exists.

After writing a bunch of pieces that paid next to nothing (thanks, Dave) it was glossy time. *National Geographic* ran this book's sixth essay, about soccer. A two-page slag on John Updike for *Time* (.com) maybe shouldn't even be in here, but it is because of how it connects to a later one, on NASA, for *GQ*—an essay that got me on planes to four states and the District of Columbia, and, as I read it over for this book, brought home the fact that no matter how ruined the earth may seem in comparison with those Stanford scientists' idea of 1930, it is still spacious and full of possibilities compared to every other planet we know about. The seventh essay in this book describes a cross-country trip made in an ancient pickup truck at forty-five miles per hour and expands on much of what's under discussion in this introduction. It's the piece that means the most to me.

NASA immersion led me back to the *London Review of Books'*

blog, which published an anecdote about meeting Buzz Aldrin. A short piece about cleaning and fatherhood precedes an essay about the restaurateur Danny Meyer and a piece about money, taste, and brands for *Fast Company*. And then back to Marfa with that *VF/ McSwy's* mash-up in conclusion. Fusion.

S ome things I'm aware of:

The arrogance of that Stanford report. The arrogance of ignoring that Stanford report. The arrogance of presuming to think for others. The arrogance of presuming others are thinking for you. The tenuousness of this introduction's Mitchell/Pynchon shotgun wedding. A wedding that, as a fantasy, bears some resemblance to the goal of writing the way you want to write—lit-mag style—and expecting to get paid for it by a glossy. Worth a try... Though when I tried it for the *New York Times Magazine* my editor there pinpointed the biggest problem with a piece we were working on like so: "that first draft was so distinctly you." The absurdity of idealizing 1930, a year that began, in the wake of the stock market's crash, a long eschewal of introspection in favor of growth. The bankrupt notion that still propels us. Another word for growth is velocity. Another word for velocity is freedom. This idea is the subject of not just the big piece about driving a pickup truck across the country at forty-five miles per hour, which begins in the Marfa of *McSweeney's* and ends in New York, but this whole book.

Zadie Smith, in an introduction to a collection of American short stories, wrote: "Underneath the professional smiles there is a sadness in this country that is sunk so deep in the culture you can taste it in your morning Cheerios."

Our mourning Cheerios.

That General Mills plant in Ohio looked like a charnel house.

Escaping from sadness is what made this country. We are all escapees. And Mitchell and Pynchon are escape *artists*. Masters.

THE REPUBLIC OF MARFA

1998

ISOLATION.

In the middle of what's known as Far West Texas, there is Marfa: a hardscrabble ranching community in the upper Chihuahuan desert, sixty miles north of the Mexican border, that inhabits some of the most beautiful and intransigent countryside imaginable: inexhaustible sky over a high desert formed in the Permian period and left more or less alone since. It's situated in one of the least populated sections of the contiguous United States, known locally as *el despoblado* (the uninhabited place), a twelve-hour car-and-plane trip from the East Coast, and seven from the West. It is nowhere near any interstates, major cities, or significant non-military airfields; it hosts an active population of dangerous animals and insects (a gas station clerk died of a spider bite the summer I first visited); and its 2,424 inhabitants represent the densest concentration of people in a county that covers nearly four thousand square miles—an area larger than the state of Rhode Island multiplied by three. The isolation is such that if you laid out the Hawaiian archipelago, and the deep ocean channels that divide it, on the road between Marfa and the East Texas of strip shopping and George Bush Jr., you'd still have one hundred miles of blank highway stretching away in front of you.

I've been in regular contact with the place since the summer of 1996—when my girlfriend, Daphne, was a reporter for the local weekly, the *Big Bend Sentinel*—visiting as often as possible, and witnessing some of the often volatile ways the town's 2,424 people come together; having coalesced, through strange endeavor and coincidence, into a sort of city-state of cattlemen, artists, writers, fugitives, smugglers, free-thinkers, environmentalists, soldiers, and secessionists—making Marfa home to what must be the most uncompromised contemporary art museum in the world; and, nineteen months ago, when a local teenager tending goats on a bluff above the nearby Rio Grande was shot by a marine patrol, the site of the first civilian killing by American military personnel since Kent State.

Marfa is the name of the titular family's servant in *The Brothers Karamazov*, the book a railway overseer's wife was reading when an unnamed water stop became a town in 1881. This frontierswoman was reading the book a year after its initial publication in Russian, the same year Billy the Kid was shot dead in nearby New Mexico, and during the extended period of border uneasiness that followed the Mexican-American war. But such circumstances are typically Marfan. The town attracts the bizarre: some of the first documentation of the area comes from Indian and pioneer accounts, in the 1800s, of flashing, mobile, seemingly animate luminescences on the horizon—the Marfa Mystery Lights, unexplained optical phenomena that are still observed from a pull-off on the outskirts of town, where a crowd seems to appear every night to socialize. And until the mid-'70s the lights were the main attraction. Then the minimalist artist Donald Judd moved to Marfa, exiling himself from what he termed the "harsh and glib" New York art scene, in order to live in a sort of high plains laboratory devoted to building, sculpture, furniture design, museology, conservation, and a dash of ranching, until his death in 1994.

Last April the Chinati Foundation, a contemporary art museum Judd founded in the late '70s and named after a nearby mountain range, invited architects and artists to come to Marfa and discuss the future of collaboration between the two disciplines. Billed as a symposium, it was more like a conflagration. Among the participants were Frank Gehry, whose Guggenheim Museum had recently opened in Bilbao, Spain (architect Philip Johnson has since declared it "the greatest building of our time"); the Swiss architects Jacques Herzog and Pierre de Meuron, engaged in a massive and controversial expansion of the Tate Gallery in London; the light and space artist Robert Irwin, who had just taken an unexpected creative detour and designed the garden for the Getty Center in Los Angeles; Roni Horn, a wily New York conceptualist who sculpts with words (she's plastic-cast adjectives that describe both emotions and weather and embedded them in the structure of a German meteorological bureau); and the pop artist (and deadpan comedian) Claes Oldenburg. This group spent two days in *el despoblado* showing slides and talking about their work, while two art historians—James Ackerman from Harvard, a hoary emeritus type, and Michael Benedikt from the University of Texas, a searing and somewhat humorless postmodernist—weighed in in a critical capacity, paid homage to Donald Judd, and attempted to shut everyone up. Daphne (her last name is Beal) had assignments to write about it for a couple of architecture magazines, and I went along. They were expecting six hundred people, and I was curious to observe what a 25 percent increase in Marfa's population might produce—the equivalent of two million ranchers suddenly arriving for a weekend in Manhattan.

* * *

Marfa sits in what seems like ground zero of an ancient impact site—a wide plain with mountain ranges surrounding it at an equidistant remove of about thirty miles. To the west lie the Sierra Vieja, to the north the Davis. The Glass, Del Norte, and Santiago (as well as an extinct volcano) are to the east, the Chinati to the south. These mountains run down to the high desert of cacti and yellow grassland around Marfa, framing an oceanic West Texas sky with nothing in the way of buildings or tall trees to interrupt it. The result is a big basin full of light and dry heat, where every object takes on a peculiar definition; shapes clarified and detailed, shadows standing out in perfect relief.

The town itself is a rectangle sixteen blocks high by twenty wide, with Mexican and Anglo cemeteries (separated by a fence) on the west end, a golf course (highest elevation in Texas) on the east, and satellite neighborhoods protruding to the south and northeast like radar arrays. It contains unexpected delfs and shadows, grand old homes behind tree-shaded lawns, century-old structures whose adobe disintegrates at any elemental provocation, and disused industrial buildings with aluminum siding that ticks in the heat. It operates in a state of oblivion to all the high-concept art that is made and displayed there. The two restaurants, Mike's and Carmen's, are full of ranchers, workmen, and border patrol. The two bars do decent business—there's no open-container law in Texas, and both have takeout windows. The streets are wide and for the most part empty.

In order to get to Marfa you fly into either El Paso or Midland/ Odessa. Of course, there's almost never a direct flight, so after landing in Dallas or Houston you get on a small twin-prop plane. When Daphne flew down to work at the *Sentinel* the editors met her in Midland. After shaking hands she ran into the bathroom and vomited. When I went down to visit I couldn't wait till landing and had to throw up on the plane.

UNFORCED EXCOMMUNICATION, FORCED COMMUNICATION.

D onald Judd, a cantankerous non-Scotsblood Midwesterner with a fondness for kilts, had all the fame, respect, and financial recompense a visual artist could hope for when he relegated his five-story cast-iron residence in SoHo to the status of a pied-à-terre and abandoned New York for Marfa in 1976.

This was a man with a hankering for space—not to say empire. A book devoted exclusively to Judd's many homes and buildings, *Donald Judd Spaces*, runs to more than a hundred pages and contains fifteen different *beds* (less than half the total). Judd held that a bed should always be convenient to a place where people might even passingly abide. When he arrived in Marfa he set up residence in two World War I aircraft hangers and proceeded to buy the bank, a three-hundred-acre former cavalry base (now the Chinati Foundation), three ranches (with a total acreage of 38,000), a mohair warehouse, the Safeway, the Marfa Hotel, a handful of light-manufacturing and commercial buildings, six homes from around the turn of the century, and the Marfa hot springs. By the early '90s he was planning on bottling the hot springs' water (which is said to contain traces of natural lithium), shipping it to New York, and selling it at Dean & DeLuca.

Judd's lifestyle was both ascetic and profligate. He bought everything he could lay his hands on with money from art he'd made with his own two hands. He had an almost feudal arrangement with Marfa, employing a workforce that for a time outnumbered the municipal payroll (and over which I've always unfairly imagined him exercising some kind of *droit du seigneur*, what with all those beds). Because of the controlled surroundings he created by purchasing whole buildings and stretches of land, his art in Marfa ingeniously extends its own boundaries to include entire rooms, structures, and vistas.

The Brothers Karamazov is a novel about a murder and a family's convoluted relations, played out in a small town. The transposition from the book's unnamed Russian village to present-day Marfa is an easy one to make. The way the brothers talk to each other— in grandiloquent outbursts of "excitement" or grave silences full of "strain"—reminds me of how Marfans communicate. Much of the town's emotion, as expressed in the *Sentinel*'s letters column, is reminiscent of that in the book. One man, writing about Marfa's segregated Anglo/Mexican cemetery, declared it "a slap in the face to humanity." A woman, dissecting an exploitative nuclear-waste agreement Texas signed with some eastern states, concluded, "We could have made this same compact with a dog."

Marfa's mood is Dostoyevsky's. The book and the town contain the same sort of devotion, and the same sort of outrage.

In Marfa, the people are restrained, disinclined to conversation, courteous, fractious, and, when they wish to be, extremely generous. There is also a good deal of public eccentricity. A woman roams the streets, roads, and surrounding desert with all her possessions tied to the back of a pack animal. Sometimes she's way out on the blacktop between Marfa and the mountains. Other times she's ambling through town, taking a short cut across the concrete apron of the

Texaco station. She sleeps out in the open, wherever she happens to be when the sun sets, and bears more than a passing resemblance to another character from *The Brothers Karamazov*, Stinking Lisaveta, who wandered Dostoyevsky's small-town back alleys, sleeping "on the ground and in the mud." Marfans call her the "Burro Lady." And she's one of many descriptions and details in the novel that apply almost word for word to Marfa. (Although, according to legend, the Burro Lady, unlike Stinking Lisaveta, does have a companion of sorts. A rogue steer drifts through the countryside—the symbol of an unpunished frontier crime. It's supposed to be immortal, and, as a sort of harbinger, it only shows itself to cursed souls: a brand burned into its entire flank, from shoulder to rump, reads MURDER.)

The town is also a place where mundane interactions unexpectedly take turns for the surreal. Daphne and I once got our car fixed by a gas station attendant who, when I told him I smelled something weird when the vehicle got hot, simply said, "Let's take a look at that *sum*-bitchie," popped the hood, rooted around for awhile, ripped something that looked like a dead snake out of the engine with a flourish (it turned out to be the AC belt), threw it over his shoulder, and chuckled "re-paired." In a travelogue by Scottish novelist Duncan McLean, something distinctly Marfan happens when the author checks out of the El Paisano, the only hotel in town:

> [I] stubbed my toes against some clunky bit of litter lying on
> the sidewalk. It went skittering away in front of me and stopped
> a metre ahead, long glinting barrel pointing straight at me:
> A GUN…. Next thing I knew I was back at the Paisano's desk,
> banging on the bell and babbling away to the clerk… it's out
> there, a pistol, come on, come on…
>
> The clerk ducked through a hatch in the counter and walked
> out of the lobby…

There, I said. See it?…

He held up a hand for me to stay, took a step forward, and peeped over my shoulder-bag.

Ha! He exhaled.

What is it?

He leant over, snatched up the pistol, and turned back towards me.

You call this a gun? he said, and laughed.

Eh… yeah.

He flicked some kind of catch, then pushed the revolving magazine out sideways.

This ain't no real gun, he said.

What then? An imitation?

He tilted up the pistol so a shower of little silver bullets fell out and on to his palm.

This here's a lady's gun, he said… Couldn't *kill* shit.

When Daphne first arrived, and was living at Chinati, a cowboy gave her a lift into town in his truck. He was a craggy guy in his late fifties who broke horses and raised livestock. When the conversation turned to why he'd settled in Marfa twenty years before, he said it was because the town had a "genius loci." It was an expression neither of us had ever heard before, and when we looked it up we found it strangely faithful to the peculiarity that animates the town. In Latin, it means "genius of the place." "Genius" (says the OED), when applied to a locale, indicates "a presiding deity or spirit."

It's true—something about the landscape, the strange goings-on, the balance between population and depopulation, lends credence to the belief that Marfa didn't just happen this way—that some unseen force presides.

* * *

RENEGADE TENDENCIES.

The *Big Bend Sentinel* arrives in New York a couple weeks after it's printed in Pecos (one hundred miles to the north, the nearest town with a printer). The core of its news is crime and the border, with a lot of art, armed forces (fighter training for the German and US air forces occurs in county airspace), sports, agriculture, and animal husbandry thrown in. The *Sentinel* covers all of these subjects with curiosity and seriousness, and after a few years of reading it, I'm starting to think it's possible to learn more about the state of the world from a carefully reported small paper than from any other source.

Here are some of the stranger, more significant recent stories:

In 1996, people with multiple chemical sensitivity, a disease whose sufferers take ill when exposed to synthetic materials, began living in the hills near Marfa and building an all-natural commune—until the members of a yearly Bible retreat (one of the oldest of its kind) arrived upwind and began their annual spraying of Malathion, a DDT-style pesticide that caused the Chemical Sensitives to become violently ill and engage with the religious group in a small war of ideology and incommunication. Compassion for the sick was ultimately rejected, because it was inconvenient to pray with the mosquitoes.

On a spring night in 1997 a band of marines on a drug-interdiction sortie (part of what locals call the "militarization" of the US-Mexico border) spent twenty minutes tracking Esequiel Hernández Jr., a young goatherd who carried a vintage World War I rifle to keep coyotes away from his flock. For some reason Hernández raised the rifle, in what evidence shows to have been the opposite direction from the marines, one of whom then shot him "in self-defense." The boy bled to death for twenty minutes before the soldiers summoned help. When a deputy sheriff arrived the marines said that Hernández hurt himself "falling into a well." Unfortunately, soldiers have been a constant presence in the county since the Reagan administration circumvented a law prohibiting military involvement in domestic law enforcement, and this event, though it enraged the populace, has had little long-term impact on the situation. Last fall the Defense Department, which still denies any wrongdoing, paid the Hernández family close to $2 million and washed its hands.

Over the last four years the Texas Low-Level Radioactive Waste Disposal Authority has attempted to push through legislation for a nuclear dump just over a hundred miles west of Marfa, on a site that, aside from being both a geological fault line and a watershed for the Rio Grande, is inhabited by an impoverished, uneducated populace, key members of which proved amenable to various forms of bribery. The dump looked like a neatly done deal until an unlikely group of zealous activists (one of them Gary Oliver, the *Sentinel*'s excellent— and legally blind—cartoonist) galvanized the entire six-county area of Far West Texas, as well as a large delegation from the Mexican government, and the measure was defeated. It seemed like a miracle.

A few months ago a local man survived a gas explosion that blew off his roof and knocked down the walls of his house—a story I followed from mystery occurrence to medical emergency to amazing recovery to possible criminal prosecution (he was trying to gas himself, which made the property damage negligent), and, lately, into the real estate column.

About every other week there's a four-hundred-pound bale of marijuana found on the roadside, an ad taken out by the county informing someone they are "Hereby Commanded" to appear in court, or a violent fugitive on the lam. (Fugitives are another Dostoyevskian touch. In *The Brothers Karamazov*, there is "a horrible convict who had just escaped from the provincial prison, and was secretly living in our town.") The bank in Van Horn, about a hundred miles to the west, went through a period in 1996 when it was robbed every few weeks.

Former Marfa sheriff Rick Thompson is serving a life sentence for smuggling more than a ton of cocaine out of Mexico—he's referred to as "the cocaine sheriff." The Unabomber, whose brother owns property in the area, carried on a lengthy and passionate correspondence with a Mexican *campesino* just over the border.

The *Sentinel* also contains an outspoken, thoughtful, varied, occasionally bombastic opinion section, with letters from the likes of "Crazy Bear," George "Pepper" Brown (who for some reason is the honorary mayor of Wellfleet, Mass., though he lives near Marfa, and writes letters to Robert Halpern, the *Sentinel*'s editor, that all begin "Roberto, amigo"), and many members of the large Mexican-American community—names like Lujan and Cabezuela are characteristic—published side by side with a sort of rustic philosophical-observation-cum-chitchat-column called "Wool Gathering," by Mary Katherine Metcalfe Earney. "Wool Gathering" is filed from the retirement home and can take some strange turns. One meandering edition about a pleasant visit to Delaware and Philadelphia, seeing lapsed Marfans, ended like this: "On the return to Dallas and in between planes, I was stabbed in the hand by an angry woman…"

On the back page there's a section for classified ads and public notices. There's a column for mobile homes, a column for garage sales, a column of miscellany ("about 20 goats, all sizes"), and a half page of real estate. Daphne and I often check to see what houses are going for (usually around $60,000 for a few acres and a couple bedrooms). We imagine moving down to Marfa, becoming some sort of ranch hands, reporting for the *Sentinel* or the daily paper in San Angelo, a town of one hundred thousand about two hundred miles to the northeast, which used to pick up her stories, and living in the "Judd way," which we've convinced ourselves involves a pure and ascetic harmony with the surroundings—coupled with culinary infusions from Dean & DeLuca.

In fact, Donald Judd, for all his land-grabbing, became something of a holy man. His masterpiece in Marfa is an installation of one hundred milled aluminum boxes—each of the exact same volume (about that of a restaurant stove), but with wildly different interiors, full of sloping metal planes and odd angles. The boxes fill two former artillery sheds that he opened up to the Texas plains with huge windows along their sides, and capped with Quonset roofs. During the day the sheds fill with sun and the boxes warp and change and reflect the landscape. At night they turn liquid in the moonlight. In the distance, between the sheds and the far-off silhouette of the Chinati mountains, Judd placed fifteen rectangular boxes, each about ten feet tall, which further link the site to the landscape. This was the artist's favorite (Karamazovian) story about the piece: after a tour, a Jesuit priest turned to him and said, "You and I are in the same business."

And Chinati, just outside town, also seems pulled from *The Brothers Karamazov*, resembling the "neighboring monastery" that "crowds of pilgrims… from thousands of miles, come flocking to see." with Judd—or the spirit of Judd—the presiding elder, called Zosima in the book, responsible for the "great glory" that has come to the place.

By the time he died, Judd had changed from a sculptor into an almost monastic figure. He was living in deep seclusion, on the remotest of his ranches in the high desert, without electricity, close to the border, surrounded by books on art, philosophy, history, and local ecology. "My first and largest interest is in my relation to the natural world," he wrote during this period. "All of it, all the way out. This interest includes my existence … the existence of everything and the space and time that is created by the existing things."

* * *

DESERT PICNICS.

I mmediately upon leaving town the temperamentality of the desert landscape asserts itself. There's an old cowboy poem about a "place where mountains float in the air," which is likely a reference to the mirages that the dry Marfan climate is adept at producing. A local man recalls seeing "the entire [nearby] town of Valentine appearing in the morning sky." Another claims to have seen "the apparition of a Mexican village in the still-light sky just after sunset." It rarely rains, but when it does the sky is transformed, going from its usual big serene blue to the purple-black of a deep bruise—and letting loose so much precipitation that water suddenly runs in rivers through the streets. You can see it all coming a hundred miles off, like a train down a straight line of track. At night there's a great heaping feast of stars, and meteor showers—"like confetti" is how Daphne puts it—are a regular event.

Sometimes the sun is so bright that you can't see. I first noticed this while driving back from Balmorhea, a town with a vast WPA spring-fed swimming pool (and ranch-hand brothels) over the mountains about fifty miles north of Marfa. It's typical in Far West Texas to drive one hundred miles just to have something to do, the way the rest of the country goes to the mall, and in Balmorhea Daphne and I'd run into some other people from Marfa and spent the day talking in the shade. Coming back, Daphne drove and I stared out the window. As we started coming out of the flatland, up through the Davis Mountains, where the two-lane road twists through a canyon and the desert terrain gives way a bit, I noticed a tree, a salt cedar or something—the first green I'd seen since leaving the pool—standing out with a sort of fluorescent brightness against the canyon's brown rock and scrub. When I pulled off my sunglasses the color disappeared. With an unshielded eye the tree looked pale, burnt, and exhausted—almost translucent. The sunlight was so strong that it was shining right through it. But when I put the sunglasses back on the light receded and the tree reappeared—standing out like it was on fire.

Besides the sparse trees, which are more common in town, the terrain supports myriad cacti: yucca and cholla in abundance, but also the odd horse crippler (a nasty, horizontally inclined weed that looks like an unsprung bear trap); nopalito, or prickly pear, a succulent with flat pads that are despined and sold in fruit bins outside the gas stations; ocotillo, a subaquatic-looking plant with wavy tentacles and sharp thorns that suggest an octopus crossed with a blowfish; and lots of juniper, greasewood (aka chaparral), and mesquite. The cholla is a thicker, less primordial variant on the ocotillo (it looks like coral if you squint), and the yucca has leaves like a pineapple's, each about two feet long. When yucca bloom, a seven-foot rod shoots out of the center and bursts into a brilliant yellow flower that stands out brightly, like a flare in the landscape, sunglasses or no.

There are four roads out of Marfa. One leads to Valentine, a comatose place with a post office that receives bags of mail in early February from all over the country, to be reposted before the fourteenth. A second leads to Shafter, a ghost town waiting for either the governor's order to abolish it or the price of silver to hit six dollars an ounce (it's now at $5.30), so as to make it worthwhile for an interested mining concern to retap a vein that was abandoned during World War II. The third road leads to the area's only movie theater, in Alpine, and the campus of Sul Ross State University, which offers degrees in Range Animal Science and is the birthplace of intercollegiate rodeo. The last leads to Fort Davis, a Wild West boutique town with an observatory dedicated to the spectroscopic analysis of light.

Technically, there's a fifth road, through Pinto Canyon, which leads out of Marfa to the southwest, in the direction of Judd's ranches, and winds up on the border in a town called Ruidosa (Noisy): though "town" is an exaggeration—there isn't a single amenity in Ruidosa, besides the road, so it's more like an encampment. Leaving Marfa via Pinto Canyon you see a sign that reads, PAVEMENT ENDS 32 MILES. My one experience driving the length of this road was unnerving in the extreme. About an hour out, halfway between Marfa and the Rio Grande, having seen no other cars, we decided to stop where the road crossed a dry creek bed. This was long after the pavement had ended. The scenery looked a lot like the ocean floor. The temperature was in the nineties. We'd packed a picnic of avocado sandwiches, Lone Star beer, and some local cheese called *asadero*; we spied some tired-looking mesquite—the only non-cactus shade in sight—and figured to have lunch under it. After shutting the car off we trudged about four hundred feet down the dry creek bed (I was thinking *flash flood*, which is something the area's known for). Away from the road— which was only a spit through the wilderness at this point—we set down our cooler and got out our food. We started to eat without saying much of anything—the silence was so immense it suppressed any conversational impulse.

The picnic was scuttled fifteen minutes later when we heard the sound of someone trying to hotwire our car. The starter whined, but the engine wouldn't catch. We looked at each other for an instant, and then jumped up and started tearing back up the creek bed, afraid of being stuck out there more than whatever we might find. I got to the road first, in a gasping, adrenaline-choked rush, and found the car sitting where we'd left it, and with no one in sight. Daphne ran back, packed up our stuff, and we got the hell out of there, fast. Whoever was out in that desert on foot, crossing into the US, had to want a car with Texas plates—*bad*. All we could think was that they gave up trying when they heard us crashing down the creek, thinking to avoid a confrontation: even if the motor had caught, the car was headed toward Mexico, and with the road disintegrating into sharp rubble and cacti a foot to either side, there was no obvious way to turn it around.

For the symposium, we came in from the south, via Shafter, and, after checking into the Thunderbird Motel, dragged some chairs outside and watched the motor court fill up with rental cars. The Thunderbird's amenities include an inexhaustible ice machine, so we filled a cooler we'd brought and drank beer on a concrete walk beneath an overhang for half an hour. Then we went to check out the town. Rob Weiner, Judd's erstwhile assistant (who shadowed the artist as he drew, designed, and wrote in a variety of bed-holding work spaces), remained in Marfa after his employer's death, becoming deputy director of Chinati. He stopped his car in the middle of the street to say hello and tell us that we might be able to stay in a foundation building later that weekend. Making people fall in love with Marfa was Weiner's mission. He oversaw Chinati's artist-in-residence and internship programs—choosing new inhabitants for the town. Considering that a significant sampling of these people decided to remain amongst Marfa's 2,424 people (a number so small any new arrival was noted), it seemed to me that Weiner was picking up where Judd had left off—creating in Marfa a work of art that was not graphic but demographic.

An ad hoc Chinati Foundation store was selling books by or about all the lecturers in the symposium as well as on the work of artists Judd admired and "permanently" installed in Marfa (Claes Oldenburg, Dan Flavin, Carl Andre, Richard Long, Ilya Kabakov, and John Chamberlain). Browsing, we fell into conversation with our first non-Marfan, a reporter from the *Houston Press* named Shaila Dewan. She had driven from Houston and was camping out in the Marfa trailer park.

"Gehry is God," she told us.

Not in Marfa, I thought. *God's Judd*.

After that we went by the paper to see Robert Halpern and his wife, Rosario, who were closing an issue but invited us to dinner with the newspaper staff and Rusty Taylor, the chief of police, all of whom had recently been involved in a violent episode of Marfa's history.

In July 1996, a photograph in the *Sentinel* showed a tall, lean, bald-on-top man with a circle of white hair above his ears wearing a T-shirt that said ASK ME ABOUT THE REPUBLIC OF TEXAS. This was Richard McLaren, described by his neighbors as "capable of tremendous violence," a man who, arguing a legal technicality in an 1845 annexation document, considered himself chief ambassador, consul general, and sovereign of the independent nation of Texas. McLaren had become a bullying presence in the hills north of Marfa, given to threats and harassment, filing false liens against property, passing bogus scrip, and accumulating weapons. That day he and his followers were having a picnic in celebration of "captive nations week," a propaganda occasion established under Eisenhower in the late '50s to foster dissent against Communist dictatorships. In the background could be seen two police cruisers: Rusty Taylor was keeping an eye on the situation.

Less than a year later, in the spring of 1997, three R.O.T. conscripts, dressed in camouflage and carrying assault weapons, stalked through the mountains from McLaren's trailer home to the house of his nearest neighbors, Joe Rowe—former president of the local neighborhood association—and his wife, Margaret Ann. When they arrived in the yard they opened fire on the house, sending shrapnel into Mr. Rowe's shoulder, then burst through the door and struck him with a rifle butt, breaking his arm. With the Rowes subdued, the intruders made some long-distance phone calls, took all the food they could carry (leaving forty dollars as compensation), and brought their hostages back to McLaren's trailer. Then the group issued a communiqué describing the action as reprisal for the arrest earlier that morning of another Republic of Texas member, Robert Scheidt, on charges of carrying illegal weapons. McLaren declared war on the United States and named the Rowes as his first prisoners. Police in Marfa agreed to release Scheidt in exchange for the Rowes, and a trade was made that left the group isolated in their trailer, several miles up a dirt road, surrounded by SWAT teams and Texas rangers.

McLaren had prepared for such an occasion by digging a series of bunkers and stockpiling more than sixty pipe bombs, a dozen or so gasoline cans, ten rifles, several pistols, and five to seven hundred rounds of ammunition. He swore to fight to the end and issued a grandiloquent statement evoking the diary of William B. Travis, commander at the Alamo in 1836: "Everyone has chosen to stay and hold the sovereign soil of the Republic and its foreign missions. I pray reinforcements arrive before they overrun the embassy." He would wage an Alamo-style fight to the death. He would kill as many officers as possible. As police reinforcements continued to arrive, McLaren got on the radio and broadcast: "Mayday! Mayday! Mayday! Hostiles are invading the Republic of Texas embassy. We have hostiles in the woods."

After a few days, though, McLaren began to soften. He conceded that he could surrender if the rules of war were applied and the US agreed to treat him under the rules of the Geneva Convention, allowing an appeal to the United Nations. This eventually led to his signing a "Texas-wide cease-fire document," essentially an unconditional surrender, with a proviso that the embassy be respected, which he understood to mean that the Republic flag, a lone yellow star on a blue field, would continue to fly—it was lowered and replaced by the Texas flag, in what a local fireman described as an "Iwo Jima–style ceremony." McLaren and four others laid down their weapons (though, arriving in Marfa, one of them shouted, "I was captured, not surrendered, and I'm ashamed I didn't die"). Two other members went renegade and retreated into the hills with rifles and small arms. They were pursued by hounds, all of which they shot. Helicopters then tracked the pair into more remote terrain, and when they were fired upon, police snipers shot back and killed one man. The other, Richard Keyes III, who had left the employ of a Kansas bathroom-equipment manufacturer just weeks before these events, managed to escape. He evanesced. Come summer he was still at large. One newspaper called him "a West Texas version of D. B. Cooper," the '70s hijacker who parachuted out of a 727 with $200,000 in ransom money and was never heard from again.

But a reporter for *Mother Jones* magazine *did* hear from Keyes, or a man claiming (quite credibly) to be Keyes. He defended the kidnapping of the Rowes, and noted that after the attack they'd subsequently called a doctor, who'd refused to help, because "he was concerned about a house full of armed fruitcakes." Touching on the fact that the assailants had left the Rowes payment for food and phone calls, the man declared, "They were fully compensated for what happened, except for the fact that they had a rather bad day." He also said that he was safely outside the United States, which turned out to mean that he was still in Texas. After five months on the run, Keyes was captured in Houston.

As for McLaren, before the surrender he made sure that his international cease-fire agreement also included a conjugal visit with a woman he'd married a short time before, in a service binding only under the laws of the Republic of Texas. She was also under arrest for her involvement in the siege, so, following arraignment by the Marfa Justice of the Peace, Cinderella Gonzalez, the two were put in the same cell.

In the lonely days that followed, while awaiting trial, McLaren took to writing florid letters to the *Sentinel*, calling his "challenge

SEAN WILSEY

to gain national independence… the best-executed legal presentation that has ever been accomplished in the 20th century." He also described his predicament in Marfa as that of a "prisoner of war" being held in the "king's jails." More than a few locals have expressed disappointment that he was not killed during the siege.

As Daphne and I left the *Sentinel* and stepped onto Highland Avenue, the main street in town, we could see the old courthouse, with its cupola, coffered ceiling, and yard of sprawling almond trees. It's crowned by a statue of justice, which, legend has it, lost her scales sometime in the '20s after a hungover cowboy, fresh out of jail and reunited with his six-guns, shot them out of her hands, yelling, "Thar *ain't* no justice in this goddamn county."

CONFLAGRATIONS.

The next morning, six hundred artists, art historians, architects, critics, journalists, and a few townspeople assembled under the corrugated tin roof of a former ice plant in a neighborhood called Salsipuedes ("get out if you can"). The place was so full that they'd borrowed extra chairs from the local veterans society with phrases like AMVETS SALUTES USO POST 65 WITH PRIDE stenciled on their backs. Opening the proceedings, James Ackerman, the art historian from Harvard, tried to temper the Judd idolatry by describing the artist as a man "at war" with architecture, given less to collaboration than to "fulminations against architecture in our time."

A big man was seated across the aisle from me. It was Frank Gehry, looking a lot like somebody's Palm Springs grandfather. He was wearing old loafers that needed a shine, a white button-down shirt, gray suit pants, and a sport jacket. When the architect Jacques Herzog—thin, hip, dressed with a Swiss meticulousness, completely in black, Gehry's aesthetic opposite—got up to give a detailed lecture, I watched Gehry. Herzog explained the process of "tattooing" photographs to concrete in order to give his buildings variegated surfaces. He'd been talking for half an hour when an El Paso–bound train came by and drowned him out for a minute. I glanced over at Gehry. He seemed aggravated. When Herzog resumed lecturing and began a long series of slides on the expansion of the Tate Gallery, Gehry, brow furrowed, started fidgeting with a pencil. The next time I looked, he was up and gone. Herzog continued lecturing for a few minutes until the director of Chinati suddenly cut him off. It seemed like Gehry had heard enough from his competition and put an end to it.

That afternoon, an ornery vibe intensified, and some Judd-style fulminating commenced when the artists took the stage. Robert Irwin, opening his lecture with a sustained tangent about art history, endeavored to make it clear that he didn't believe in anything beyond modernism. "*Post*modernism: if that isn't a red herring I'll kiss your ass," he hollered. He then proceeded to slam Richard Meier, the principal architect on the Getty Center project, saying, "I chewed him up and left him for dead… Though you'd never define a collaboration in that way."

It was around this time that I heard a groan. It wasn't Gehry, but Shaila, from the *Houston Press*, who had fainted from the slowly intensifying heat. Daphne had to help her outside. When Shaila filed her piece she would blame the incident on side effects associated with her stay in the Marfa trailer park and its limited culinary options: "the smell of my own road fare farts."

And during all this commotion Irwin didn't ever slow down. Animated with a sort of giddy, profane enthusiasm, the artist reveled in some of the stranger details of his work. He described his relations with his horticultural consultants on the Getty Center garden as

"spending a lot of time going to nurseries and hugging each other."
As evidence of his attention to minutiae he said that he'd made
certain that benches in the garden would "feel good on your ass." He
then explained that he'd fashioned the stream that runs through the
garden with heavy stonework because "I didn't want it to look like
some gay bathroom." With this a disapproving rumble came over the
ice plant. (Later, when questioned about the gay bathroom comment,
Irwin was both chagrined and cagey. "I don't get out much. I'm an
artist," he explained.)

The next speaker, Michael Benedikt, the postmodernist, riveted
Irwin through steel-rimmed spectacles and said "Modernism is male
and macho. And that's the problem with it."

After castigating Irwin, Benedikt called the work of making art
a "religious project" and delivered a lecture that delved into the Old
Testament. In Benedikt's mind the burning bush that Moses encountered in the desert was, like successful art, "burning with its own
authenticity." Then we were released for dinner at Chinati.

As I stood in line for food I heard a man behind me tell his companions, "We need to maximize returns for the whole Marfa concept."
This was Judd's old lawyer, John Jerome. Dinner was brisket and
Shiner Bock beer in the Arena, a former army gymnasium that Judd
rehabilitated. It's difficult to say what exactly the "Marfa concept"
might be. For Judd it meant control: of his surroundings, of his
art, of the company he kept. As the Russian installation artist Ilya
Kabakov noted, "When I first came to Marfa, my biggest impression
was the unbelievable combination of estrangement, similar to a holy
place, and at the same time of unbelievable attention to the life of the
works there. For me it was like some sort of Tibetan monastery; there
were no material things at all, none of the hubbub of our everyday

lives. It was… a world for art." (Although I don't think that's what Jerome meant.)

But Kabakov's presence in Marfa alters the concept significantly. The Russian, whose installation stakes out different aesthetic territory than all the other major pieces in Marfa, was an underground artist in the Soviet Union who began to exhibit in the West only in the late '80s. In the early '90s Judd invited him to come to Marfa and do a piece. Kabakov was "astounded." The haunting result is "School No. 6," a replica of an entire Communist-era Russian grade school—desks, display cases, lesson plans, Cyrillic textbooks, musical instruments—installed in a Chinati barracks, exposed to the elements, and encouraged to decay. "Of course there was nothing more awful than the Soviet school, with all of its discipline, abomination and militarization," he has said of the work. "But now that that system has collapsed and left behind only ruins, it evokes the same kind of nostalgic feelings as a ruined temple." It also has its serene, even spiritual overtones. As he describes it: "The entire space of the school is flooded with sunshine and quiet. Sunny squares lie on the school floor. The blue sky is visible in the empty apertures. From all of this, the neglect reigning all around does not seem so cheerless and depressing." The installation plays the trick of turning Marfa into Russia. And Kabakov's description of its mood is akin to one in *The Brothers Karamazov* wherein the youngest brother, Alyosha, repeatedly recalls his mother's face, but always in "the slanting rays of the setting sun (these slanting rays he remembered most of all)."

Kabakov has said that "everything that we see around us, everything that we discover in our past, or which could possibly comprise the future—all of this is a limitless world of projects." In my mind the statement pairs with Judd's declaration of interest in the natural world, "all of it, all the way out." A sociable take on the same artistic impulse that led Judd into isolation.

So Kabakov is also part of the "Marfa concept."

And the concept—no matter which of the seminal events or legends in the town's history one follows—always connects with light.

Light is Marfa's last name. Marfa *Ignatievna*—meaning daughter of Ignatius, which, as my paperback copy of *The Greatest Baby Name Book Ever* explains, derives from the Latin *ignis*, meaning fire. Ignatievna means "daughter of fire." According to Dostoyevsky, the character is "not a stupid woman," and early in *The Brothers Karamazov* she gives rise to "a strange, unexpected and original occurrence"—the birth of a boy that her superstitious husband fears, calls a "dragon"—fire-breathing, I'm guessing—and refuses to care for. When the baby dies, Marfa takes it stoically. Dostoyevsky endows her not only with intelligence, but fortitude. She's a sharp, stoical lady—a desirable pair of qualities in a frontierswoman. And since the woman who named the town after this character had to have been reading the book in the original Russian—the first translation, into German, wasn't until 1884, and the English version didn't appear until 1912—she could not have been unaware of the name's significance in this light-crossed place.

After filling our plates with brisket Daphne and I sat down at a discomfitingly long and wide table with Rob Weiner and Jeff Elrod, a young artist in residence at Chinati. Both men were voluble enough to bridge the distances inherent to Judd's furniture. We discussed Patrick Lannan, a philanthropist whose eponymous foundation was funding the renovation of two homes it had bought to house writers selected to receive residencies in town. An English poet would be arriving in a month. Weiner said that Chinati had just received its first NEA grant, toward the repurposing of six U-shaped army barracks to house a piece that light artist Dan Flavin had planned with Judd and completed designing after Judd's death, when Flavin was on his own deathbed, in 1996. There was also talk about Robert Irwin maybe taking a spare building and making an installation.

After dinner the evening migrated to Lucy's Bar, where Frank Gehry was given a wide, semi-awestruck berth. Ray, Lucy's owner, even allowed him to stand in an off-limits-to-customers spot beside the bartender (blocking the sink). Eventually the architect left for the dilapidated old El Paisano Hotel, where he was the most famous guest since James Dean was in residence during the shooting of the film *Giant*. As Lucy's started to break up, people either headed home or out to see the Marfa Lights.

The Marfa Lights, not unlike Frank Gehry, are a fairly aloof phenomenon—mostly appearing at a hard-to-quantify distance from a roadside pull-off, near the site of an old military airfield. To most observers they look like a distant swarm of fireflies, changing direction and flashing on and off in random patterns. But there are wild exceptions to this aloofness. In various first-person accounts, collected in a mimeographed pamphlet on sale at the Chamber of Commerce, the lights are animate and even intelligent. Per witnesses they metastasize, hide behind one another, change color, bounce across the desert "like basketballs," line up for aircraft "like runway lights," and pursue lone motorists between Marfa and Alpine. (Robert Halpern told me about a guy who was descended upon and pursued by a pair of Marfa lights, blazing furiously, all the way to the town limits, after which he swore that he would never leave Marfa again, and hasn't.) Though the most reliable place to see them is the viewing site, overlooking a vast swath of desert between Marfa and Alpine—where a weather-beaten historical marker details various explanations for the phenomenon ("campfires, phosphorescent minerals, swamp gas, static electricity, St. Elmo's fire, and 'ghost lights'")—the lights have been known to stray as far away as the Dead Horse Mountains, sixty miles to the east, the hills near Ruidosa, an equal distance to the southwest, and the Davis Mountains, the location of McDonald Observatory, one of the country's most sophisticated stargazing facilities, thirty miles due north. According to Marfan Lee Bennett, who wrote the town's entry for the Texas State Historical Association's *Handbook of Texas* as well as some of the boosterish material promoting the annual Lights Festival (an excuse for yearly outdoor concerts), even the observatory is mystified by the lights phenomenon: "One night they trained one of their telescopes on the viewing site until they spied some of the glowing lights. Everyone working that night saw them. They pinpointed the location. The next day, they traveled to that exact spot, certain they would find the source. What did they find? Grass, rocks, dirt. That's it. Nothing else."

Though this history may be a little casz with the facts, serious scientists have visited the site over the years, eventually arriving at one or more of the hazy explanations engraved on the historical marker. Folktales stretching back to the nineteenth century explain the phenomenon as everything from restless Indian spirits to the spectral campfires of perished settlers. Most often close-up observers compare the lights to combustion. "It was a ball of fire," said a motorist of the light that kept pace with her car for ten miles on the way to Alpine. "I saw three big balls of fire lined up," reported a woman of lights she witnessed hovering by the side of the road outside town. A former Alpine resident once stopped at the viewing site on a spring night and saw thirteen lights "coming through the field like little fireballs... and rolling out onto the road." Hallie Stillwell, an Alpine rancherwoman and justice of the peace, observed some on her property to "die down and then come up again, brighter. They looked like flames." Less comforting information comes from a recluse living off in the hills around Shafter, who calls them "agents of Satan" and claims that "they walk up the side of the mountain" near his house; and a bit of hearsay in which the lights are supposed to have incinerated a truck belonging to a pair of investigating scientists, rendering the men, in the words of a Sul Ross University English professor, "idiots from that day on."

Lee Bennett also contributes this story to the Lights Festival material:

> I'm the local historian. So when someone in town dies, the families usually give me pieces of history that may have been collected by that person. Well, a special lady on a ranch west of town had kept a little tiny notebook of writings about the local flora and fauna and the general environment out here. But one entry especially caught my attention. She wrote in her own handwriting about driving down an old canyon road—a good 20 miles from the usual viewing site—many years ago. She was rather new to the area, and when she looked to her right she saw Chianti Mountain. "Isn't that a pretty big mountain?" she asked. Her friend replied that it was one of the highest around. "And there's a road coming down it?" she asked, amazed. Her friend looked at her strangely and answered, "There's no road coming down off Chianti." "Then why do I see lights coming quickly down that mountain?" The entry went on to describe several lights that shot down the side of the mountain, directly toward them. They danced in the canyon and moved right up to the hood of the car. In her own words she wrote, "I felt so special. We were never afraid. In fact, we had sort of a warm feeling."

There have also been a good many lights posses—debunkers who go out to "get them" and always return humiliated. In the '70s a corporation that figured the site for a uranium cache funded various futile investigations. In the '80s a science professor from Sul

Ross University gathered a large party of students and volunteers to converge on the lights, with walkie-talkies and spotter planes coordinating their maneuvers. But whenever a group got close the lights would go dark or move rapidly out of range. A geologist from Fort Worth named Pat Keeney visited Marfa on business and became fascinated with the lights. Hoping to find their source, he conducted a series of experiments in order to rule out car headlights and other man-made luminosities, and then managed to triangulate the area of the remaining unexplained lights. He subsequently returned with another geologist, Elwood Wright, and together the two drove out on a small ranch road where they encountered a pair of lights moving nearby. Keeney published this account of what happened next:

> They looked like they were moving at about a hundred-fifty
> to two-hundred miles per hour, but of course I had no way of
> measuring that. The lights spooked some horses, almost ran into
> them. Those horses started kicking and running through a cactus
> patch, trying to get away. The lights came to the edge of this road
> and stopped. Several times I had seen lights around this old hangar
> they had on the airbase. Well, one of these lights took off for that
> hangar, but the other one stayed there by the side of the road. It
> kept moving around a bush, kind of like it knew we were trying to
> get near it. It seemed to possess intelligence—it was like that thing
> was smarter than we were. It was making us feel pretty stupid. It
> was perfectly round, about the size of a cantaloupe, and it moved
> through that bush like it was looking for something. When the
> light stopped moving, it would get dimmer, but as it moved, it got
> brighter. Finally, it pulled out in the middle of the road about twenty
> yards from us and just hovered there. I had left the engine running,
> and Elwood said, "Put it in gear and floorboard it. We'll run over
> it." All of a sudden it got real bright and took off like a rocket.

Marfa mayor Fritz Kahl dismisses most accounts of up-close encounters as "asinine stories" (though he has a certain deference for Keeney). Many years prior to his mayoralty Kahl was a military flight instructor at Marfa Field, and he took after the lights one night in a World War II fighter trainer. Unable to ever get close, he banished them from his thoughts (as most saner Marfans have). "The best way to see the lights is with a six-pack of beer and a good-looking woman," he says today.

> Still, the lights are out there, and on most weekends (as on the first night of the symposium) people assemble by the roadside while the sun goes down, and stay on into the evening. Only after midnight does the crowd thin out and return the road to the circumstances under which most reports of close encounters have occurred.
>
> Some say that the place was bewitched... during the early days of the settlement; others, that an old Indian chief, the prophet or wizard of his tribe, held his powwows there before the country was discovered... Certain it is, the place still continues under the sway of some witching power, that holds a spell over the minds of the good people... They are given to all kinds of marvelous beliefs; are subject to trances and visions, and frequently see strange sights, and hear music and voices in the air... stars shoot and meteors glare oftener across the valley than in any other part of the country.

This is not Marfa. It's Westchester, New York, as described by Washington Irving in *The Legend of Sleepy Hollow*. And for the late-night driver traveling an empty road between Marfa and Alpine it is easy to identify with Ichabod Crane, with Paisano Pass, where the lights tend to disappear, subbing in for the church bridge in Sleepy Hollow where the Headless Horseman "vanished in a flash of fire."

*   *   *

On the last day of the symposium, the big boys, Gehry and Oldenburg, spoke. And the odd, inflammatory statements continued. "I'm for an art that doesn't sit on its ass in a museum," Oldenburg declared. He and his wife and collaborator, Coosje van Bruggen, took turns at the lectern, one talking while the other hit the button for the slide projector. Van Bruggen described the typical architect's ideas about the position sculpture takes in relation to architecture as "nothing more than a turd on the sidewalk." Like Irwin the day before, they seemed all fired up. Among their slides was a sketch of two giant copper toilet floats the artists had proposed be installed on the Thames, near the location of Jacques Herzog's Tate Gallery (for which they expressed unequivocal disdain). By the time Gehry took the stage there was tension in the air.

"Don Judd hated my work," said Gehry, who seemed to find perverse pleasure in the fact. It may have been the spare setting that provoked him, but he made a point of defending the Guggenheim from the charge of upstaging the art it displays (the antithesis of anything that can be said of the unadorned spaces of Judd's Marfa installations), insisting that "artists want their work in an important place." (Again, not the "Marfa concept.") Gehry then talked about his other recent commissions, like a seafood restaurant topped with a fish that he'd deliberately turned to face the windows of a neighboring five-star hotel. "The owner told me he didn't want 'em looking up the *asshole* of a fish," Gehry explained. Future projects included the Condé Nast cafeteria in New York (a sketch conveying Gehry's idea of a Condé Nast employee showed a leggy woman in a short skirt and shades, blowing a kiss), and a massive gateway for the city of Modena, Italy. Modena's mayor originally offered a design budget of $1 million for the project, "but you get a few people back and forth and that won't hardly cover airfare," said Gehry. "And I ain't gonna stay in no El Paisano Hotel in Modena."

At the end of the lectures the participants gathered together around one of those long, isolation-enhancing Donald Judd tables to discuss each other's work and riff on the theme. It didn't take long for the ideological lines to clarify. Irwin disparaged critics who engage in "ass-kissing." Coosje van Bruggen lit into Jacques Herzog for his Tate Gallery expansion, calling the whole thing "a pity." Pissed off, Herzog glared out at the audience and said, "It's not bullshit." But before he could go on, he was interrupted by the artist Roni Horn, who stole the moment by remarking, "All this architecture is really about sex." The audience banged its steel chairs, and a beaming Gehry raised his fists above his head like a prizefighter.

"And on that note," Horn said, "I'm going back to New York." Everyone applauded as Gehry and Irwin strode off stage with her, trailed by Herzog (waving a dismissive hand at van Bruggen). The remaining artists soon followed. "The panel has defected," said the moderator. The only ones left onstage were the academics, who were still talking to each other—via the microphones.

That afternoon, once everyone had left town, Daphne went running and I went back to Lucy's Bar. I heard a local guy tell the bartender he'd "never seen so many people in black." The bartender told him, "We had the most famous architect in the world in here!" I ordered a Lone Star and heard the bartender tell another customer, "We thought we'd sell a lot of Mexican beer—but all they wanted was Lone Star."

Something in Marfa had *riled up* a lot of architects, artists, and academics. Six hundred of us had been treated to tongue-lashings, dressing downs, fully amplified upbraiding, storming, and railing— not what anyone had expected out of a symposium. In this vexed atmosphere rumors were circulating about an old feud between an art photographer and the Judd estate breaking into a full-blown multi-million-dollar lawsuit (broken in the *Sentinel* the next week).

On the surface, of course, Marfa had hosted celebrated artists and architects. But the way it struck me was that *they* had hosted *Marfa*. Marfa had *got into* them. They'd been possessed. And they had behaved accordingly: cantankerously, radically, wonderfully, badly, generously, absurdly; *in extremis*. Like Marfans.

Some other notable people who've come through Marfa:
  Katherine Anne Porter
  John Waters
  Denis Johnson
  Dennis Quaid
  Martha Stewart
  David Kaczynski
  W.S. Merwin
  Neil Armstrong
  Gwyneth Paltrow
  James Caan
  Selena
  Elvis

I wish I could say that the place nourishes artists. It may. But I think it does something stranger. The relationship seems less friendly—more volatile. (I can imagine it destroying some.) Katherine Anne Porter, who lived there as a girl (Judd's son, Flavin, now lives in her house), loathed it. Elvis played a dance nearby and never came back. A cave in the wilderness near the town of Terlingua was a refuge for

David Kaczynski, the Unabomber's brother. And W.S. Merwin, who is fascinated with the lights, would rather no one else know about it.

It seems that the best places for artists are places that *are* themselves; have a certain innate self-confidence—burn with that authenticity that Benedikt was talking about. And Marfa *is* what it is. Less Kabakov's "world for art," perhaps, than a provocative place for all kinds of impulses: creative, destructive, uncharted—by all means authentic.

And it's got better things to do than become aware of its un-self-consciousness. Within the next year there may be a hundred-man crew of silver miners in nearby Shafter, drilling on a ten-to-fifteen-year timetable and eating at Carmen's next to the likes of Seamus Heaney, A.R. Ammons, or William Trevor—all three men are on the small list of Lannan grantees eligible for Marfa residencies. The Entrada al Pacífico, a trade corridor opened up by NAFTA, is altering the regional economy, with border crossings in the county up 100 percent in the last year. Hydroponic tomatoes are being cultivated in massive greenhouses just outside the city limits, turning Marfa into a desert town that exports water, just as Judd wanted. (It's a disquieting sight: huge glass-and-steel superstructures, sucking away at the aquifer. Though there's undeniably something Marfan about it.) The border patrol is bolstering its forces in Marfa. Newcomers have bought back the hot springs and a handful of other buildings from the Judd estate, restoring the former to public use. An ATM was installed this January (the one Marfa had a few years ago was decommissioned because it never caught on—but this one may). Things are happening. By no means moribund, Marfa is a viable town on its own terms. As Robert Halpern told me by e-mail the other day, "Pretty much most of the folks who are moving here as well as us locals are reading from the same sheet of music: A town has to change and grow or it dies. Marfa will survive in spite of us all."

And, of course, "mystery lights" is not a bad description of these people who continually pass through Marfa: people like Irwin, Kabakov, Judd, and Peter Reading, the inaugural Lannan grantee, an oft-inebriated Englishman with a tab at Lucy's who likes to kick around Chinati muttering about how much all the damn boxes cost, or, in characteristic Marfan style, provoke his benefactors by bragging of his residency, "I am required to do nothing. This suits me." But many others also seem to find their way to Marfa. A few weeks after the symposium, a *conjunto* accordionist, Santiago Jiménez Jr., who, along with his brother Flaco, is one of the more revered traditionalists on the Tex-Mex scene, paid a visit. He walked around town playing for old folks, the community center, veterans, whoever wanted to listen. Fantastic pictures of him doing sessions with local musicians kept appearing in the paper. I don't know how long he was around, but he seemed to just stay and stay and stay—through about four issues of the *Sentinel*, becoming a part of the town. And then he winked out and was gone.

For our last night, Rob Weiner at the Chinati Foundation said we could move out of the Thunderbird Motel and into a foundation building. Fortunately, part of Donald Judd's philosophy about beds also obtains to having one in most every gallery. We wound up in the John Chamberlain Building, a thirty-thousand-square-foot former mohair warehouse full of sculptures made out of crushed cars. "You'll find it interesting," Rob said. At two a.m., I awoke with a start. The windows were shaking, the air vibrating, and roars and whistles seemed to be coming straight from the bathroom. It got louder and louder until I was sure something was going to come crashing through the door. "Get up!" I shouted to Daphne. "It's the ghost of Donald Judd!" And the El Paso–bound train shot by.

NO WORK FOR ME

2002

A few days after the World Trade Center was destroyed I heard on the radio that Cantor Fitzgerald, which had traded bonds on its 101st, 103rd, 104th and 105th floors, had over six hundred missing employees, and needed volunteers to help run a support center for their families. I put my name on a list. They asked me to come to the ballroom of the Plaza Hotel on Monday, September 17, by which time "missing" had changed, in everyone's minds, to "presumed dead."

I got to the Plaza at nine, and a tall, blonde Englishwoman, dressed completely in white, told me to stand by the two elevators that brought people to the ballroom and be a "greeter." She said I should say "Can I help you?" when people arrived. I was to make sure they signed in, so we knew who had come; I should try to answer any question asked of me; and if people were overcome with emotion I should find a professional counselor, who would be wearing a name tag with an orange circle on it. My name tag had a blue circle on it. There were plain name tags for the victims' families.

During the first hour I mostly greeted other volunteers. Also Plaza Hotel employees, priests, rabbis, and psychotherapists. During lulls I would read from one of four cork boards, which displayed handwritten notes to lost family members, phone numbers of people who had extra beds in their homes, a safe list, locations and times of numerous memorial services, an announcement stating that this was the last day the center would be open but that a website and hotline would continue to be available, and several copies of a laser-printed message which read: "Massages are available from Margaret in the back of the ballroom."

The first grieving person to arrive was a big man in his late fifties, wearing a yellow-and-green polo shirt stretched tight over his stomach. I realized that he was one of the people we were all here for because the words "Can I help you?" seemed to sink into him, rather than leaving him unaffected, or making him conventionally polite, or annoyed. He was pierced with sadness and gratitude by the question. He had not been to the support center before and he was dazed and needed us to tell him what to do.

At around eleven, two other volunteers were made greeters. One was a twenty-one-year-old who had just graduated from Tulane and moved to New York. He was wearing a white T-shirt, an unbuttoned and untucked blue Oxford, baggy denim cargo pants, a necklace of small, white shells, through which he'd threaded a dangling pair of sunglasses, and an off-white baseball cap. He said: "I'm unemployed. So it's not like I have anywhere else to be. I worked here two days last week, too."

I said: "Wow."

He said: "The worst thing I saw was a guy who was sitting on the stairs with his head in his hands because he'd quit the Friday before it happened."

The other new volunteer was a young woman wearing white

jeans and a white tank top who had two parallel black pen marks running up and down her nose. She told me she'd dropped out of college and come to New York looking for a "fashion industry internship." She was from a small town in California. She kept losing track of what she was talking about as people spilled out of the elevators and said who they'd lost and great washes of sadness and empathy passed over her face. She said: "I graduated from high school in '99. My generation—we've had nothing. We really want to participate in something. We want to help. You had"—a second's pause—"Vietnam."

I said: "I missed Vietnam. You graduated high school in '99? How old are you?"

"Twenty."

"I was your age in the Gulf War."

I wanted to ask about the pen marks on her nose. But I was worried they might not be pen marks, but unusual pigmentation.

"Well—we all really want to do something. That's why I'm here."

They had to be pen marks.

We started talking about the president. I said: "Everyone thinks we need to support him, but we should probably just impeach his ass fast."

She nodded in agreement.

A group of four solemn, middle-aged black women arrived. One of them said: "We've come to get the picture of our son. Where is it?"

They looked at me as though I would know. I could not tell them where this precious thing was. I could not tell them that this was my first day and that I did not even know anyone's name. I knew the CEO of Cantor Fitzgerald was Howard Lutnick and that was it. Hundreds of pictures of missing people covered a wall in the ballroom about a hundred feet long. The wall looked like a quilt. But they were all color Xeroxes, and these women were looking for a real photograph.

I imagined that it was a baby picture. I could see my mom doing that. More people were coming and we had to greet them. I told the women it was certainly on the wall in the ballroom. I felt them thinking: *A lot of good it did leaving his picture here. He's still gone.*

The girl and I started talking about the likely military response.

She said: "I have a friend in the Navy and he told me that we just bomb all the time, in all these places, whenever we feel like it, and it's all completely secret."

I thought unpatriotic thoughts about America. How we'd all been living in a bubble of ease for the last ten years while bombing. How, thanks to our droneish work ethic, the attack was on big office buildings full of prompt people eager to earn money. Were this Spain no one would have been in those buildings. Why couldn't the US be opposed in values by someplace that wanted us to take long siestas and eat for hours at midday—and would stop at nothing to undermine our current system of insufficient sleep and bolted sandwiches?

We were joined by a man in his late twenties called John, with long curly hair and very blue eyes. He said: "Bush looked good today. He just talked to reporters at the White House and he was really on a roll. Speaking extemporaneously for a few minutes at a time. He's good at that kind of back-and-forth. It takes him a few days to get a handle on situations. But now he knows what's going on and he's really impressive."

We were silent. Then he said: "Have you heard the international reaction to what's happening? I have an Icelandic friend. You know, Iceland? This guy said that on Tuesday a group of four or five Algerians and Tunisians—people who work in the canneries up there for a few months at a time and make five thousand dollars and then leave—were spotted jumping around in their yards having a little whoop-up, you know, after hearing the news. So this got around and a bunch of Icelandic guys went over and beat them till they had to scrape them off the ground. Like almost to death. You know the Scandinavians." He laughed.

"I don't think that's a good thing," I said.

The twenty-year-old was silent. Her nose pen strokes looked like the Twin Towers combined with the Leaning Tower of Pisa. Maybe she had put them there on purpose? John said: "It's bad if attacks on Arabs are unprovoked, but if people are celebrating they've got it coming. I'm telling you, if someone did that right next to me on that day I don't think that I'd be able to resist just beating them. To death or close to death."

At this point I was sent to find a Plaza security employee to help someone park their car. I found a burly-looking man in a suit and when I asked if he was security he dropped what he'd been doing, tensed, and strode down the corridor in the direction I'd come from, looking from side to side and barking, "What's the problem?" over his shoulder.

"Nothing. No problem. Something about parking," I said.

When I returned to the elevators I saw John talking intensely to the twenty-year-old, who was listening and nodding in just the same way she'd been listening and nodding when I was talking to her.

The others were sent out to Kinko's, and I was briefly alone. Then a young Asian man dressed in an immaculate gray suit and gray tie joined me. He was wearing a name tag that said "Kristina."

I asked him how he happened to be here.

"I had a friend who worked there," he said.

"I'm sorry," I said.

"It's no big deal for me. It's not like I'm in his family. They're really suffering."

"How did you know each other?"

"We met in college, through a mutual friend I knew in high school. Yeah, man, Sean—that was his name." He shook his head and smiled. "He was a total derelict." Pause. "What's crazy is that he's got an identical twin and I don't think anyone here knows about that. He's just like him. And he's coming out here now. Man, when the people at Cantor see him it'll blow them away. He's just like Sean."

We were silent for a second. It occurred to me that all the people who might recognize Sean's identical twin had probably perished.

"Now he's gonna have to rage twice as hard for both of them," Kristina added.

Meanwhile, sad people were arriving in numbers that would soon overwhelm the shrinks. The sad people were black, white, Irish, Latin American, English, South Asian, East Asian. But they all looked the same. All of them looked like they never again wanted to see pain inflicted on anyone. In even the most trifling acts—signing their names, drinking water, walking—they were slow and gentle. Time after time I had to hold the elevator doors for them so they wouldn't get caught. The sad people who came in groups would put forward the least sad among them to speak. The saddest were almost impossible to speak to; their sadness made them far too distant. Saddest of all were those who were alone.

A young man stepped off the elevator and advanced five feet toward me. I said: "Can I help you?"

He was wearing baggy gray cargo pants, a gray-blue, too-big, crew-necked shirt with dark maroon pinstripes, loafers, a gray-blue backpack with both straps on, wire-rim glasses. Everything about him was muted. And he could not speak. "Yes," he whispered. Everyone else in the elevator stood behind him, waiting, not wanting to walk past.

"My friend," he said even more softly, with barely any air in his lungs. "I'm. I'm. I'm." He choked up.

I touched his arm and said: "It's OK. You're in the right place."

Kristina seemed desperately to want to do something. He

paced distractedly around us, letting people from behind filter past ungreeted. Then he stepped in decisively and asked, with efficiency and cheer: "Can I bring you something to drink?"

The young man moaned, and then started to cry. Everyone around us hushed. Not knowing what to do I asked the man to follow me. Kristina said he would try and get a counselor. I guided the man over to a long table where we were signing people in, and said: "There are other people here, too. Other people who have lost people. You're not alone. Please just write down your name so we know you're here."

Holding the pen so tightly his fingers went white, he started to write, very slowly: "R-o-b-e-r-t L———."

I uncapped a blue magic marker and carefully copied what he was writing onto a name tag. Once he had a name tag everything would become normal. It took fully thirty seconds to write the tag. Then I tried to peel it and realized that I had been writing on the waxy reverse, not on the sticker side. This seemed like a monstrous fuck-up. No one could bear any further delays.

I flipped the tag over and wrote his name again, causing some of the blue ink from the not yet dry side to seep into the tablecloth. I placed it on his chest.

A counselor arrived. She had a red bob. But she didn't approach us. Instead she stood a few feet off, like a meter maid. I kept looking at her while stroking his back. She kept standing there. I tried to telegraph the message: I've got the blue dot, you've got the orange dot. They've given us these dots for a reason. The red-bobbed woman kept standing still, but eventually nodded, and I moved back to the elevator.

*   *   *

After people were signed in a dark-haired woman in her fifties took great care to pin a red-white-and-blue lapel ribbon on each new arrival, like she was dressing children, or putting the finishing touches on a wedding party. The grieving ones offered the least resistance.

Bellhops and waiters from the Plaza—all either Eastern European (as in one particularly jolly, paunchy, white-haired man with a name tag that said "Rolf," who ushered a bunch of young waiters into the elevator saying, "Age before beauty!"), or Latin American, or South Asian—kept taking the ribbons and sneaking off. They loved them. They'd sidle up, palm one, along with a fake-pearl-tipped straight pin, act as if they'd just remembered some important task in a distant part of the hotel, and hustle off into the elevator, hands attaching red-white-and-blue to white coats. It's possible that every waiter in the hotel made his way up to the landing outside the ballroom, where we were set up.

The black-clad security man approached me when the lapel-pin woman had left her post for a moment. He said, "I hope this isn't an imposition." Pause. "But could I possibly take one of those ribbons?"

"Sure. Of course!" I said.

He took one and moved to go.

I said, "Don't forget one of these," pointing to a straight pin.

"Yes," he said.

I picked up the straight pin and raised the ribbon higher than he was holding it, up to his button hole, and attached it to his black suit.

Soon the ribbon supply was exhausted. Volunteers were employed to replenish it. We had the three colors needed to make the flag but lacked staples to put them together. Two people with blue dots were dispatched to Staples to buy staples. When they returned a young woman took them and sat Indian style on the marble floor cutting strips to the proper length and clamping them together like an art project.

* * *

The tall, blonde Englishwoman in white—almost everyone had decided to wear either all black or all white (I had gone for black and brown)—asked me if I could stay for another shift. She lent me her cell phone so I could make calls to arrange this. I got a friend to walk my dog.

A tall, elegant, Arabian-looking man strode out of the elevator and said: "I'm from the Bubble Lounge." The Bubble Lounge is a champagne bar in Tribeca. He was dressed in what looked like a very expensive blue button-down shirt. He reached out and shook my hand. "I just wanted to offer space or money or whatever I could. You guys were in there all the time and this really hurts us, too."

Kristina was still thinking about Robert L. "I can't believe I offered that man a drink. I'm an idiot." He looked pained.

I said: "That's actually what they told us to do earlier. Offer something to drink. It's OK."

It occurred to me that the question "Can I bring you something to drink?" was part of the very fabric of the Plaza Hotel's ballroom. I changed the subject.

"What do you do?"

He said: "I've been working out of my home with a company that has Cantor as one of our clients."

I imagined him not wearing his beautiful gray suit, but in sweat pants in Brooklyn, doing a spreadsheet and getting a joke e-mail from Sean at Cantor Fitzgerald.

"But now I'm applying to graduate business programs. I'd like to go to Pepperdine, in California. Man, that'd be the life. California. The weather! I want to just be on the beach, you know."

The idea of anyone ever going to Pepperdine again seemed patently ridiculous. We were going to send more blue-dot people to Afghanistan and make more people without dots. And then they would quietly send more of their blue-dot people over here.

John, the Bush supporter, stopped to talk with us for a moment. He introduced himself to Kristina.

"Who's Kristina?" he asked.

Kristina said: "Kristina? That's my girlfriend. Why?"

A dark-skinned woman with a cane stepped out of the elevator. She had long black hair and looked like an aging Spanish flamenco dancer, or a Portuguese fado singer. She was wearing black, many, many layers of black—long skirt, sweater, blouse—dangly jewelry, and ample, dusky makeup. She looked like a professional mourner. She had come to offer her services.

She spoke softly, almost inaudibly. "I saw what Mr. Lutnick said on TV last night and… help… moving… need to tell him… understand… must talk with him about… special… called to do."

I said he wasn't here at the moment. She clouded up and whispered a repetition of the above, with more urgency.

I said: "Why don't you talk to the blonde woman in white over there? She should know more about when he's coming and what to tell you." She drifted across the marble and stood in front of the volunteer registration area.

The woman at the sign-in desk next to me asked, nervously: "Did she maybe need to *sign in*?" A person who looked like they needed to sign in was someone who looked like they were troubled or suffering or about to lose control.

Two empty-faced women, like bombed-out buildings themselves, stood near us, their eyes unfocused. They looked like mother and daughter. One was a slightly smaller, younger version of the other. Their faces registered pain in the same way. They wore red hearts pinned to their sweatshirts. I stepped around Kristina and asked: "Can I get you anything?"

"No. We're leaving," they said, and continued to stand still as elevator doors opened and closed and people came and disappeared.

Kristina and I resumed our conversation about graduate school. He had replaced his "Kristina" name tag.

I said: "Pepperdine, dude!"

He said: "Man, the beach!"

I said: "I really hope you end up there."

"Unfortunately, most of the schools that I've applied to are in the Northeast," he said.

I wondered what his girlfriend thought.

A serene, dark-haired man in his mid-thirties named Steve, who by some miracle of public transport was one of the only surviving Cantor employees from the New York office, came up to us and said: "Everyone's asking me: 'Who are all these wonderful people?' 'They're just regular people, volunteers,' I tell them. You all are doing an incredible job."

I saw Robert, the man who could not speak, reading the message board.

I approached and saw that the back of his head, where the arms of his glasses wrapped behind his ears, was pulsing. I'd never seen this part of the body register emotion. It was vivid. People kept coming. More than Kristina could deal with alone. Here was my excuse. I was afraid of getting too close to Robert. I decided to let him be.

People got out of the elevator. The man I still thought of as Kristina and I delivered our phrase. "Can I help you?" I said repeatedly.

A dark-haired woman in her late thirties, beautiful, drawn, steely, matter-of-fact, said, "My husband is gone from the World Trade Center," and walked right by me.

Seemingly the same woman, but thirty years older, said: "My son is missing from the 104th floor of the World Trade Center."

Everyone always specified that it was the World Trade Center, apart from a well-dressed man in his mid-thirties who said, simply: "My brother was a Cantor Fitzgerald employee." With a look of great cordiality on his face he waited for me to explain the forms we had. He signed in. An older, tired man with a face full of broken blood vessels, who looked like a Scottish golf pro, had to be his dad.

Standing behind two older black women who looked like her mother and aunt was a teenage girl, pretty, sassy, wearing a huge Stars and Stripes Cat in the Hat top hat, beneath which her face was hollow, empty, crushed. One of the older women said: "My daughter was a temp. I think she was there that day. We haven't heard from her." The Cat in the Hat girl stared blankly in the direction of the message board.

Five Spanish-speaking women wearing clothes that suggested they had just come from cleaning a building on the night shift pushed the youngest in their group to the front. She pointed to an older woman and said: "Her son. He worked as a caterer there. She thinks he was there. She has not heard from him." She looked at me as though I might at least be able to put the question to rest.

A tall, thin, handsome man, speaking with a Midwestern accent, said: "I'm from Howard Lutnick's hometown and I just came out to see him."

An Upper West Sideish woman with huge curly hair and a long jacket, over a cardigan, over a dress, said, her voice thick New York: "I've brought back the CEO's wife's cell phone. She lost it. This is it." She waved a silver, plastic, folded-in-half object at me.

There was a man who was so bent over he looked like a Muppet without a puppeteer—with his sunken, sagging cheeks and days of stubble, he looked like Fozzie Bear in particular. He stood behind two women, one of whom said: "My son was in the World Trade Center and we haven't heard from him."

I said: "Can I help you?"

A tall man with a clerical intensity said: "Yes." He was wearing a black FDNY ball cap and a blue FDNY sweatshirt. He made blink-less eye contact, with bloodshot eyes, through steel-framed, circular glasses. "I've been here before. I've signed in and registered and been given a name tag—twice. Now I just need information. Benefit forms. Social Security."

A group of neat, slender, composed, preppy, South Asian men in shorts stepped off the elevator. One said: "I am looking for my brother who was employed by Cantor Fitzgerald."

I touched everyone who looked like they'd let me.

We gave them all name tags as quickly as we could. Name tags seemed to make us all closer. "Cantor is a family," people with dots on their tags said, and it seemed like the truth, not the corporate speak it would've been a week before. We all milled around with our name tags, doing the opposite of what strangers usually do when gathered in a hotel wearing name tags. Touching, crying, talking truthfully. I began to love the name tags and feel strongly about their necessity. Others needed them. Out on the streets, everywhere.

The professional mourner, apparently satisfied, left with a look of peace on her face.

The Bubble Lounge guy came to say good-bye and give me a firm, extended handshake. He seemed to love me because I was a Cantor employee. I was strong and helping my company in a time of need. I didn't tell him I was none of these things, that the real employees were off trading bonds. The Bubble Lounge did not need to know about this.

Muted Robert walked slowly into the elevator. His name, in my handwriting, was still where I'd pressed it.

The Englishwoman in white invited me to a memorial service in the ballroom before my shift ended. Kristina would take over the elevators. I went in and sat down at a table marked "104th Floor." From either end of the ceiling hung two crystal chandeliers, and in the center of the room was a disco ball. It was beautiful. I stared at it until I realized what it was and why it was there—weddings—and was then able to look away. Onstage there were black priests, Irish priests, Latino priests. Old, white-haired rabbis; young, red-headed rabbis. An older priest spoke. A young woman sang liltingly and badly, in a way that brought out the pathos all the more. A female rabbi read something. A Social Security representative with a wide tie that was a narrow American flag ran a little DMV in the corner.

I went to say good-bye to the Englishwoman in white. She asked me if I would volunteer in the future. I said I would.

She took my number. "We'll call you," she said. "I imagine there'll be lots to carry on doing." Then, as an afterthought, she said, "I'll give you my mobile number, too," and I wrote it down on a blank name tag.

On the subway I realized that I was still wearing my name tag. Out of vanity I did not remove it. Back home I stuck the other name tag, with the Englishwoman's number on it, to a bookshelf by my desk.

The next day I took a train to Vermont to visit Daphne (my wife), who was at a writer's colony. In a rural station a female Amtrak ticket taker, black, mid-thirties, kind-faced, confessed: "I'm worried that they're gonna start going for the trains—the terrorists. The ones that are still living here—being all nice!"

I didn't hear from Cantor Fitzgerald. Over the next few weeks life began, eerily, to resume. Normal things happened and then strange things happened. Sometimes simultaneously.

One night, within sight of the late-night-ballgame glow of the Trade Center site, I saw a blonde, loudly drunk woman who reminded me of a similarly drunk, blonde woman I'd met on September 11 and then forgotten about. I'd gone up to my roof and found some neighbors there whom I'd never spoken to before: two young guys, and this modelish-looking woman. They were passing round a bottle. It was dark. We were watching what looked like a high-plains tornado of smoke and debris blow steadily into Brooklyn. It had just been announced that Manhattan south of Fourteenth Street would be closed to everyone but residents, and by way of starting a conversation with these neighbors/strangers I told them this news. The blonde, drunk girl began to dance around the roof, with the smoke behind her, singing: "No work for me-ee! No work for me-ee!"

After the 11th I was feverish, like so many people, with the desire to do something. But also with the competing desire for all of this just to go away. After working that one day at the Plaza the worst of the fever abated.

Eager-to-help people were pouring in from all over the US. I walked my dog. I continued not to hear from Cantor Fitzgerald.

A few days after working at the Support Center I was skateboarding down Amsterdam Avenue from 125th Street, moving along the edge of a housing project. Three young boys, just shy of being teenagers, were playing around on a patch of grass next to the sidewalk. One saw me, straightened, and as I passed he ran out and punched me.

I stopped.

"What are you doing?" I asked. Silence. He didn't seem to expect that I would speak to him—more like he would hit me and I would disappear. "Why did you do that?" I was laughing. "You don't even know me!"

He looked shy then, and started half-laughing himself, embarrassed. I said, "These are difficult times. We all need to stick together."

"OK," he said. He walked up and held out his hand in a gesture that occupied some gray area between a high five and a handshake. We touched. Then someone yelled for him, and he ran away fast.

I originally thought that the attacks resembled Pearl Harbor, but I then started to research the 1906 earthquake in San Francisco. Almost everything was the same, in specific details and general surreality. The quake, like the planes, hit without warning: at 5:12 in the morning, when people were asleep in bed and, unable to escape, were buried in the wreckage. When the shaking stopped people thought the worst was over. It was a beautiful, severely clear day. No one anticipated that fire would sweep the city, leveling five hundred blocks, just as no one anticipated that the Towers would collapse. In the end, a few more than three thousand San Franciscans were killed. The majority of the bodies were unrecovered, incinerated in temperatures in excess of 2000°F. Witnesses remarked on the beauty and grandeur of the fires. The city was closed, but people came from all over the country to volunteer, sneaking or talking their way past military checkpoints. Buildings were dynamited. There was ash everywhere. Eugene Schmitz, the previously vilified mayor, became an acclaimed national figure. Flyers like this one covered the city:

> Missing Mrs Bessie O. Steele Age 33, dark hair, brown eyes, 5 ft
> 5 in., weight 135, slender; Helen Steele 6 years old, brown eyes.
> Donald Steele 2 years old, blue eyes. Mrs. H.O. Wheeler Age 55,
> iron grey hair, eyes grey, 5 ft 2 in., heavy set, weight 150 lbs.

The fire chief was killed. People fought fires with wine. Refugees wandered through the streets with parrots on their shoulders and birdcages full of cats. Camaraderie formed and then evaporated. Nobody knew what to expect. Aftershocks struck, and it seemed like the whole thing was going to happen again. There were rumors. Someone said the same thing was happening in New York and Chicago in a pan-American doomsday. Afterward people bragged that they'd been a part of it. There were massive fund-raising benefits featuring famous actors. Money poured in.

In the aftermath, Pauline Jacobson, a staff writer for the *San Francisco Bulletin*, wrote:

> Have you not noticed with your merest acquaintance of ten days
> back how you wring his hand when you encounter him these days,
> how you hang onto it like grim death as if he were some dearly
> beloved relative you were afraid the bowels of the earth will
> swallow up again… Some take it that we are such "brave, brave
> women," such "strong, strong men"… Bah! That's spreadeagle,
> yellow journalist rot!… To talk of bravery is previous. Wait till
> this novelty has worn off, this novelty of having been spilled
> out on the world like so many rats caught in a hole, like so many
> insignificant ants on the face of the earth, petted objects of charity
> and of kindness, the focal point of all the world. Wait till we have
> settled back into the old trying grooves of traditional civilization
> with the added trying struggles inherited… It is then time to bring
> out one's adjectives of bravery and courage.

On October 3 I visited a website (part of NYC.gov) that listed all the firemen who had died. There was also a bereaved letter from fire commissioner Thomas Von Essen, who had briefly become a celebrity for his suffering. I was used to seeing him grim and choking back tears, but on the site, in his official photo, he was smiling. I started to cry in huge gasps. I went through a good deal of toilet paper reading his ultimately forgettable message. Then reading his bio. Then reading about other firemen. It was the first time I had ever felt such overwhelming emotions about a public event.

I found myself watching TV and finding everything on TV to be at once knowing and false. Knowing seemed to be the new tone we had adopted in the face of the vastness of everything we didn't know.

Heading uptown on an express train, mid-December, I was standing in the center of a semi-crowded car doing what I thought was a pretty impressive balancing act: holding an umbrella, a backpack, a skateboard, the overhead grab bar during sudden decelerations, and ripping open and reading a bunch of Christmas cards. I was pleased because it was a bumper mail day for me. I did this for four stops, from Houston to 34th Street-Penn Station, at which point, as I was about to open the final envelope, a man in his early forties, who had been sitting directly in front of me the whole time, caught my eye and shouted, in a thick West Indian accent, and with great, pent-up hostility: "I goalie dewlap in that Marilyn mafia!"

I looked at him closely. He was wearing a herringbone cap, a perfectly smooth, black, weatherproof jacket, and very blue blue jeans, with cargo pockets.

I said: "What? Me?"

He said the same thing again, and this time I could make out the words *don't*, *like*, and *face*. He was saying that he didn't like my face. My obvious enjoyment of my Christmas cards was galling to him.

"I'm not sure what you're saying," I said again. All the people sitting with him on the bench had turned to stare. They seemed to dislike me and my Christmas cards, too.

NO WORK FOR ME

He said the same phrase a third time, with anger and now a bit of panic in his voice.

I looked at the man next to him, who was Filipino, in his fifties, and wearing a khaki raincoat. His expression was impassive. "I'm sorry," I said. "I still don't understand you."

Then the man said, very slowly, and with a great deal of force and deliberation: "I Don't Like You Opening That Mail In My Face!"

And I realized that he believed my Christmas cards might be contaminated with anthrax.

"I'm sorry," I said.

I shoved the last, unopened letter into my jacket pocket.

"I didn't know you were worried about that."

"Yees," he hissed. "I'm *worried* about *that*."

A friend told me to go see a show of tabloid press photographs from September 11 that hadn't been published because they were too graphic. The suppression of these images, which showed the real results of violence, it seemed to me, only led to more violence.

The show was at a small basement gallery in the East Village. All the wall space had been used.

There was a photo of an EMS squad standing in the perfectly clean and empty plaza in front of tower number two (all the wreckage must have been falling on other sides) about to enter the building. A label said that the building fell ten minutes later and the entire group was lost.

There was another such picture of a group of firefighters, one of whom was smiling grimly, just before they entered a building, and the building collapsed.

But two photographs of specific victims stood out indelibly and above all.

The first showed a human head at the center of a pit of rubble and debris, with a group of firefighters gathered around. Almost all the hair on this head had been burned off. The eye sockets were empty, and the skin was charred. Race, gender, age were all impossible to determine. The head was also much bigger than it should have been, and the expression on the face was strangely neutral.

My reaction was to look away, but as this seemed to deny the dead even more respect, I looked back. The pit was full of pipes and concrete and may have also contained, buried further down, the person's whole body. All the rescuers were looking away, even though this was obviously the reason they had gathered there. The head was like a movie prop or Halloween mask. And at first I thought maybe it *was* a Halloween mask, from some nearby magic shop that had also been destroyed. That was the kind of small business that used to exist in the old alleys in this part of downtown.

I looked more closely, leaning into the picture, which felt like leaning into something radioactive, and I noticed the ears: delicate and undeniably human. These were a real person's ears, with strange curls and cartilage. I looked at them for as long as I could stand it.

Then, as I was leaving, I saw the second indelible picture: a clean-shaven man in a blue shirt and khakis, just a focal adjustment shy of being recognizable, falling through the air headfirst, body rigid, arms folded like a pharaoh's, the uninterrupted, waterlike facade of one of the trade towers filling the entire background. His body was at a slight diagonal to the vertical of the building. It seemed like the man had chosen this falling pose on purpose. It was full of surrender. It also had a cinematic quality to it. The photograph was almost identical to the promotional poster for the '80s Robert De Niro movie *The Mission*, an airbrushed rendering of a man plunging over a massive waterfall somewhere in the jungles of South America, rigid because he was tied to a cross, and frozen at the exact same angle as this man, but about to enter a huge, white plume of mist. Here it was in reality. With no white mist, but concrete and steel at the bottom of the sky.

For months I looked at the name tag and phone number next to my desk and told myself I would call the Englishwoman in white soon— if I didn't hear from Cantor Fitzgerald in the next week, or two weeks maybe. But I was delaying. Finally I grabbed the tag off my bookshelf and called the number before I could really think about it.

After a couple of rings a female voice with a bright English accent said: "Hello."

I said, nervously: "Hi. My name is Sean. I worked as a volunteer for Cantor Fitzgerald at the support center back in September. You gave me your number, and it's actually the only contact number I have, and I've been wondering if there was still any volunteering going on, still anything to do."

"Oh," she said. "I actually live in Chicago now." She paused. "You should look on the website for information. Have you looked on the website?" I remembered that many people at the support center had talked about how when the center closed the website would carry on.

I said I had seen the website some time ago, but would have another look. I did not mention that the website, with its bottomless links and emphasis on bond trading, offered no information except how to donate money. There was a silence.

Then I asked, awkwardly: "When did you move to Chicago?"

"I've been here for four weeks now."

"Are you still working for Cantor Fitzgerald?"

"No, someone else," she said ambiguously.

I felt strongly that I was intruding on her resumed life. What the hell was I doing?

I said: "I'm really sorry to bother you. You probably don't remember me."

Without hesitation she said: "No! I do! You're the soup guy!"

For a moment I thought about what this might mean. Then I said: "No…"

"You do work in a restaurant, though?"

"No. I was a greeter for a day at the Plaza. I stood by the elevators, and you asked me if I could do more in the future."

"You were there with your friend!" she said happily, like she'd put it all together. I could hear some outdoor, city-type noise behind her. I imagined she was standing by Lake Michigan in the same all-white outfit she'd worn that day at the Plaza.

I said: "No, no. I was by myself." There was some white noise in the background. "But of course there were so many people there. I'll check the website again. And I'm really sorry to bother you."

Then, as I was about to hang up, she said, her tone gone sweet: "If you're ever in Chicago, give me a call."

And we said good-bye.

USING SO LITTLE

2003

*Clop*p. Ssh… RRRaaaaooooowwwwwwrrrrrrrrrrrrrr—
reeeeeeeeeeeeeeeeppp—rrraaaaoooooowwwwwwrrrrrrrrppppppp—
tic!—rrraaaaoooooowwwwwwrrrrrrrrrrrrrrr—
reeeeeeeeeeeeeeeeppp—*tic!*-schrapp!—

BAM!-COMBP!—RRrraaaaoooooowwwwwwrrrrrrrrrrrrrrr— —
TNK!—rrraaaaoooooowwwwwwrrrrrrrrrrrrrrr…

Skateboarding, from the outside, looks more like a metaphor than a thing in and of itself. Take the following pictures from old magazines: a girl in jeans, high tops, and T-shirt, arms outspread for balance, high up on a half pipe with a floppy white prom bow in her hair. A boy sliding his board along a handrail four feet above the pavement while wearing only a right shoe, because his entire left leg is in a cast. Another kid all in black, but with white socks, sliding along the lip of an indoor pool, with delicate blue tiles at its edge (most of them ripped out by skating), rubble in the background, a toilet seat in the foreground, and a big skylight, with what looks like a knotted sheet hanging from one corner, providing both access and illumination. Sleeping bags in the bottom of a pristine pool behind an unsold, newly constructed suburban mansion—full of boys sleeping off a day of skating.

Skateboarders sprang up in the same moment as the modern city. Dirt and cobblestones disappeared and there we were! A 1952 photograph of the Children's Aid Society's Anything on Wheels derby shows a gang of kids from the Lower East Side of Manhattan, a handful of rogues (all out in front) with steel rollerskate wheels bolted to planks. The first skateboarders. They are girls and boys, black and white, from the city's poorest, most paved neighborhood, and they outnumber the spectating adults in the photograph by thirteen to one. The boy whose father takes him swimming, the girl whose mother takes her to the theater, children whose parents do things with them—these are not skateboarders.

It took off for real in the 1970s, a combination of surfers without waves and pools without water, drained by the California drought. Now, as the world becomes more like America, more paved and less natural, skating improves. We already outnumber football and baseball players in the US. We'll overtake global soccer next. Despoilment is gorgeous to a skateboarder.

The steepest hills in San Francisco—where I grew up and learned to skate—lead up to and around Russian Hill, which isn't a hill but a series of hills. From North Beach, at the bottom, you can see Russian Hill's hills rolling—planed into paved geometry, but rolling underneath. The steepest of these crests is in the middle of Filbert Street between Hyde and Leavenworth. The roadway midblock seems to disappear, like an incomplete section of elevated freeway. It looks as if the city is dangling nine hundred feet in the air. When you drive a car up to the lip it drops too steeply even to see ground past the end of the hood. The drop is demarcated by two yellow-and-black signs that say: STEEP GRADE AHEAD BUSES AND LARGE TRUCKS NOT ADVISABLE AND SHARP CREST 10 MILES PER HOUR.

My best friend, a boy now dead whose name was Blane Morf, got a skateboard while I was away at an Eastern boarding school. When I came home for summer vacation—on probation for a straight D-minus average, largely attributable to the fact that I was hazed mercilessly for being from San Francisco (making me a "fag")—I discovered that he was a skater. Since there weren't many other skaters, Blane didn't know any other skaters. And even if there had been, the kind of personality that's drawn to skateboarding is the kind of personality that's not given to sociability.

Skateboarders are lonely. Skateboarders are not well loved.

I was lonely and not well loved!

I tried his board. He taught me a few things. It was no fun watching while the other skated, so he begged me to get my own. I got some money out of my mother (guilty about boarding school), went down to the skate shop, and bought myself a skateboard. Then I climbed to the top of Russian Hill.

At the crest of Green, where it meets Leavenworth, is the lower of the summits of Russian Hill. Green then slopes down again, leveling off midblock on its way to Jones and my house, behind which is the higher summit, at the end of Vallejo. By San Francisco standards, this bit of slope isn't a hill, because it kinks back to horizontal after about half a block.

I set down my board, stepped on, pushed off. My plan was to roll the whole slope and use the flat to slow down gradually before the intersection. I had no backup plan.

The acceleration was instant. In a matter of seconds I was moving faster than my legs had ever taken me. After thirty feet I was moving faster than I'd ever moved outside of a car. Faster. Without thinking I locked my legs at the knees and stood as if I were trying to look over a fence, the instinct—a terrible instinct—being to get as far away as possible from the rushing tarmac. My knees should have been bent, body low, arms out to the sides. The board started rocking side to side, trucks (the metal suspension/steering system) slamming back and forth, fast, hard left, and then fast, hard right. It felt like the board was possessed and wanted to throw me off. I had what's known among skaters as the (dreaded) speed wobbles. And once they start there's no way to stay on.

I bailed just before the bottom of the slope and tried to run it out, knees aching when I hit the ground, going so fast it was like a wind was pushing me from behind. I kept my feet for ten feet and watched my new board rocketing down the block toward the intersection. Then the speed shoved me over. I pitched forward, screamed "Fuck!" with more emotion than I'd ever expressed in public (skateboarding, like learning a foreign language, offers a whole new personality), and as I heard my voice echo off the buildings I slammed onto the street, hands first, torso second, thighs third, calves and feet up in the air behind me—and began to slide.

This was like bobsledding! I had all the speed of a bobsledder. But without the sled, or snow. There was just me and some fabric and the concrete.

I was no longer going down the center of the street, but, since my last step had been off my right foot, I was plowing into the oncoming left lane, toward the parallel-parked cars on the far side of the street, my destination the front tire of a dark-blue two-door Honda. I braced for impact, closed my eyes, missed the tire, and instead went under the driver's-side door—a deeper dark filled my head—and kept going, calves banging against the car's plastic frame and flopping back down, head dinging off something in the undercarriage and then down to the street, until I was wedged under the trunk, between gas tank and pavement, my cheek jammed up on the curb.

The curb is the piece of the city that skaters are most often concerned with. Mine was cold, and I could smell it: oil and salt. I also could taste it in the back of my throat. Piss. I'd never looked properly at curbs until I learned to skate, and I haven't looked at them the same way since. Steel-edged ones make for long, fast grinds (slides on your trucks). Regular ones make for loud, sloppy grinds. This one was plain and clean and angular, no rounded steel edge (coping, as skaters and masons call it). I was feeling a strange mixture of sensations: pain, embarrassment, isolation, and a pleasurable sort of intimacy with the hidden parts of the city. I felt like I had just survived a rare experience. I was glad to be still. I thought that beneath a Honda might be a good place to lie low for a while and nurse my wounds. I had never crawled under a car on the street before. There was something good about it. There was un-burned-off morning fog under there.

Then—*shit!*—I remembered my board. I scrambled back out.

I stood, but I couldn't move. The slide beneath the car had ripped my pants off. I stood on top of Russian Hill in my underwear, ankles cuffed together. I pulled my pants back up. They were full of holes. My shirt looked like someone had thrown acid at me. My chin was sore. The skin was grated off the palms of my hands. I started to run.

A man and two women, all middle-aged, him in a light brown suede jacket, came running toward me. The women hollered: "Oh my God!" The man bellowed: "Are you OK? Are you OK?"

"Yeah, yeah—I'm fine! *Fine!*" I said, angry, and then I ran faster, chasing my board, which had made it across the intersection, my hamburger hands throbbing, holding up my trousers, feeling slow compared to moments before. I'm proud to say that I got on and pushed the last twenty feet to my house.

* * *

For the next four years, being from San Francisco meant being from the world capital of skateboarding. The city where *Thrasher* magazine was published, and half the photos in it were taken. After sliding beneath the car I came out in another city. I'd never understood skateboarding before that fall. Skating is a feeling. If you really want to get it, you have to do it.

The magazine—which has been around since 1981, starting up at the lowest point in the history of skateboarding, with no hope of making any money—almost succeeds in conveying skateboarding, without skateboarding. Every skater used to read *Thrasher*. To *thrash*, according to *Webster's*, means "to dispense a beating" (to curb, ledge, handrail, coping); "to move in an uncontrolled, restless manner" (inevitable on a skateboard); or, in sailing, "to move against the wind." All are correct. And there is no higher honor that can be accorded a skateboarder than to be considered a thrasher.

Thrasher used to sneer at those of us who carried our skateboards. So for years I would skate up hills, which is much harder and slower than sprinting up them. They also used to disparage skaters who didn't skate every day. I never understood these people. Obviously you should skate every day. And think about it every minute of every day. I never went anywhere without my skateboard. I watched less TV than my parents. I skated in my room when it rained. There were days of fulfillment and frustration as a skater, days you fell down and days you landed, but nothing felt better than the way you'd sleep at the end of a day when your feet had hardly touched the ground— drifting off, board beside your bed, reliving it as you went under, still feeling the motion in your body, like the way you feel the rocking of a boat after you've come ashore, and then dreaming about doing it all over again.

At the height of my skateboarding abilities—and I was never better than average—I would fly down hills, turn the board sideways and slide the wheels to decelerate, then pull the slide all the way round into a 180, ride backwards, then kick-turn forwards again, then do another slide, plant one leg and boost ("boneless") off a notch cut in the hill for someone's garage, fly, replace my foot on the board, land, roll, pop off the curb into the intersection at the bottom of the hill, and weave through traffic to the next block. There are various stopping methods: stepping back on the tail, taking the board from level to a 45-degree tilt and then skidding wood on concrete (acceptable then, distasteful now); dragging your rear foot while maintaining balance on the board with your front one; or, most elegant and difficult, turning the whole board sideways and putting the urethane of your wheels into a long, controlled slide.

The skateboard is the most versatile urban conveyance. In a crowded city, no one on foot or bike or in a car can ever hope to keep up with you. Up and down stairs. On buses and trains in an instant. Kick it up into your hands and it's a club to ward off danger; throw it back down and you're gone. In a paved landscape skateboarders are both dangerous and invisible, inhabitants of the interstices—rats, the city a series of tunnels and chutes, skaters perfectly adapted.

One summer day, a year after I'd started skating, a few months after I was kicked out of the boarding school, Blane and I were cruising down Market Street. Market is a long, wide, diagonal slot through the city to the bay. We were moving through the edge of the run-down Tenderloin, SF's skid row, and I was feeling confident from the good skating I'd put in the day before. Blane was about ten feet ahead.

Market Street is like a river for skateboards. It slopes slightly, heads toward the bay, and requires almost no effort to ride to the end. It takes you past run-down buildings and drunks in the Tenderloin, canyons of skyscrapers and businessmen in the financial district, and then both mixed in with tourists at the end, as it empties out like a waterfall into the basin of the Embarcadero Plaza, at the edge of the bay, where all the city's skaters used to gather. Market's sidewalks are polished brick and so beautifully laid as to be almost seamless (again, only a skater or a mason would notice). The seams are just wide enough to make a lot of noise without slowing you down. When you click over them they send a wall of sound ahead: the unmistakable skateboard rumble of rolling urethane interrupted by wood tails hitting cement and occasional squeals of wheels going sideways into slides—Market being so easy to slide, the polished brick offering much less friction than tarmac or cement. Cloppssh... RRRaaaaooooowwwwwwwrrrrrrrrrrrr—reeeeeeeeeeeeeeeepppp—rrraaaaooooowwww wwrrrrrrrppp... The noise put us in a trance. We'd push off for more speed, the decibels would spike, heads would whip around up ahead, conversation would go back and forth.

After a few minutes we passed a dirty brick building. A punk kid—skinny, bitter expression, tight, pale face broken out with zits, black pants pulled close to his legs with glimmering silver safety pins—stepped out of its doorway, looked at Blane, sneered, cocked his head at me, and said: "Skaters suck."

Then he kicked back and smirked.

I looked him in the eye and said: "*You* suck." This was something I would never have said as a pedestrian.

His face fell in surprise. "What?" he said, jerking straight. "What did you say?"

"You suck," I repeated.

He faded into the doorway. It had been such a righteous burn I figured he'd combusted in shame.

Then, as I drew level with the doorway, he reemerged. And four skinheads in flight jackets and Doc Martens popped out behind him. The punk pointed at me and shouted: "Get him!" All four leaped and missed.

Blane and I started flailing our legs—kicking way out in front of our chests and all the way back behind us—and propellering our arms, crouching down low, doing all we could to move our boards as fast as possible. They started running in their heavy, many-eyed boots, awkwardly, as though they were tripping down a flight of stairs, over and over again. We pushed hard, going for all the speed we could get, our skateboard sounds amplifying and people in front of us now turning and scattering, their faces registering unmitigated fear of the spectacle that was thundering toward them—which, through my own terror, I was just able to register as totally cool.

Their boots weren't stopping. They weren't just trying to scare us. They kept shouting: "Come back here!" We skated harder, and their shouts, as they explained how they were going to kill us (first pummelling us down to the sidewalk with our skateboards, then kicking and stomping), started to get strained. A skateboard, with sixty-millimeter wheels that require minimal impetus to complete a revolution, and so get up to speed—is probably faster getting off the line than any other vehicle. Much, much faster than sprinting or bicycling or skiing; or, for the first two seconds (an eternity), a Kawasaki Ninja or an F-16. We skated harder—we were going to get away. Unless we hit a big crack and our wheels got caught.

From the point of view of a sixteen-year-old in 1986, skinheads were the most terrible force in America. Arousing sufficient anger to provoke pursuit: this was an honor, like being in a movie, or the pages of *Thrasher*. There were fabled skinhead murders, and whole

San Francisco neighborhoods—the Haight—under their dominion. We were skating for our very lives. A single skinhead possessed the might of an entire high school. But four of them? If we won, made them look weak, it would be truly awesome. Like having skate-granted superpowers. Our skateboards made us better than them. And skateboards were what had provoked them. They were envious.

After a couple of blocks I dove down a stairwell for the mono-line subway that runs the length of Market Street—useful as a sort of skateboard chairlift to get you back up so you could flow down Market again—kicking my board up into my hand without stopping, flying/falling down the stairs, then leaping the turnstile as though SF were NYC while Blane ducked into a dusty sports memorabilia shop. On the platform there was silence, no sound of pursuing boots, and then a train. In the sports memorabilia shop Blane feigned interest in an autographed San Francisco 49ers Super Bowl game ball (there was nothing skateboard related). When Blane later told me he'd been familiar with the players who'd autographed the ball, and that he'd actually enjoyed the sports memorabilia, I realized that his commitment to skateboarding had been surpassed by my own. After fifteen minutes of browsing he got the owner to see if it was safe to leave (a store proprietor would not have helped a fully committed skateboarder), and then skated away to the Embarcadero.

We arrived at the same time, told our story to the twenty or so assembled skaters in an adrenalized rush, and then a semi-homeless skate-rat kid, whom I considered a friend, stepped out of the pack and said: "You shouldn't go messing with skins. You're gonna get our asses kicked." Everyone was silent. Then he smiled, a chip-toothed skater's grin (one that I would copy after slamming directly onto my upper incisors a couple weeks later), and shouted: "You suck!"

And so I went deeper into the other San Francisco.

* * *

A lot of letters were sent to *Thrasher* about running, or being hurt, or persecuted, or lawless, or luckless—written by skaters with names like Erik Tunafish, Kenny "Gator Bait" Walsh, Bug, Chunk, Skinard, Duckie, Schmoe, or, frequently, Incarcerated Skater. Skaters were lonely and harassed and unsupervised and rolling around all over America with nobody but each other to talk to. (Or locked up in sufficient numbers to justify a skaters' prison.) In a stack of the magazine, dating back to the 1980s, I found the following shouts of ignorance, confusion, joy, despair, insanity, and rebellion. From Kinston, North Carolina: "Hey, we live the fast life—it rules being a skater... Ever since I picked up a board my entire life has changed up. Right now it isn't really so great. I am locked down in a reform school for flipping out at school and for threatening my teacher." (Soon I would be, too.) The Deep South: "Me and the other skaters from the neighborhood built a halfpipe. While we were having a session, a bunch of Klanners pulled up in a pickup and threw a Molotov cocktail on the ramp. No one was hurt but the ramp burnt to the ground. The cops won't do anything because half of them are in the Klan." Lake Zurich, Illinois: "I went to the local 7-11... the manager hit me in the back of the head with a can of beef jerky." Colorado Springs, Colorado: "We were having lots of fun and then... our neighbor, 'William,' started drinking beer and staring at us. Then, out of nowhere, William started up a chainsaw and cut my [ramp] into six pieces." Westtown, New York: "I have been riding skateboards since 1976... I'm glad that skateboarding is a crime. I love being a fucking outlaw asshole." New York City: "I'm in a body cast and I can't wait to get out so I can skate again." Fort Grant, Arizona: "Fuck your 'zine and everything about skating. I'm sitting in Arizona State Prison for two years because of it." Redwood Shores, California: "I'm a

12-year-old skater… I have a problem. My parents don't really like to buy me shoes. I just wanted to know if it could happen—if I could get some shoes. If you guys could get me some free shoes, that would be great! If not, I'd understand." Melbourne, Florida: "Sometimes in conversation with acquaintances the question will come up, 'What do you miss most about freedom?' Without the slightest hesitation, I say: 'Skateboarding.' The looks I get in return are shocking to say the least. 'Dude, what about chicks? Beer? Parties?' Obviously these people have never spent all-nighters ollieing the gap in downtown." (To *ollie* is to simultaneously jump and kick the board so that it stays attached to your feet. To fly.) Wichita Falls, Texas: "I was skating with my friend Sam at McDonald's. We were skating the curb out front when a lot of parents and their kids went in for some kind of party. They were giving us bad looks. About five minutes later Ronald McDonald came out in his clown suit. He started griping and telling us to leave. I fell down and my board hit the curb and flew up and hit Ronald McDonald in the dick (groin)… Ronald McDonald is now firing assault charges on Sam and I. Wish us luck." Garland, Texas: "One day I came home and saw my mom's underwear on the ground by her door. I walk in her room and who do I see, but my black art teacher Mr. Woodron banging the hell out of my mom. The next day I asked her if she liked black guys. Expecting her to say no, she said yes and three months later my mom and my art teacher got married. Shows you how far lust for artistic men goes." (Much as San Francisco's counterculture is counterbalanced by a behind-the-scenes conservatism, the most surprising photos and stories in *Thrasher* seemed to come out of Texas.) Jacksonville, Florida: "Today is my birthday and the only thing I found in my mailbox was the March issue of *Thrasher*. Thanks for remembering!!"

Parents read *Thrasher*, too. The magazine, one wrote, "offends and harasses the educated reader." Another was confused. "My

15-year-old boy loves to skateboard. That's great. It's good, clean fun. Also good exercise. But tell me, what… the following topics have to do with skateboarding? 1. As-hole 2. F-uck 3. Sexy Lover 4. Warrior from Hell 5. Demonic Wizard 6. Cannibal Women 7. Lou Ferrigno getting laid…" This parent concluded, "Until today, I have allowed this trash in my home. But no more!"

Thrasher's editors would usually print an italicized response to each letter, signed "*T-ed.*"

> My best friend Sean is on death row for shooting both his parents
> while they slept. We perform rituals covered in blood, sometimes
> mixed with wine and urine. In 1989, five people were arrested in
> Mexico in connection with the slaughter of twelve people who
> were sacrificed and cannibalized by a satanic cult. One of the
> people arrested was my sister. We make sacrifices from hamsters to
> humans. If Satan calls us to sacrifice one of our own, then we do…
>
> Diana, the moon Goddess
>
> South Bend, IN
>
> *Hamsters? T-ed*

> I'm 17 and have been skating for almost 3 years now… Without
> it I don't know where I'd be. I have my good and bad days, but
> lately my days have been shitty. I've fucked both my ankles,
> and I'm too shook to try anything close to being big. Past few
> months I've also had real hard times to deal with, problems
> with my homies and the law. I've always been able to forget all
> my problems when I go skating, but these even haunt me when
> I skate. Fact is, skateboarding's all I got, and the thoughts of not
> being able to enjoy it keep me up every night… I want that feeling
> of putting everything I've got into my tricks, and wanting to push

them to the limits. I'm scared to not be a part of skateboarding; I don't know where I'd turn to. I tried to express my feelings in words, but they can't compare with how I feel, and probably many others. Can you give me some advice on this? Always loyal.

Curtis Dilley
Wilmington, NC

Try aromatherapy. T-ed

One time me and my friend were walking through our local mall and saw some people talking about God and stuff… I yelled, "God sucks!" and they looked at me like they wanted to kill me. This stupid lady who was their leader or pastor or whatever sat down next to us and demanded that we go with her to some church place. When we said no, she tried to force us. Then my friend yelled, "Security, this woman just touched my penis!" She got arrested… Another job well done by the local, apathetic, skateboarding losers…

Preston Deane
Harrisonburg, VA

Walking? T-ed

When a locked-up skater begged for a free subscription—"I'm hoping my years of devotion… along with the *Thrasher* tattoo I got on my arm at age 17 will pay off… I'm at your mercy"—he was told "*It sounds to me like yer dick is in yer hand. T-ed*." When the author of a long screed ended by asking, "Do you want to skate and have fun, or bake cookies with your mommy?" T-ed replied, "*There is nothing wrong with cooking with your mother.*" The succinct retort was something I was trying to master. That's why I'd told the punk kid he sucked. I was trying to be T-ed.

* * *

I loved *Thrasher* most when it claimed the unskateable for skaters. With each new issue I turned first to the cooking column: "Skarfing Material," written by "Chef-Boy-Am-I-Hungry," who declared his elevated taste by illustrating the first installment with a photograph of a 1975 Sebastiani "Proprietor's Reserve" Cabernet Sauvignon (a wine, in its '74 bottling, that reviewers on *cellertracker.com*, "the world's most complete database" of wine, described as "beautifully balanced and offering lots of pleasure"). Skarfing Material exploded and deflated food writing as if it could somehow see, in the early 1980s, what the genre would become. It still feels avant garde today. The Chef, skater that he was, always moved unpredictably between the low and the high. His ingredients included "Perrier from France," pheasant, fresh okra ("okra winphrey"), Cornish game hen, anisette liqueur ("if you're a recovering alcoholic or straight edge skip the anisette"), wine, fish stock, Velveeta, M&M's, Oreos, marshmallows and chow mein noodles (together), and "as much ice cream as your gut can take." He frequently called for "wieners." He once suggested that "While you let them cool, you might want to get some food coloring for some special hot dog colors."

Skarfing Material existed because nobody was cooking for us. The Chef cared. The Chef was, in his lawless way, wise. An early column offered a wide-ranging denouncement of McDonald's (illustrated by a kid projectile vomiting in front of the golden arches), and was full of facts about meat consumption and industrial agriculture that—more *Thrasher* prescience—were a couple decades ahead of their time. The Chef traveled to Europe ("I am in Italy, oh Italy"). He described how to "build" a salad, and suggested we purchase specialized cooking equipment, like steamer baskets and tongs, "If you can afford them." The Chef was the father I wanted.

As he wrote:

"O.K. this is what I did. I went to a grocery store across town, where I've never been before and I stole a whole bunch of groceries without getting caught. Now you don't have to do this because most of you are too impressionistic and would probably get caught." Recently, a skater I know taught a free class to inner-city kids at Asphalt Green, a recreation center run by the New York City Parks Department in upper Manhattan. When she brought her students a bag of apples they reacted first with confusion—"What *is* this?"— then joy—"It's delicious!" As the Chef had written several decades before: "What's wrong with fruit? Sometimes it seems as if humankind is losing its taste for fruit. Try to eat some everyday, besides, it's cheap... Some varieties come with a free sticker."

This was the voice of *Thrasher*: wily, dirty, broke but unbroken, dictionary checked out of the SF public library (*pietism*, *penultimate*, *suffragette*, *prosy*, and *magnum opus* fall right out of the column), a mélange of prose styles to match the incompatibility of his ingredients:

> Let me show you something... show you how to make...
> TORTELGAGGA-NAG-NAG with a zesty NO IF, AND, OR
> BUT SAUCE § The flea, upon reaching the blue tattoo of the
> naked lady surgeon, suddenly turned back to the right. I sensed
> the flea had some class. § Italy. This place is something else. Bad
> timing on my part landing here because everyone here is fully
> pissed-off at the United States for jacking those Achilles Lauro
> hijackers from the Egyptians who, I hear, are pissed-off at us
> as well, screamin' "air-piracy." A couple days ago a few high-
> ranking government officials quit their posts because they weren't
> stoked at all on this government's move releasing the alleged
> mastermind of the whole ship-hijacking ordeal from custody. And
> today Italy's government just went "pfoohfpuh!" § He had a gun.

Of course he had a gun, these days every finger is a weapon. Even
the simple kiss. § I hunched tighter in my fetal curl, determined
never to leave the womb's safe haven. I felt her giggle—sadist—
and heard the refrigerator door open. "Oh, I know it's crazy, but
I want some… PICKLES IN A PIG BLANKET" § PINHEAD
ABSTRUSE CASSEROLE This tasty little recipe for four is
dedicated to my old school buddy, Vinny Gordenzola, who, only
months after successful electroshock therapy, is now managing a
bank in Bonsall, Ca. and has plans to win the State Lottery.

At least one column was purportedly written from prison.
When readers complained that recipes were too complex. The Chef
derided the "very uncomplex personalities who read the mag" and
published this:

He sniffs at the air. It begins to rain. He knew it would. Even as
a boy he could smell the rain coming. The distinct fragrance of
the still air, the way it felt on his face. Dogs will start eating grass
when they know it's going to rain. Though he is no dog, he too
has a sense for these things.

The rain is light so he chooses to sit and feel the tiny droplets
end their descending journey on the flesh of his travel-weary face.

Having lived through a rough, full life, he's seen his share of
good and bad times. The bad times outnumber the good, but the
good times, by far, outweigh the bad…

The rain holds many memories in its showers…

It had just stopped raining, the clouds had just parted and the
sun had begun to sparkle off the glistening earth.

The little boy stood looking out the front window of the
old green house in the country. He had just said goodbye to his
daddy, who was about to ride off on an old Triumph motorcycle

to buy him his favorite soda. After kickstarting the metallic beast, his daddy turned and waved to his son. The boy waved back, smacking his lips because he could already taste the soda pop his daddy was about to fetch for him. He watched as he roared off down the long driveway, then covered his eyes in absolute horror when his daddy could not negotiate the "T" at the end of the rainsoaked driveway and was hurtled through the air, across the country road, landing in a heap on the large stump of a eucalyptus tree.

After the ambulance had taken his daddy away, he walked the distance of the long driveway, tracing the roar of the wild ride.

Coming upon the tree stump, he stared. There, on its surface, lay the crushed corpse of a six foot long diamond back rattlesnake, which had made the unfortunate mistake of choosing to sun itself on that stump after the storm. His daddy had crushed it when he landed.

Scanning the mangled body, he noticed the rattle missing. One of the ambulance attendants must've cut it off as a souvenir. The boy felt angry, he thought that he should have that particular rattle.

The boy looked up, the sun was gone, the clouds were back, and it began to rain again. The drops mixed with his tears. He grabbed the snake and walked back to the old green house. He was hungry for...

VENOM SURPRISE

INGREDIENTS

- 1 medium sized living King Cobra (Rattlers will do. Sidewinders, Diamond Backs, take your pick.)
- 2 tbsp cooking oil
- ¼ cup soy sauce

- 1 cup mushrooms
- 1 cup water chestnuts
- 1 cup bean sprouts
- ½ cup bamboo shoots
- ½ cup broccoli

First off, you gotta conjure up the courage to kill the Cobra...
Sneak up behind it, grab it by the neck, pull that meat cleaver
out of your back pocket and chop off its head right below the
Adam's apple. Don't skin the slithering creature. Just cut it up
into 1"× 2"× ½" strips. Take 10 oz. of this meat and soak it in the
soy sauce. Put some oil in a pan, skillet or wok, heat it up, toss in
the 'bra and cook until it's the same consistency of fish. Quick fry
the veggies in a separate pan. Toss veggies in the snake meat and
salt lightly, stir a bit, then let simmer for approximately 3 minutes.
Serve. *Note: Bile from the snake's stomach can be saved and used
as a quick remedy for colds, flus or infections. Must be warmed
before ingesting.*

A typical recent letter to *Thrasher* said: "Skateboarding is going
corporate. The one thing to blame for this, I think, is that fucking
Tony Hawk video game. It's got little seven-year-old kids playing
with finger boards and saying that me and my friends suck at skating
because we can't launch off 15-foot vert ramps or do 900s" (two and
a half midair rotations).

And it's hard not to hate how skating has changed. Tony
Hawk, skating's celebrity and the man now-defunct *Big Brother
Skateboarding* magazine (Larry Flynt, briefly, publisher) referred
to, unironically, as "our ambassador," is a perfect video-game character. No pain, all precision. In the 1980s, as a teenager, encouraged by

his father, the president of the National Skateboarding Association, he won every contest and was the exception that defied the rule of the parentless, rejected, lonely, Scarfing Material–fed skater. Unlike virtually every other pro in *Thrasher*, he always wore full pads and a helmet. He was also the exception that made it big; that cashed in. Hawk, whose annual income was reported in the early '00s at $10 million, is responsible, more than anything else, for the current watered-down hugeness of skateboarding. The arrival of skaters as athletes. He was the first human being for whom skateboarding was a career instead of a last resort or a refuge. Because of the economics brought to skating by Hawk (who is in no way malign—I don't begrudge him the success he's earned), no pro will attempt something really hard without a full video crew there to document it. And to produce their video snippets these skaters go through the antithesis of the true skating experience—uninterrupted flow—and do one thing over and over and over again: killing the imagination for the image. One pro lamented this predicament in an interview with *Thrasher*: "Everyone just does one trick at a time… You might think they're super sick but then you'll see them push and it looks like they've never even touched a skateboard before." Skateboarding has been reduced to doing stunts for money.

Another pro who embodies technically perfect skating and yet is Tony Hawk's opposite (while also being Hawk's friend) is Rodney Mullen, whom I met and skated with one morning in 1986. I was rolling through an empty park in downtown SF and stopped when I saw him. He wore pulled-up tube socks and was skating with a boom box on which he was playing a cassette, recorded straight off the radio in Southern California, commercials and all, while practicing kickflips and heelflips, tiny, precise things that seemed like the work of Swiss watchmakers, with perfect balance and total concentration. We sat and talked for a while. He gave me some advice and I practiced while he watched. Then he signed a board that wasn't even his own pro model. I left with the impression that he was a gentle and modest person. He'd've fit right into a monastery. I had no idea that he had grown up on a cattle ranch, where, after completing his chores he would be left with half an hour of sunlight in which to skate. After he'd won the biggest contest in skateboarding his father had told him, "Good, now you can move on to something real."

In 2009 Mullen (then forty-three) told Tony Hawk that he always slept during the day and skated after midnight, usually in gas stations or parking lots, always alone: "*That's* like the joy for me. So if anyone watched me it would be so embarrassing."

As for pain:

> You know, everyone's done: back foot bounces off, you do the splits. And I did that kinda one too many times… A bunch of scar tissue grew and it pulled my leg into my hip so *tight* that it was grinding about thirty times a day, and the doc says, "It's gonna grind the head off the bone… You're kinda screwed." And the doctor can't cut on it because it's *all throughout you*, and it's just gonna generate more problems so, "Here's how it works: good luck." And I learned basically how to tear that stuff out, 'cause it grows like weeds in you, and you have to tear yourself. And finally you have to learn to put so much pressure on yourself it's enough to almost kind of break your own bone. And the night I broke— like, I put my leg in my wheel well of my car, and reached for under the frame of my car and just *rip, rip, rip*… Three cops at different times, 'cause it's the middle of the night, would come by 'cause the yells, they thought I was being *mugged*.

SEAN WILSEY

This went on for two years, thirteen nights out of fourteen—"I'd take a day off every two weeks"—in a process that Mullen described as "breaking myself apart, pretty medievally." Cole Louison, a fact checker at *GQ* whose excellent book on the history of skateboarding, *The Impossible,* is named after a Mullen trick, spoke to him at length about this medieval period. Scar tissue "tears out like chewing gum that's kinda old, dry, and it'll stretch and stretch and stretch and that's when you're just giving up—and then a 'pop.' If you've ever broken bones you get a heat sensation, then a little nausea, then you get this crazy high." One evening Mullen was bouncing in the wheel well when he heard a sound "Like a tree branch. And my body hit the ground—not all of it, because I'm stuck in the wheel well, but the rest of it. And I looked up, and there was snot and tears on my hand. And I got that crazy high and I pulled myself out the best I could, lying on the ground going, 'God, what'd I do, what'd I do, what'd I do,' and I got up… I got on my skateboard and was like 'I did it! I did it! I did it!' I went home, slept for fourteen hours. I vomited."

Rodney Mullen—self-torturing; flipping ballet moves alone in a gas station at midnight—is as close to an authentic holy man as an American can get.

Skating alone is the purest experience. The flow of skating (what Incarcerated Skater terms "soul skating") makes for bad watching. Pictures are deceptive. Videos don't convey anything. How someone looks doing it has very little relation to the experience. A skateboarder moves like a thought. While skate videos cut from skater to skater doing trick after trick, making the whole enterprise (I refuse to call it a sport—and the US Department of Labor backs me on this: professional skaters are officially product spokespeople, not athletes) into something resembling an automobile plant at full capacity, welding chassis after chassis with skater robots. There's something inhuman about the way this most human and interior of activities has been put on display. The removal of all the trial and error and experimentation. Slo-mo can unpack a trick and make it beautiful, but the whole point of skateboarding is speed, which makes all the details invisible to everyone but the skater. Video games are better at replicating the feeling of pulling something good—like a long grind—but without the pain and practice that makes a trick more than a trick: the word *trick* itself being almost a travesty of what can be done on a skateboard.

My favorite skaters of the late 1980s and early 1990s—Natas Kaupas and Mark Gonzales—would skate the Embarcadero just for fun, not for cameras. They were street skaters. They rolled and talked to everyone, then flew back into the city in search of spots. Stylistically, Natas Kaupas (Satan Sapuak backwards; Sapuak, according to *Thrasher*, meaning "God" in some ancient language) was the most inspiring. Today everyone cites him as an influence. Physically, he could have been a double for Tony Hawk, but with grace and style and imagination—and a loner's soul, like Mullen's. Natas was best known for ollieing directly onto a wall and riding it like a wave. There were photos of him doing this for the better part of a city block. He'd jump straight from the street to the vert, roll around twenty-five feet, depending on how much speed he had, and then kick back to the flat. He also could ollie onto a fire hydrant and revolve there, like an accelerated version of the fanciest restaurant in a midsize American city. (One disbelieving pro, on seeing a video of this feat, told a documentary film crew, "I still think it was smoke and mirrors, man.") There *was* something pact-with-the-devil-ish about Natas's ability to defy the laws of physics. Shortly after he appeared in *Thrasher* his sponsor began getting calls from parents and palindromists, convinced that skaters were being lured into Satanism. Natas swag was banned in schools and taken off shelves in shops. The name actually means "birth of Christ." It's Lithuanian for Noël—the nativity.

Compared to Hawk, Natas got relatively little recompense from skating (according to a letter in *Thrasher*, he ended up in porn). But he changed everything. In the late 1980s Hawk and the other ramp guys were just going back and forth, stuck there like hamsters, while this backwards-Satan kid found a way to take skating into the real world. That was the significance of pushing his board through the transition from horizontal to vertical and riding on walls—no ramp required. Freedom. And the humanization of inhuman landscapes with his body alone. No ramp-building schematics, spacious yard, and father's shed full of power tools required. I saw him skating at the Embarcadero that same skinhead summer and it was the most inspiring physical accomplishment I ever witnessed. He got lined up on top of a huge concrete wall, fifteen feet above the plaza. There was a launch ramp at the end of the wall, and he pushed toward it, getting up to speed, all the skaters watching in the plaza below anticipating a huge air when he hit it, and then he ollied right *over* the ramp, floated across a huge expanse of space, and landed impossibly far out in the plaza, as if to say: "I don't need your ramp. I don't need anything but my skateboard." We were all so awestruck nobody got so much as a picture.

But it's Tony Hawk everyone knows. He first pulled his famous 900 at the X Games, which are broadcast on the Entertainment and Sports Programming Network. (A recent *Thrasher* letter read: "Fuck ESPN! Fuck TV!") Thanks to Hawk most Americans think spinning in circles is the highest achievement in skateboarding. The "900" was a moment manufactured for TV. And, like the 900, a lot of current skateboarding is styleless, flourishy, has nothing to do with getting from A to B, which is what skating is, at its best: getting down the street as smoothly and quickly and entertainingly as possible—riding on (or off) walls if you have to—and never, ever, putting both feet on the ground.

Skateboarding is having filthy hands from always touching the street, and not washing them before going to McDonald's for lunch (sorry, Chef). Skateboarding is feeling that every flight of stairs is nagging you, begging you to boneless, or ollie over, or railslide down it. Skateboarding is looking into toilet bowls and fantasizing about shrinking down and skating them. It is using the word *transitions* to refer to curved areas between horizontal and vertical. It is an apocryphal mention in *Thrasher* of three skyscrapers in Manhattan with transitioned bases (Forty-seventh and Third Avenue; Forty-ninth and Third Avenue; and Ninety-sixth and Columbus)—designed by a skateboarding architect. It is a review of a new California skatepark that says: "As usual, it's behind the McDonald's." It is a California newspaper reporting on a law requiring all underage skaters to wear helmets: "Skaters… think the new law—the toughest helmet law in the nation—will signal an apocalypse for the sport. 'They're going to ruin the sport, and everyone is going to go home and do drugs,' said Ray Rusniak, 13, after hearing the news." Skateboarding is ninety-six term papers available for downloading on the *Thrasher* website. It's a Spanish woman, post-9/11, accosting a bunch of pro skaters in Barcelona to tell them (per *Thrasher*), "After meeting you, I think I agree with the people who say America got what it deserved!" It is the joy of practice over performance. At sixteen or seventeen, alone, for hours, skating made for my earliest insight into the power of sustained focus. Also: courage. I made myself do things that I was very afraid to do. I tried to wall ride like Natas. This amounted to rolling at speed into a wall—on purpose—slamming my face right into it, and then stumbling around in pain, dazed, crying, but also unable to stop laughing with joy. It's *Thrasher*'s description of Argentine pro Diego Bucchieri attempting to ollie a double staircase "that started wide on top and ended up the width of an average closet door at the bottom":

> He sized it up, shouted in Spanish a little bit to get psyched and then went for it.
>
> He packed on the first one, jumped off in the air on the second and got obliterated on the third. He was looking pretty bad.
>
> "If I don't make this one, I'm going to die," he croaked.
>
> Of course he nailed it, squatting deftly through the narrow landing and out into the plaza. Although his arm no longer wanted to work and he couldn't drive the car anymore, he was satisfied.
>
> "Stop the car. I need to get a fucking beer," he ordered. It's a smart athlete who knows when to medicate.

But no, not an athlete. Skaters are collective consciences, dervishes, holy fools in a religious trance.

Skaters are people like Jerry Hsu, as interviewed by *Thrasher*:

> *Thrasher*: "What do your grandparents know about your personal life?"
> Hsu: "Not very much. It's a pretty sparse relationship I have with them."
> *T*: "What are their names?"
> H: "I have no idea. Grandma and Grandpa?"
> *T*: "You don't know their first names?"
> H: "No, they're not English names."

T: "But you must have heard their names mentioned around the house?"

H: "No, never."

Or Ricardo Carvalho:

"We should bomb Germany," [Ricardo] declared one day at lunch… "Germany sucks, man…" We were at a loss… until he described how he had struck his head at the Dortmund contest this summer. His German doctor sent him to a mental hospital where he was forced to remain for two weeks.

Skateboarders are not role models.

Skateboarding is observing things minutely. It is tuning the world out: cutting your hand and not noticing till hours later. Looking at the world like a skater means looking down. It means rarely raising your eyes above curb level, constantly monitoring the smoothness of concrete and being alert to the presence of pebbles or grit, experiencing an instant elevation in your mood when you roll through a spot where you've successfully pulled a trick, and depression and superstition in a place where you've slammed—no matter the grime or beauty of the location in conventional terms. Skateboarding is bringing emotion to emotionless terrain—unloved parking lots, vacant corporate downtowns long after the office workers are home. I remember skating in such places and feeling I was somehow redeeming them from their daily functions, giving them a secret life.

At my second East Coast boarding school, my parents had my intelligence tested and discovered that my "performance IQ" was 90—in the twenty-fifth percentile of all Americans. Off a skateboard I was miserable, and incapable of seeing past my misery.

These days *Thrasher* seems to reside in a similar state. Chef-Boy-Am-I-Hungry left the magazine in the early '90s. I learned his real identity—a writer/designer/photographer called Mörizen Föche (aka Mofo) who produced half the stuff they published—by reading his "Industry Profile" on a job-placement website: "I need some freelance photo work so I can visit my son in Phoenix more. 'Photographer for hire' anyone? ANYONE?" As for Skarfing Material, he described it as "some bullshit department that I thought of off the top of my head" and then wrote "under the *nom de plume* 'Chef Boy Am I Hungry'... I'd make something to eat, take photos of it, make up some BS story and print it." I wanted to tell him he'd made me become a writer, and that when he left the magazine it lost depth and daring. My wife, Daphne, got to something I'd been trying to figure out for years when, after reading a particularly asinine article in the February 2003 issue, she said: "It's really not OK that these people are using so little of their brains."

"Using so little." It's the perfect indictment of everything that's wrong with—and the most succinct encapsulation of everything that's brilliant about—skateboarding. The beauty of using so little in a country that uses so much. Living for a plank and four wheels in a profligate culture. And the saddening fact that *Thrasher* has, in many ways, been failing to move against the wind. Jake Phelps, the current editor, a San Francisco skater to the bone, wrote a sort of suicide note in the March 2003 issue: "I've never felt as depressed as I do now... I try to stay focused on the mag—my life is in this mag. And its life is in me... I feel distant from the spots, skaters and special people I've known... God this is awful." These desperate words, especially jarring in contrast to *Thrasher*'s ironic dirtbag voice (it used to be ironic, big-hearted, dirtbag), were wedged into an issue stuffed with ads. An issue fifty-four pages longer than a contemporaneous *Vanity Fair*.

Feeling depressed by your success is a rare predicament for an editor in chief. (I wanted to tell him to try aromatherapy.) I figured Phelps was about to hang it up and let *Thrasher* go fully corporate. There were certainly skateboard doomsday signs aplenty. I attended a screening of *Dogtown and Z-Boys*, a documentary about the earliest days of skating, in a private theater at the Sony Corporation's New York headquarters. The place was filled with MTV celebrities and their posses. I was the only person with a plank on wheels. A guy in a long black leather jacket pointed at me, turned to a young woman, and said: "Ooh, he brought his *board*," and I felt *ashamed*.

Skating through midtown Manhattan that night, I remembered that I used to think skateboarding would never get too big because it hurt too much. Because you can't take the pain out of skateboarding. Because putting yourself deliberately in harm's way is a quick, easy, and reliable route to the truth. But what I didn't realize is that you can take the skateboarding out of skateboarding—make the act a mere accessory to its style.

Phelps, as it turned out, did not succumb. Within a few issues *Thrasher* announced a contest-cum-cross-country-trip that featured teams of professional skaters who set out from four different West Coast cities and made for New York. On the way they were required to perform various challenges and dares ("Ollie over a man or woman of the cloth"; "Make out with someone working at a fast food restaurant"; "Do a trick over roadkill"). He appeared to have found something no corporate sponsor would touch. And King of the Road, as the contest was called, has continued to evolve, as skaters continue to refuse to grow up. An older skater mused in one of the final issues of *Big Brother* (in tiny white type one suspects went unread), "I'm still riding a skateboard, and I'm fuckin' 32 years old. When I look back at other generations I feel that they were more grown up and more responsible… And here we are, we're all just riding skateboards and staying in our childhood… we're remaining skateboarders for so long. I mean, it seems like I haven't gone through some sort of rite of passage that I'm supposed to go through." Phelps's challenges took this head-on: "Find someone over the age of 40 who can do a kickflip"; "Make out with a woman over forty"; "One person cut their hair to mimic the style of someone suffering from sever [*sic*] male pattern baldness."

Returning from Thanksgiving with my pregnant wife I got us moved to a better seat because a flight attendant on JetBlue, ten years my junior, saw my *Thrasher* sweatshirt, saw me writing, and thought I must write for them. When she told me this I asked if she skated and she said, "No. I just like skaters and the music. *Anthrax*."

I had a baseball cap over my disappearing hair.

The last time I saw Blane Morf was in the summer of 2000. I lived in New York, and he lived in the small town of Blue Lake, in far Northern California. I went out to visit for a few days, and in the middle of remembering how we used to jump the fence and skate the playground of Yick Wo Elementary School (I once got so much air there that I snapped my board in half; and I wish I hadn't cared that nobody saw me but Blane), he said, "Wait! I have to show you something!" and got a ladder. He climbed up to his ceiling, pushed open a hatch, rooted around, and returned with an object I never thought I'd see again—my Natas Kaupas pro board. I'd lost it when I got sent to reform school.

Seven months later I got the news that Blane had died. He hadn't shown up at the brewery where he'd worked. A colleague found his body in bed—heart failure. I went out to San Francisco. Without Blane I found the experience of moving through the streets, and riding the bus, isolating in the extreme. I wondered if I was the one who'd died and this perfect-yet-so-lonely city was my punishment or reward. When Blane's mother asked me to speak at his memorial service I talked about skateboarding, and how, because of the rolling nature of our friendship, I couldn't go anywhere in San Francisco without being reminded of him.

Skateboarding is the most lasting gift a friend ever gave me. I now skate on that same Natas Kaupas board, every freezing, New York, wish-I-was-in-San-Francisco day.

Back in the mid-1990s, the last time skating could claim to be in any way marginal, an Iranian-American pro skater called Salman Agah wrote in *Thrasher*, somewhat disjunctively, but all the more truthfully for his ollies over syntax and logic:

> One of the many things I love about skateboarding is the freedom to ride whenever and whatever I want. There is no practice, no conditioning, at least, not consciously… Some of us are driven by our hearts, some by reputation, and some by money. But regardless, no matter what the motivation, the dance that we do compares with nothing at all. Am I exaggerating? I think not!… If you don't know what I mean, get on your board in San Francisco, shoot the hills, scare yourself to death, and then tell me your heart is working involuntarily!

SOME OF THEM CAN READ

2005

Over Thanksgiving in Florida Daphne and I told her parents that she was pregnant. There was a lot of toasting and crying, and then we all went to bed. The next morning I woke to find a rat had gnawed through the power cord of the laptop I'm writing this on. Come spring, back in New York, we read parenting books. Daphne was due in July. Under the rubric "advice to fathers" one said: "Keep the nest tidy. An upset nest yields an upset mother—and baby. In the postpartum period seeing one dirty dish unglues Martha... TIDY is your memory word for the day... Feel like a servant and waiter? You are." I also began reading about rats. Mature rats and newborn babies are approximately the same size, and the former make terrifyingly good reading for an expectant father.

The first thing I read was "Rats on the Waterfront," the mother of all New York rat pieces, by the great reporter and fabulist Joseph Mitchell:

"The brown rat is hostile to other kinds; it usually attacks them on sight. It kills them by biting their throats or by clawing them to pieces, and, if hungry, it eats them… All rats are vandals, but the brown is the most ruthless… Now and then, in live-poultry markets, a lust for blood seems to take hold of the brown rat. One night, in the poultry part of old Gansevoort Market, alongside the Hudson, a burrow of them bit the throats of over three hundred broilers and ate less than a dozen. Before this part of the market was abandoned, in 1942, the rats practically had charge of it. Some of them nested in the drawers of desks. When the drawers were pulled open, they leaped out, snarling."

In 1944, when Mitchell wrote his rat piece, there were three distinct varieties of rat thriving in New York City: the brown rat (*Rattus norvegicus*), which lives in burrows and stays close to the ground; the black or ship rat (*Rattus rattus*), which is fond of attics and eaves and seagoing vessels; and the roof or Alexandrian rat (*Rattus rattus alexandrinus*), a subspecies of the black. In the intervening years, winter by winter—that being the season in which they're forced to live in closest proximity—the brown rat has killed off the other two. The black and the roof rat, all but extinct in New York, have gone to Los Angeles. Gendy Alimurung, an *LA Weekly* reporter, is entertainingly obsessed with them: "Rats! Rats burrowing through see-through plastic garbage bags. Rats scampering in a line across the edge of the dumpster like pedestrian traffic. Rats poking their noses through holes in the walls. Old rats. Young rats. Baby rats. Thrashy rats. Ugly, dirty scratchy rats. Funny, jumpy cute rats."

And then there is Robert Sullivan's delightful and revolting *Rats*, the most exhaustive compendium of rat facts yet set down. Facts such as: wherever there are human beings, there are rats. Asia is where the rat originated, and where you can find it on restaurant menus. Rat populations increase in times of war. New York City battled an epic rat infestation at the World Trade Center site after 9/11, and was obliged to fill the ruins with poison. A third of the world's food supply is consumed or destroyed by rats. Rats have eaten cadavers in the New York City coroner's office. Rats have attacked and killed homeless people sleeping on the streets of Manhattan. In the mid-twentieth century New York City fires classified as "of undetermined origin" were thought to have been started by rats. (In Florida I discovered the damage to my laptop's cord when sparks shot out of it. Shortly thereafter my father-in-law trapped a rat—in the house.) There are more rodents currently infected with plague in North America (mostly in rural western states: Wyoming, Montana, Colorado, West Texas) than there were in Europe at the time of the Black Death. Whenever we see a rat, it's a weak rat, forced into the open to look for food; the strong ones stay out of sight. Brown rats survived nuclear testing in the Pacific by staying deep down in their burrows. There have always been rats in the White House (though the Nixon administration had a particularly light infestation). Exterminators will always have work. "Rats that survive to the age of four are the wisest and the most cynical beasts on earth," an exterminator told Mitchell. "A trap means nothing to them, no matter how skillfully set. They just kick it around until it snaps; then they eat the bait. And they can detect poisoned bait a yard off. I believe some of them can read." A pest control technician—as they're now called, *exterminator* having a deceptive air of finality—told Sullivan that a "sniper with a night-vision scope" is the only way to kill a rat of the semiliterate kind. The Department of Homeland Security, as part of its post-9/11 bioterror-alertness effort, catches rats and inspects their fleas to see if terrorists have released the Black Death in New York City. A male rat will continue mating with a female rat even if she's dead. A "dominant male rat may mate with up to twenty female rats in just six hours," Sullivan says.

He goes on:

> Male rats exiled from their nest by more aggressive male rats will
> also live in all-male rat colonies and have sex with the other male
> rats. The gestation period of a pregnant female rat is 21 days,
> the average litter between eight to ten pups. And a female rat
> can become pregnant immediately after giving birth. If there is a
> healthy amount of garbage for the rats to eat, then a female rat will
> produce up to 12 litters of 20 rats each a year. One rat's nest can
> turn into a rat colony of 50 rats in six months. One pair of rats has
> the potential of 15,000 descendants in a year.

As Mitchell more concisely puts it, "rats are almost as fecund as
germs."

I often move through the city in the most ratlike of ways, on a
skateboard—rushing along curbs with a squeal, always close to the
street. So my rat revulsion is tempered with respect and identifica-
tion. And after a decade and a half in New York, I've collected a
few rat stories. My friend Paul, a fisherman, told me that an aqua-
culturist acquaintance seeded the entrance to Brooklyn's Gowanus
Canal with oysters. They established a bed and briefly flourished.
Then they all died—not for lack of oxygen or from overexposure to
pollutants, but because rats jumped into the canal, dove fifteen feet
down, and ate them all.

My friend Cressida, who lives uptown on 108th Street and wears
open-toed shoes in the summer, always walks home in the middle
of the street on trash-collection days to avoid the rats that dash
back and forth across the sidewalk, running like commuters from
their basement dens to the heavy black bags set out along the curb.

On the other end of Manhattan, Brad and Mary's al fresco dinner in the tented garden of a pan-Latin restaurant was interrupted by the squeals and thrashings behind one of the tent's side panels of a particularly vicious rat fight, which culminated in victor hurling vanquished over a nearby table (at which people were eating). In the late nineties my friend Eli and I had dinner at a trendy downtown pizza place (John F. Kennedy Jr. was at the next table). After we'd finished, and I was halfway out the door, Eli called me back, in a strangely delighted tone of voice, to show me the dead, foot-long sewer rat (gray, oily belly distended, chest flattened, long yellow incisors bared in anguish) that had been under our table—under our backpacks, in fact. "That's one big dead rat!" Eli said as I fled for the street, leaned between two parked cars, and retched.

Colin used to work as the superintendent of a run-down, medium-size building in a Dominican block on the Lower East Side. One of his duties, which he hated, was to cart out the building's trash—always full of foraging rats. The previous super was known for putting on a big pair of steel-toe-capped boots so he could leap into the trash barrels and stomp the rats to death. Colin usually left them alone. One time, though, he managed to trap a rat in an empty barrel. Then he found a heavy iron rod in the building's courtyard and dragged the can out onto the street, where a group of Dominican men were playing dominoes. The rat squeaked and threw itself against the sides.

"What you got in there?" a man asked. "A rat?"

"Of course," Colin said.

"What're you going to do with it?"

"I'm going to beat it to death with this iron rod."

Everyone immediately stopped playing dominoes and followed Colin out into the middle of Rivington Street. He tipped the barrel over on its side, brandished the rod, and pulled off the lid, expecting the rat to come running out to meet its fate. But rats are cautious.

This one stayed put, stared at its captors, and took mincing steps side to side. After about fifteen seconds Colin adjusted his grip on the bar, and that's when the rat made its move: it dashed out of the barrel through the legs of one of the domino players—"They all screamed," Colin said—and disappeared into an empty lot.

Gary had a rat infestation in his building. "We killed a lot of them," he told me excitedly. "Mostly mothers and babies!" I can think of no other mammal about which such a statement could be made with the same guilt-free pleasure.

Most of the live rats I've seen have been in the subway. Train workers call them "track rabbits." Sullivan describes a subway station near Madison Square Garden:

> People come down from the streets and throw the food that they
> have not eaten onto the tracks, along with newspapers and soda
> bottles… The rats eat freely from the waste and sit at the side
> of the little streams of creamy brown sewery water that flows
> between the rails. They sip the water the way rats do, either with
> their front paws or by scooping it up with their incisors.

Recently, a track worker called Manuel, who moonlights as a handyman, helped Daphne and me paint what would soon become our child's room. Manuel painted in silence until I asked if he ever encountered rats in the tunnels. "I see them all the time! They're big, and they're brave. They scare me. The other night I was spreading concrete when I looked up and there was one about a foot long, staring at me. When I waved my shovel at him he stood up on his hind legs and snarled."

"What did you do?"

"I decided to go on a break."

With New York to themselves, the city's brown rats continue to adapt in ever more unusual ways. Sullivan records the reaction of the city's head exterminator on discovering a pack nesting in the trees of a Brooklyn park—unprecedented behavior for the ground-loving *norvegicus*. My first thought on reading the passage was: *pity the squirrels.* As for the head exterminator, he got on a walkie-talkie and shouted: "Hey, Rick! *There's rats in the goddamn trees!*"

Rats—fast, tireless runners—will also make use of public transport. Subway workers have reported rats boarding trains to ride a few stops down the line. They are most numerous in the older stations in the lower parts of Manhattan.

What no employee of the city government would deny is that we kill an astounding number of rats. "We kill more of them than anyplace else," mayor Rudolph Giuliani once said. "We probably lead the country in rat killing." While in office he held a "rat summit" and gave the city a "rat tsar." But no matter how good we get, rats will always be better at killing their own.

The peg for Mitchell's piece (initially entitled "Thirty-Two Rats from Casablanca") was the city's close brush with bubonic plague, when "an old French tramp, the *Wyoming*, in from Casablanca, where the Black Death has been intermittent for centuries," falsely claimed to have carried out rat fumigation and was allowed to dock, first in Brooklyn, then in Lower Manhattan, then in Staten Island. Eventually some longshoremen noticed the *Wyoming* was infested. The ship was quarantined and fumigated, and thirty-two rats were collected and combed for fleas. The fleas were pulverized, mixed with a solution, and injected into healthy guinea pigs, which died of plague. It's hard to read this story and not think about terrorism, and the impossibility of screening every container shipped into the United States. I had to wonder what inspired Mitchell to write about rats in the middle of the Second World War. Could he have suspected a biological attack?

I got in touch with one of Mitchell's friends—who wished to remain nameless—and asked her. She gave me a definitive no, saying that the writer's interest in rats didn't have anything to do with biological warfare, and if he had thought there was a story there, he would have written it. I asked her if he maybe hadn't wanted to alarm the public. She said no. He was a reporter. He reported. Then I started thinking about what Mitchell had in common with Sullivan, and decided it was fatherhood. (Daphne was seven months pregnant and I was thinking about children all the time.) As it turns out, Mitchell had become a father shortly before he started working on the rat piece. Sullivan, too, has young children, and makes a few oblique, amusing references to fatherhood in *Rats*. His wife asks him to strip and scrub down before coming near their children. He is especially disturbed by the fact that rats bite babies on the face, because they smell traces of food there. Mitchell's friend told me she'd worked in child welfare when she was a young woman, and had treated a baby that had been bitten by rats, which made her "grow up fast."

The only other domestic-rat fact that seems seriously to disturb Sullivan is that they occasionally emerge in toilet bowls, after crawling through sewer pipes, and bite people's genitals. My friend Lou once walked into a ground-floor restroom and surprised such a rat, which dove right into the bowl and was gone.

A few weeks before our child was born I called 311, the City of New York's Citizen Service Center, to get the latest statistics on the rat population. The operator told me I needed to speak with someone at the Department of Health and Mental Hygiene. This, she said, was where "all rat questions go." After she transferred me, a man answered the phone immediately, in a bored voice.

Must not be a lot of rat questions, I thought. "I'm trying to get a grip on the rat situation in the city," I said. "Specifically the number of rats we've got here." There was silence. "The most recent information I could find was in the *New Yorker* magazine," I went on. "An article that said there were twenty-eight million rats in New York City."

"What!? Twenty-eight million rats?! That cannot be!'

"Four per person," I said.

"That sounds more reasonable," he said. "I'll check your figures with rodent control."

I asked if he could also check whether there were any vestigial traces of black or Alexandrian rats in the city. He said he would. A few hours later another man called me back and left a long message: so long I saved it to listen to properly at a later time. Soon afterwards, Daphne and I were walking down our block when a small, blurry shape came galloping out of the Catholic cemetery surrounding Old St. Patrick's Cathedral, straight at us.

Daphne, a few days past her due date, shouted: "What?! Oh my God!"

I thought: *Oh, fuck—a rat! A rat's going to send my wife into labor!*

But it wasn't a rat, it was a squirrel (possibly driven from its tree by rats), which chattered as it leaped the curb, ran under our legs, circled us, and then ran back across the street. A few hours later we were at the hospital. Our son, Owen Taylor Wilsey, was born after a twenty-seven-hour labor. He weighed seven pounds nine ounces, had no hair, could not see farther than twelve inches in front of his face, had no peripheral vision, could not feed himself, was startled by any metallic or staccato noises, and would not be able to hold his head up for three months. A rat can hold its head up from birth.

*　*　*

At home, presents rolled in. We got a pair of baby pajamas that opened at one end and were covered in pirates: we called them the rat bag.

A few weeks later, I listened to the congratulatory birth-of-our-child calls on the answering machine.

From my mother: "Sean! You're a father! Hooray! Let's hope he doesn't have too many of our crazy genes."

From my drawling uncle Charles, in Houston: "Owen Taylor is a very masculine name. Very male."

Then "Hi Sean. Or Mr. Wilsey. This is Sid from the New York City Department of Health and Mental Hygiene, returning your call. Let me know if this message suffices. We understand that you have an estimate of the number of rats in New York City; but, quite frankly we don't have an estimate, nor have we ever given one out, as far as I know, on the number of rodents in New York City. There are a number of variables that play into how many rodents there might be at any given time, such as weather changes—during cold weather the number of rats declines—or the availability of food sources and other things, like exterminations and baiting trends in New York City, all of which may alter the size of the rodent population in the city at any given time. Plus, quite frankly, we don't have someone going around taking a rat census. So we've not given out a number, a guestimate, or an estimate for the populations of *Rattus norvegicus* in New York City. The brown rat, or the Norway rat, is the only rat in New York City at this time. On that point you are correct. Thank you sir. Good-bye."

Since Owen was born I have sent numerous requests to the Department of Health and Mental Hygiene for more rat information. Among other things, I'd like to know if they still inspect ships for rats, what the command structure is in the case of a major rat-related public health emergency, and the size of the biggest rat ever found in NYC. But they have been unresponsive. A child suffocated in an outer-borough day-care center, the media went crazy, and the head of the department was fired. They have no time for rat inquiries.

My other rat source, Manuel, has regularly called me looking for odd jobs. I haven't been much help, but I've learned a little bit of his life story. He came to America not for money—"There is plenty in Ecuador," he says—but because he'd been in command of a detachment of paratroopers guarding the Ecuadorian president. He was ordered to fire on an unruly crowd, and refused. Then he had to flee to escape prison. He's not afraid of much—except rats.

"Sean, how is your son?" he asked the other day.

"Getting bigger. Holding up his head." Pause. "And the rats, Manuel, how are the rats?"

"Numerous! Getting bigger, too! Ten inches! Thirteen inches! All over Brooklyn. None of us want to work in Brooklyn."

I continued not to hear back from the Department of Health and Mental Hygiene, until I got a letter marked:

THE CITY OF NEW YORK
DEPARTMENT OF HEALTH AND MENTAL HYGIENE
125 Worth Street
New York, NY 10013-4089
Vital Records, CN-4

I figured they'd decided to put their answers in writing.
I tore the envelope open, and found my son's birth certificate.

THE WORLD I WANT TO LIVE IN
2006

There are many beautiful things about being an American fan of World Cup soccer—foremost among them is ignorance. The community in which you were raised does not gather around the television set every four years for a solid, breathless month. The US has never won. You have not been indoctrinated into unwanted-yet-inescapable tribal allegiances by your soccer-crazed countrymen. You are an amateur, in the purest sense of the word. So when the World Cup comes around, you can pick whatever team you like best and root for them without shame or fear of reprisal—you can spend the month in paradise.

That's what I do. The world of the World Cup is the world I want to live in. I cannot resist the pageantry and high-mindedness, the apolitical display of national characteristics, the revelation of deep human flaws and unexpected greatnesses, the fact that entire nations walk off the job or wake up at three a.m. to watch men kick a ball. There are countries that have truly multiracial squads—France, England and the United States—while other teams are entirely blond or Asian or Latin American. There are irritating fans: "USA! USA! USA!" (Blessedly few.) There are children who hold hands with each player as he walks onto the field. National anthems play. Men paint themselves their national colors and cry openly at opposing victories. An announcer shouts "GOOOOOOOOOOOOOOOO OOOOOOOOOOOOOOOLLLLLLLLLLLLLLLLLLLLLLLLL LLLL! GOL GOL GOL!" on the Spanish-language channel you're watching (it's the only way you can see the game live). A Slovakian tire salesman, an Italian cop, or a German concert pianist—having passed the official fitness test and psychological examinations—will moonlight as referee. There are two back-to-back forty-five-minute segments without commercials. To quote the book every traveling athlete finds in his hotel room: "Rejoice, and be exceedingly glad: for great is your reward in heaven." Or, as my copy of *Soccer and Its Rules* says: "Are you ready? Ready to cheer the players to victory, marvel at their fitness, speed, and skills, urging them to win every tackle for the ball, ready to explode at a powerful shot? Ready for the excitement of flying wingers, overlapping backs, curling corners, slick one-two passing and goals scored with panache? Ready for another moment in a fantasy world?"

I am ready.

I mark the passage of time in World Cups. I started watching when I was old enough to be a young player, and still imagine myself as the unlikely substitute who comes in and scores.

My first Cup was in 1990, and I rooted for Cameroon. Cameroon had Roger Milla, who was an old man (thirty-eight, that year) and ran only when it mattered. He did not need to run. He was wily and stylish enough to walk around the field scoring off defenders young enough to be his children. When Cameroon went out I switched allegiance

THE WORLD I WANT TO LIVE IN

to Italy. I was in Venice, and Italy was the host nation. I got swept up. When the *Azzurri* made it to the final four, young men jumped into the canals, risking death by infection in order to express their triumph. Then Argentina kicked them out in the semis, despite allegations of cheating. (Ever since Argentina's star, Diego Maradona, punched a ball into the goal to win a match against England, then claimed it was won "a little bit by the Hand of God, another bit by the head of Maradona" Argentina has been the cheater's favorite team.) Finally West Germany—with seemingly immortal attackers like Lothar Matthäus (veteran of five World Cups), and clinical defenders like Olaf Thon (nickname: the Professor)—shut down all Argentine forays and won the whole thing. Tragic but inevitable.

The next World Cup was in America. The world looked to the United States and the United States did not notice. The only part of the tournament to get much attention stateside came when a Colombian defender scored a goal against his own team, flew home in disgrace, and was shot dead in the street by a fan who shouted "*Gol! Gol! Gol!*" as he pumped bullets into the body. So far as I know, no one has ever done this to an Olympic discus thrower.

Italy was still my team, despite the Italians' boring soccer. Italian soccer watchers, I discovered, make better watching than Italian soccer, which entails getting a single goal and then locking into defense for the rest of the game. The Italians even have a word for it: *catenaccio*, which means "door bolt," or, if you're a more literal translator, "ugly chain." That year they ugly-chained it all the way to the final, lost on penalties to Brazil, and I decided to abandon them. Seeing your team go out on penalties is particularly demoralizing when you've watched them make it there without any flying wingers, curling corners, slick one-two passing, or goals scored with panache. The *Azzurri* had chintzed their way into the final. I'd supported them through a string of draws and one-point victories, watched them shut down Brazil for two hours, and then watched them lose. Even the misery was tepid.

Next cup I switched to England. I was converted by watching a young David Beckham score an impossible-looking goal from a direct free kick, then get ejected from a game for kicking an Argentine player after the whistle was blown. There was something irresistible about a player whose talents were undermined by the fact that he was foolish enough to do this right in front of the ref, against a team as good as Argentina. I was hooked: Beckham was a brilliant imbecile, and England was my squad. Of course it was the Argentines who continued to the next round.

So I switched to France. France was the host, and their team was a mélange of skin tones and shaved heads the likes of which had never been seen before. *Les Bleus* came up against *Gli Azzurri* in the quarter-finals, won heroically in a penalty shoot-out, then went on to win the whole thing, using their home-team advantage to beat psyched-out world champion Brazil. Bliss!

But it was the 2002 World Cup, held jointly by South Korea and Japan, where it all came together for me. I watched the games in New York, on Telemundo, the Spanish-language channel ("GOOOOOOLLLLLL!"), and split my allegiance between Japan, England, South Korea, and Turkey. Japan had great hair, a player who wore goggles, and another who taunted the opposing side *in Italian*. England—with grown-up Beckham (now captain) and my new favorite striker, Michael Owen—was dangerous and disciplined and incredibly unlucky. South Korea humiliated Italy with great determination and well-deserved good fortune. The Turks were ruffians: egregious foulers who made for the best watching of the tournament. Inevitably, Brazil won. The final was against Germany, but the best game of the tournament was the one when Brazil knocked out England with a gorgeous goal by Ronaldinho ("little Ronaldo") scored on a direct free kick—from midfield. Deus ex machina. A beautiful way to lose.

When the Cup was over I wasn't ready to stop watching. I *needed* more international soccer. I tried Mexican and European league games on the weekends, but it just wasn't the same. What was at stake? Soccer only mattered when you knew an entire country sat rigid with anxiety in front of its television sets, national hopes and paranoias on full display, yearning for release; when players were playing out of love of country, not money. The team with the biggest payroll is almost always going to win in league games. Not so in international soccer. GDP is meaningless. China is a nonentity. America has *always* lost.

So I took advantage of my American ignorance. I went on eBay in search of a historical World Cup and was soon deep in discussion with a fan whose screen name hearkened back to the victorious West German team of 1990: "Olafthon1" (the Professor must have got there before him). Olaf1, a sort of monastic scholar of soccer, wrote me a number of e-mails that read like doctrinal encyclicals, and advised me on which World Cup I should retroactively attend. After settling on 1970—the first one to be televised in color—he warned me that there were two missing games, Uruguay–Sweden and West Germany–Morocco. The former was no great loss, but the latter, he said yearningly, was not only magnificent, but no longer existed, and "nobody can get it." *West Germany–Morocco*, I thought, *lost for all time*. And it's a measure of my zealotry that I later found myself daydreaming about a world space agency that could send out a probe to overtake and intercept the original broadcast and bring it home to Earth. Traveling at light speed, West Germany–Morocco passed beyond the etheric magnetic sphere of our solar system in just over four hours, placing it, at the time of my imagining, thirty-six years, three hundred and sixty-four and one quarter days and twenty hours later, 3.40586297e+17 miles from Earth.

The 1970 World Cup was held in Mexico, beginning the same month and year that I was born. I had no idea who would win. When it arrived I slipped the first of twenty-five VHS tapes into the VCR I for some reason still owned—Mexico–Soviet Union, 5/31/70—and proceeded to watch the entire tournament, drawing it out over a couple months. The great games (Czechoslovakia–Brazil), the boring games (Uruguay–Israel), and the weird games (Morocco–Bulgaria). I watched the whole thing alone, like West Germany–Morocco, deep in nostalgic space.

The quality was surprisingly good. The fans all looked like farmers. The ads at the edges of the fields were for alcohol, tires, and cigarettes. The players wore short shorts and short haircuts. Though not Brazil's Rivelino, who sported a shag and a mustache, and, from my amateur's perspective, played better than Pelé. Despite what history remembers as a legendary performance, Pelé looked to me like a man who spent most of the tournament hobbling to his feet after being preemptively fouled, while Rivelino and Jairzinho got the goals. Some of the players on the Swedish team worked *day jobs*. And then there was the commentary: innocent, avuncular, genteel:

"My word, he's got a kick like a mule!"

"Rubiños was left like a foundering whale."

"No danger to this big, handsome Belgian goalkeeper. This boy last year was only eight stone. Now he's nine stone. Look what football's done for him."

"The little men from the tiny republic—they're not beaten yet!"

* * *

Friends who turned down invitations to watch got into the habit of asking me how the 1970 World Cup was going, who was doing well, if I wanted to place a small bet on the outcome. I detected some mockery, *the mockery of infidels*, but I did not care. I turned to Sweden–Italy for solace, as others might turn to the Bible—which itself, if you looked, had some apropos passages: "Blessed are they which are persecuted for righteousness' sake: for theirs is the kingdom of heaven." And: "When thou prayest, enter into thy closet." Watching the 1970 World Cup by myself, in a dark TV room, doors shut at my wife's request, was like living in a closet, in heaven. It was lonely. But knowing the politics and history that surrounded these countries in 1970 made for the best cultural/historical/sociological—yea, sacramental—experience of my life.

I resisted rooting for Brazil. Rooting for Brazil in soccer is like rooting for America in war. I went for the underdogs, the teams from countries that no longer exist: Czechoslovakia, West Germany, the Soviet Union. Brazil won, of course, providing me, in my own private 1970, with several of the most rapturous moments I've ever had in front of a television screen. They won me over. But they weren't the only great team. England was almost as good, if mostly in the elegance of their defense. The West Germans were heroic in their determination. Franz Beckenbauer, the original sweeper, or attacking defender, played in the semifinal with a dislocated shoulder, his arm strapped to his side. And Italy, when sufficiently pressed, and pressed they were, proved capable of inspiring soccer, beating Germany 4-3 in an epic, two hour semifinal—a task that left them sapped for the final, which Brazil won easily, deservedly. They've taken home the trophy in three of the five World Cups I've seen. After 1970 I finally understood why. As Nick Hornby has written about the champions of 1970: "In a way Brazil ruined it for all of us. They had revealed a kind of Platonic ideal that nobody, not even the Brazilians, would ever be able to find again… 1970 was a half-remembered dream they had once had of themselves."

Soccer's worldwide popularity isn't surprising when you look at what has always motivated humanity: money and God. There's lots of money in soccer, of course. League soccer (like capitalism or war) is basically the childlike desire to make dreams come true, no matter what the cost, played by men with enough money to combine commodities like the best Brazilian attacker, Dutch midfielder, British defender, and German goalie and turn them loose on whatever the other billionaires can put together—an unfair situation that describes much of the world these days. But God's there, too.

What is soccer if not everything that religion should be? Universal yet particular, the source of an infinitely renewable supply of hope, occasionally miraculous, and governed by simple, uncontradictory rules ("Laws," officially) that everyone can follow. In fact, if only for this last reason, soccer's got it over on religion. Unlike God's Laws or Allah's Shari'a, soccer's Laws are all laws of equality and non-violence and restraint, and all free to be delayed in their application or even reinterpreted at the discretion of a reasonable arbiter. What the ref says goes, no matter how flagrantly in violation of dogma his decisions may be, and despite the fact that he earns his living as a concert pianist, a middle school math teacher, a tire salesman, or commissioner of penitentiary police—to name the professions of four men who reffed in the '06 World Cup. My official rulebook, after presenting a detailed, Olafthon1-style enumeration of soccer's seventeen Laws, concludes that the ref can throw out any of them in order to apply what it rather mystically calls "the spirit of fair play." Spirit is the only real Law within the boundaries of the soccer field (boundaries that themselves are allowed to vary according to the realities of any given playing situation—unlike, say, the earth's location at the time of Galileo).

The religious undercurrent in soccer runs especially deep in World Cup years. Teams from across the globe converge on the host nation in something of an unarmed, athletic Crusade. As in the Crusades, the host nation tends to repel them. There's a weird power in home-team advantage. Hosts always find a level of success disproportionate to their talents on paper, triumphing over stronger sides, as if exerting a gravitational pull on the game, causing it to be played the way they want to play it, as if, to carry this metaphor to its inevitable conclusion, God were on their side. These unexpected heroics can make for great watching—especially for the impartial amateur. One of the best contests I've ever seen was 2002's second-round matchup between cohost South Korea and three-time world champion Italy. This was farther than Korea had ever advanced, and nobody expected them to do any better. But with the stadium in Daejeon, near the geographic center of South Korea, filled with over forty thousand people, seemingly all wearing red shirts and banging kettle drums, the national team played with such vehemence that they took Italy into overtime. Christian Vieri, the *Azzurri* striker who usually spent quarterfinals just a quarter step off offside, was actually playing defensively, and sweating. Ahn Jung-Hwan, the Korean midfielder who eventually won the game with a golden goal, was also sweating, more than I'd ever seen an athlete sweat: great silvery explosions kept flying out of his hair every time he headed the ball. The Italian players were running as hard as children—all after him. The whole game felt possessed. It was David and Goliath—for two hours. The Italians, a team of dour and disciplined professionals, rather than breaking the opposition's flow, as they'd been trained to do, were being forced to play the game like the South Koreans: running, running, running, running, and—when Jung-Hwan rose up and headed the ball with neck-jerking, spray-showering force in over tired old Paolo Maldini's head—losing.

I turned off my TV and was surprised I couldn't still hear the celebrating.

South Korea kept on going, through the quarterfinals, all the way to the semi, which they barely lost to Germany. For a while they were the world's team. We all wanted to play soccer like South Korea. But it only took one loss for them to collapse, as if the spirit had abandoned them. They gave up the first of three goals in the third-place game against Turkey in a record eleven seconds—the fastest score in World Cup history. They'd been propelled as far as they could go, by belief alone, and then they were done.

America advanced past the group stage when the tournament was in the US. An epic rout will surely occur when the Cup is hosted by Brazil, whose dominant style of play, for some mysterious reason, is less like the chaos and Catholicism of Brazilian culture than the force and resourcefulness of American capitalism: opportunistic, well defended (Brazil has appeared in more tournaments and conceded fewer goals than any other nation), ready to avail itself of all loopholes, overwhelming in its force and originality. If American life is geared to profit, Brazilian life is geared to goals. Seeing the Brazilian national team on the field is to see a country's very soul distilled into eleven guys with no last names.

But, demographically, how deep can the pool of talent in Brazil really be, when compared to India or China? Shouldn't countries with bigger populations inevitably produce a higher percentage of great athletes? Shouldn't India, as the populous former colony of the nation that invented soccer, be the dominant practitioner? (Instead they play cricket.) Or isn't athletic talent directly correlated to nutrition—shouldn't the best-fed country win? Japan then!

No. Though the fact that the World Cup could even take place in Japan and South Korea was a victory. In less than half a century South Korea went from barring the Japanese national team from passing its borders for a World Cup qualifier to cohosting the tournament with its former occupier. We might live to see the Cup cohosted by Israel and Palestine.

I mean this. Soccer's universality is its simplicity—the fact that the game can be played anywhere with anything. Urban children kick a can on concrete and rural kids kick a rag wrapped around a rag wrapped around a rag, barefoot, on dirt. Soccer is something to believe in now, perhaps, like its central piece of equipment, empty at its core, but not a stand-in for anything else.

In 1990, Pelé predicted that an African country would soon win the World Cup. Shortly after the 1990 tournament I visited Africa with an Italian tour group that used me as an English translator. This was Zambia, where the main industry is copper mining and every copper mine has a soccer team. I tried ridiculously hard to become Zambian. I memorized the difference between a Hyena print (oval, with a heart at the bottom) and a lion print (round, with a squashed nose at the bottom). I learned the lion call. I found out how to call someone a liar in the local dialect ("Boza!"). I ate dinner, with my hands, out of a shared plastic bucket with half a dozen villagers.

Hands in our food, we talked about soccer. Zambia was about to play Zaire in the neighbors' first post–World Cup match, an early African Nations Cup qualifier, and the Zambians were full of optimism. The future of soccer was going to be in Africa.

A few days later I was in the capital, Lusaka. Having missed the big match by a day (Zaire won), I decided to watch a league game between a mining-town team, the Konkola Blades of Chililabombwe, and the Red Arrows, the Ministry of Finance squad. These were the young players who had a chance to make the next Zambian national team and win the World Cup in 1994. Or that's what Pelé and I thought.

I took a cab to a stadium outside the city, bought a ticket, and sat in the concrete bleachers. After carefully scanning the crowd it seemed fair to conclude that I was the only white person interested in Zambian league soccer. Then, as the bleachers filled up, the space around me remained empty, in a zone some twenty feet across, like a penalty box. I felt like a goalie. But I didn't really think much about it. When the game started I got caught up in the fever of it and stopped wondering why nobody would sit with me.

The Arrows wore red and the Blades wore blue. It was attacking soccer, running soccer, the sort of soccer you see when both teams want to win but neither has an advantage of age or experience or talent or fan support. The players were exuberant and serious. No score at the half. I went to the bathroom, figuring I might lose my seat, and not caring: I could squeeze in somewhere. When I came back, the empty space was still there, so I sat in its center again.

A few minutes after the restart, at around the fifty-minute mark, I noticed a shift in the crowd's attention, a collective wavering that amplified into a change in focus. Suddenly everyone on the other side of the field was looking in my direction, and the rows in front of me started turning around, too. Soon even the closest spectators, right at the edge of my empty radius, turned and looked at me. Then they started moving away. The whole stadium was looking at me, and I couldn't pretend it wasn't happening. I started to feel very, very uncomfortable.

I had missed some cue. Was I wearing the wrong color shirt? Did I look like a fan from some hated place? Was it simply that I was the only Caucasian in the stadium? The space continued dilating around me. I thought I was about to be a casualty of soccer violence.

I mumbled "hello"—*boza*, my only vocabulary word, seemed like a bad idea—to a man who was looking straight at me but for some reason wouldn't quite focus his eyes on mine. He didn't answer.

Then I saw something in my peripheral vision, close to my back. I turned around. A tall man in a yellow track suit was looking over my head at the game. The peripheral object was his knee. I was virtually in his lap. Where had he come from? On either side of him sat several other men in identical track suits, their knees equally impressive. I'd been so engrossed in the game that I hadn't noticed their arrival. More began to sit beside me.

This was the victorious Zairian national soccer team. They had stuck around Lusaka, come to see the local league game, and now sat remarkably still, with no tension in their bodies; a stillness that seemed to come of spending their lives running. I stared. They didn't care. Everybody else was staring, too. When they'd all sat down around me—the space had apparently been reserved for this purpose—the crowd applauded. We all watched the game together.

When the Arrows and the Blades ended the game in a scoreless tie, the crowd jumped onto the field. The Zairians got up to go. I stayed for a while. I have never been in better company. I was on a national team. A boy in shorts kicked the game ball into the goal, then leaped in celebration.

FIFA, which stands for Fédération Internationale de Football Association (founded in Paris on May 21—my birthday!—1904), soccer's governing body, is the most powerful international authority on earth. It oversees all of global soccer, setting tournament dates, choosing host nations, and ranking countries. These rankings are much touted, constantly fluctuating, and meaningless. In the run-up to the 2006 World Cup, the US beat Mexico and England lost to Northern Ireland, a team ranked near the bottom in the world, just above Hong Kong—but it's a telling fact that one of the terms of the Chinese takeover of Hong Kong was the nonabolition of the Special Administrative Region's own national soccer team.

What makes the World Cup most beautiful is the world; all of us together. Watching the 1970 tournament, leaping up at goals, shouting in solitude, I wished more than anything that I'd actually been there in the stands, knowing what I could only know about those countries with thirty-two years' hindsight. It's the rare sport (let alone religion) that allows for both knowledge and wonder.

Every four years the joy of being one of the couple billion people watching thirty-two countries abide by seventeen rules fills me with the conviction, perhaps ignorant, but like many ignorant convictions, fiercely held, that soccer can unite the world.

SCANNING UPDIKE

2006

At BookExpo America, before what looked to me to be the breakfasting majority of America's booksellers and editors, John Updike prophesied the digitization of all print into an online "universal library." It was prophesy by proxy, as the first guy to float the idea was one of the editors of *Wired* magazine. But Updike conveyed the premise with conviction. Then he told the audience that digitization was a "grisly" scenario, one that would lead readers to download and cut books into playlist-like "snippets"—treating novels like albums. The word *snippets* was delivered with an East Coast snap, teeth into an apple.

Watching this performance I didn't believe that Updike thought there was any correlation between the tracks of a recording and the paragraphs of a book. It was propaganda. And much more personal. Here was a writer who hadn't actually been edited for decades; his *own* state of solipsism/removal causing him to describe the act of cutting his stuff as "grisly." As if universal electronic access to books might mean that readers would tackle the editing themselves.

And Updike, close to death, looking back on a century-spanning career—comprising perhaps twenty thousand bound-between-covers pages—was watching his immortality slip away.

Readers want what they are reading to have already undergone the sort of editing that allows a book to be the most intimate, immersive, pleasurable art form yet invented.

In 1998 I downloaded Constance Garnett's public-domain translation of *The Brothers Karamazov* and searched it for references to a character called Marfa Ignatievna. My goal was to better understand why a Russian-speaking railroad executive's wife had taken the name of a character who "obeyed" yet "pestered" her "honest and incorruptible" husband, and given it to a small town in the most remote part of the lower forty-eight states. Having a searchable version of the novel—which I also owned and knew—provided me with what I never have enough of as a writer (especially a writer with children): time. Writing, for me, is all about finding the time to write. A universal library of scanned and searchable books would be the greatest imaginable gift to writers and readers alike.

Who will DJ *The Mill on the Floss*, Sister Souljah's *The Coldest Winter Ever,* and one of Mr. Updike's golf poems into a grisly new work?:

> I shall be a clever woman, said Maggie, with a toss.
> O, I dare say, and a nasty conceited thing… a bad bitch…
> [Who] handles her business without making it seem like business.
> Only dumb girls let love get them delirious…
> You slide you eyes down to his zipper, check for the print.
> Inside you scream…

their genitals hang dead as practice balls,

their blue legs twist;

Where, now, are their pars and their furor?

Emerging from the shower shrunken, they are men, mere men, old
	boys, lost,

the last hole a horror.

Only another writer.

We have most to benefit and the least to lose from bookscanning.

Publishers, on the other hand...

After Updike made his closing statement—"booksellers, defend your lonely forts"—*Publishers Weekly* claimed that a "standing ovation" took place. In fact it was a reluctant standing ovation. A single woman stood immediately, while most others sat for as long as possible, until her solitude grew uncomfortable, and they joined in to relieve everyone's embarrassment.

TRAVELS WITH DEATH

2008

To better understand the comedy and poverty of the United States, I decided to cross them very slowly.

In the fall of 2002, in the company of a dog and an architect, I drove a 1960 Chevy Apache 10 pickup truck, at a maximum speed of forty-five miles per hour, from Far West Texas to New York City—2,364 miles through desert, suburbs, forests, lake-spattered plains, mountains, farmland, more suburbs, the Holland Tunnel.

A year before this drive the planes had hit the towers, twenty blocks from my apartment. And in the months before and after that my best friend from adolescence had died, my senior-most aunt had died, the man I'd long thought of as a father and my actual father had died. Death had come up fast and refused to pass me by.

And then, just a few days before I set out, another death: Geraldine Simmons Crumpler, a woman who'd raised me more than either of my parents, whom I saw and spoke to and corresponded with regularly, was suddenly hospitalized in San Antonio for kidney failure, and gone within a day.

Wanting to see the country, not wanting to obstruct the freeways, I had to stay on back roads. Where I began back roads were the only roads available. This was the town of Marfa, Texas, sixty miles north of the Mexican border, surrounded by one of the few untouched landscapes remaining in the lower forty-eight—a high desert formed in the Permian period and left more or less alone in the 250 million years since. All roads out of Marfa lead across empty yellow grasslands, through blue sage and cactus-covered mountains, where the traveler's only company is the weather. A hailstorm once blackened the sky behind me, caught up, dented my hood, starred my windshield, covered the pavement in ice cubes, and moved on into the distance. At night the stars glowed like phosphorescence in the sea and were as abundant as static on a broken TV.

Driving slow both satisfied and ran contrary to my instinct to flee. And, pleasingly to my mind, it made fun of the two main preoccupations of our entire country: velocity and ease. Not that I didn't appreciate velocity in particular. On a road trip a few years prior I'd tried to set a car's cruise control at 140 miles per hour. Another time, on a jungle road between Oaxaca and Veracruz, Mexico, I pulled out of my lane to overtake a truck, while another truck was coming straight at me, cutting it so close I actually heard the oncoming driver's voice as he screamed in panic.

Now I would piss off and get passed by everyone, including a guy hauling hay, and a wide-load trailer pulling a house. I almost passed a school bus in Arkansas,

but, when the half-asleep driver spotted me, he sat up and floored it. I would be the slowest person in America.

M y traveling companions were a dog named Charlie Chaplin and an architect named Michael Meredith. Michael and I became friends in Marfa—where the minimalist artist Donald Judd exiled himself in the 1970s from the "harsh and glib" New York art scene— in 2000, when he was in town designing a house for Judd's longtime companion, Marianne Stockebrand, and my wife Daphne and I were guests of an arts foundation, each working on a book. Michael left for a teaching job back east, and Daphne and I stayed on—that's when I saw the truck, in front of the post office: boxy, banged up, covered in sky-blue house paint, half-smashed windshield a lattice of stars and linear cracks, like a flag. A Mexican man in his sixties walked outside with his mail (smoking a cigar, wearing a cowboy hat) and drove it away. I biked around town till I found it parked out by the cemetery, around the corner from the beauty parlor. Jesse Santisteban, the owner, said I could take a closer look. The doors had handmade wooden armrests, and the seat belts were canvas and chain link. There was orange shag on the floorboards. He opened the hood and showed me the spot in the engine compartment where he'd signed it like an artist. I asked if he'd ever thought of selling. He said, "Never thought of selling." Then he told me he had kidney stones and needed an operation. Without even thinking I offered him $1,200.

"Guess I'll sell it," he said.

After going to the courthouse and making it official he handed over the keys (on a green plastic fob that said LAUGH, LIVE, LOVE, AND BE HAPPY!) and warned, "Don't take it over forty-five or it'll throw a rod."

A friend later explained, "That's a polite way of saying the engine will explode."

Daphne and I also acquired a puppy around the same time, Charlie, whom we took back to New York a couple months later. I left the truck, which Jesse agreed to look after. I didn't think much about it till two years later, when I got a letter saying my insurance policy had been canceled because I had "neither possession nor control" of the vehicle. I called Jesse, who said all was well. Well, sort of well. There was maybe some seeping brake fluid. He mumbled something that sounded like "Butterwutchdat." And I decided I had to drive it back to New York. Michael agreed to meet me in Marfa.

Charlie (now quite big) and I flew back in order to assess/drive this piece-of-folk-art-cum-death-trap, which had never gone farther than the nearby town of Pecos, across the country, seeing America in a way almost nobody gets, or wants, to see it.

I booked the trip and coordinated schedules and then I got the news: the woman who'd raised me was dead.

As Geri's youngest son, Verne, put it, "Mother looked upon you like you were one of hers and my brothers and I have always followed the mention of your name with something like, 'Yeah, that our Lil invisible brother.'" But after a humiliating conversation with American Airlines on the topic of "bereavement fares," my ineligibility for one, and the nonrefundability of my ticket to Far West Texas, I decided to stay invisible. I'd dodge everyone else's grief and mourn—or avoid mourning—alone. In slow motion. Behind the wheel.

And the route I'd planned would take me right past Geri's grave.

* * *

At nine a.m. on a Wednesday, I honked the horn in front of a small adobe, where Michael had spent the night with some friends. It was a clear sound in the dry air. Michael burst out of the house. He looked harried. Renderings for the place he'd designed for Stockebrand had appeared in *Architecture* magazine and attracted a Texan I'll call Don Harris, who'd written Michael and asked if he would come to San Antonio to discuss the construction of "a house with no walls." We were headed there first.

On the phone we'd planned out the trip as follows: always take back roads, eat only in non-chains, never hurry, spend a day in San Antonio with Mr. Harris so Michael could design another house (potentially his first to be built), write songs to perform at an open mike in Nashville. Charlie would ride in the bed of the truck, and we would have the cab. I tied his long leash to the truck's roll bar so he'd know not to jump out.

Michael looked like an architect—thin, with thick glasses, black pants, and a white shirt, the two colors separated by a belt with a brushed-steel buckle—without an architect's manner. He loved junk food, slept in his clothes, mumbled and mixed slang and mock formality when speaking. He'd met Charlie, but this was his first look at the truck.

"Hello Charles," he said, then remarked, "I like the shotgun rack."

"Yeah," I said. "It's also good for keeping umbrellas."

He stared. "*No*, man. *Umbrellas?* What kind of wuss-ass keeps umbrellas in his shotgun rack? If we do that we're not even worthy of this truck. We'll be a laughingstock." He shut the door

SEAN WILSEY

and looked out at the road through the splintered-flag windshield. Fifteen up-and-down cracks, thirty-one left-to-right ones, scattered constellations of stars. The motor vehicle code in our destination state read: "No crack of 11 inches long or longer is allowed if any part of the crack is within the area cleared by the windshield wiper." I'd have to deal with it when I got there—no 1960 Chevy windshield replacements were available in Marfa.

"Can you drive like that?"

Hard to say. But if we made it to New York we'd be breaking the motor vehicle code fifty-two times. Then he noticed the stick shift.

"Oh, shit, man, I didn't sleep all night because I was worried about that. I can't drive stick."

"What?"

"Sorry, I didn't think it would be a stick shift. I mean, it's American. Everything's easy in America."

"It's from 1960."

"I'm sorry, man."

I figured I could teach him. There was nothing to hit out in the desert. Then he told me we had to be in San Antonio by nine a.m. the next day to meet Don, his potential client. San Antonio was just under four hundred miles away. I'd been thinking we'd reach Del Rio, half the distance, following along the Rio Grande.

"You know we can only go forty-five."

"What? C'mon—you're joking, right?"

"No. Really. Look at this thing," I said. Michael took in the ancient interior and medieval seat belts. "Can you call and say that we'll be there around noon?"

"I only have his e-mail. I just told him we'd be there. But come on, *fifty*? We can definitely do fifty."

After a pause I said, primly, "We'll just keep driving till we get there."

* * *

With every year of adulthood, there are increasing numbers of relationships that are central and time-consuming and financially imperative but have nothing to do with friendship.

I thought, ridiculously, that the truck was my friend—a near-dead one that, if I could get it back to New York, would allow me to get one over on death. Its very oldness transformed taking a long time to travel into a sort of time travel.

Geri Crumpler had taught me the meaning of friendship. She was—in the convoluted tradition of black women occupying the center of certain white households—my family's cook (my mom sent her off to study with Jacques Pépin). It was an odd arrangement for San Francisco in the early 1970s. Though she did much of her cooking for my mom's then-best friend, Alex Haley, the author of *Roots* (and "Uncle Alex" to me). I have a framed snapshot of Geri and Haley standing with their arms around each other on the aft deck of *Lord Ligonier*, the slave ship used in the ABC miniseries based on his book.

When I was a child Geri'd laughed at my jokes before anyone else. Cardiac arrest seemed imminent when she'd fall into a chair at our kitchen table, panting, "Oh, Sean-Sean!" Then I'd bring her water. After she died, at age eighty-two, I was singled out in a San Antonio paper's obituary as her "embraced son" and included in a list of her close family. The executor of her modest estate later told me, with recrimination, "lots of people attended, on short notice." These attendees included the third of her four sons, just released from prison after a failed robbery and subsequent shoot-out. But I couldn't face the absence of a woman who'd given me more love than any other. There was more than just cowardice to this; there was also pure selfishness, which was really *un-self-knowingness*. Or maybe I should just say cluelessness.

Shortly before she died Geri gave me a copy of *America the Majestic*, a book of recipes and photographs of landscapes like the ones I was planning to drive through. Her inscription read: "Dear Sean Hope you will enjoy this, an when you use it, that it will remind you of our happy days together in the Kitchens of the Past. Love, Your best Friend Geri."

Now, on this drive, when it was too late to make amends, I wondered if I even knew how to be a friend.

From the Marfa grasslands, east through the Glass Mountains, we made the town of Alpine, twenty-five-odd miles away, in forty-five minutes. The gas gauge fell by a third. Afraid there wasn't a lot of fuel in the next leg we decided to buy two ten-gallon jerry cans, along with tools, water, and food.

I should mention here the weird coincidence that we were driving our way through a book I'd never read: John Steinbeck's *Travels with Charley*, wherein—I've now read it—the author and his dog, Charley, lit out on the back roads of America, in the fall of 1960, in a new GM pickup, in order to "rediscover this monster land." In the fall of '02 we were heading out in a 1960 GM pickup (same body style; quite possibly the same assembly line), with a dog named Charlie.

Fleeing death was also Steinbeck's objective. As he put it, a "second childhood falls on so many men. They trade their violence for the promise of a small increase of life span. In effect, the head of the house becomes the youngest child. And I have searched myself for this possibility with a kind of horror. For I have always lived violently... I've lifted, pulled, chopped, climbed, made love with joy and taken my hangovers as a consequence, not as a punishment.

I did not want to surrender fierceness for a small gain in yardage."

He died shortly thereafter, in his mid-sixties, of heart failure (brought on by nonstop smoking and drinking). But before that, in 1962, the year *Travels with Charley* was published, Steinbeck was awarded the Nobel Prize for Literature. Anders Österling, one of the Swedish Academy's judges, a lover of what he once characterized as "taut and sonorous prose," devoted more time in his presentation speech to Steinbeck's travelogue than any other of his books. This made me wonder if Österling had actually read it. As Steinbeck wrote in *Travels*: "I had forgotten how rich and beautiful is the countryside… the lake country of Michigan handsome as a well-made woman… high overhead the arrows of southing ducks and geese. There Charley could with his delicate exploring nose read his own particular literature on bushes and tree trunks and leave his message there, perhaps as important in endless time as these pen scratches I put down on perishable paper."

Shut your mouth, old man! hollered a voice in my head.

Of course there'd been another old man to whom I'd wanted to address such sentiments. Steinbeck's bluster reminded me of my late father, who, for sixty-five of his eighty-two years, kept a Class A, three-axle, commercial truck rating on his driver's license. At the end of his life Dad had a fleet of Peterbilt and Kenworth sleeper tractors that hauled black-and-white trailers with WILSEY emblazoned of their sides. They were easiest to spot between the hours of ten p.m. and two a.m. heading east on I-10, I-40, and I-80. Though the violence and fierceness of my father the trucker ends there. His trucks were full of blossoms. Dad was the second-largest shipper of fresh-cut flowers in the US. Four out of every ten weddings and funerals in the country got its flowers

off the back of a Wilsey truck. In his late fifties, the same age as Steinbeck when he took his drive, Dad learned how to fly a Hughes 500D turbine jet helicopter, and throughout his sixties and seventies routinely flew himself across the country from San Francisco, where I grew up, to the East Coast. He made thirteen crossings, usually with an employee or friend, and never, despite repeated requests, with me. (Steinbeck knew his son would "probably never forgive" him for not being allowed to come along. Such thoughts never even occurred to my father, who, in a gesture that struck me as a sort of taunt, sent me one copilot's lengthy description of the 1994 crossing: "He headed east, then north along the squall line looking for a break. There wasn't any… At dusk, in pouring rain, he landed the helicopter in the parking lot of a Ramada Inn. He went inside and asked the astonished manager if he had a vacancy, if he would please park his helicopter outside over night, and if he might purchase a comb and tooth brush."

Even if *Travels with Charley* is not a book of taut and sonorous prose, Steinbeck is precise and prescient about America, throwing off observations about how "there will come a time when we can no longer afford our wastefulness—chemical wastes in the rivers, metal wastes everywhere, and atomic wastes buried deep in the earth or sunk in the sea." And in a letter Steinbeck wrote to Adlai Stevenson he makes the dead-on observation that as a country we "can stand anything God and Nature throw at us save only plenty. If I wanted to destroy a nation, I would give it too much and I would have it on its knees, miserable, greedy and sick."

Michael and I were careful with each other that first day, rolling slowly and courteously through the desert. Around lunchtime we'd made it eighty-four more miles. We stopped outside the town of Sanderson and filled up the tank again.

A lean old man touched his cowboy hat, pointed at the truck, and said, "'65?"

Michael replied, "Yep," and the man walked away.

I said, "It's a '60, actually."

Michael said, "Yeah, but why bother correcting somebody? He doesn't care what year it is really, he just wants to feel like he *knows* something—now he feels good."

We were on a slight downhill—a good place to learn stick, so I let Michael drive. The truck got going after a few stalls, and we rolled through the Chihuahuan Desert. Getting cocky, he tried to sneak it up to fifty and I shouted him down as he struggled with the loose steering, veering into the oncoming lane—me scared and hollering "Watch out!"; him apologizing, "Sorry, sorry, I got a trick leg!"— until a rank of orange plastic drums, like buoys in the sea of the desert, shunted us to the side of the road. Two border patrol agents asked where we were going.

In this context, Michael in his architect's uniform and me in a skateboard sweatshirt and Kangol hat, we made no sense as anything other than a gay couple. They looked at our IDs, walked off to confer, and seemed to be snickering.

We waited in total silence. Eventually they handed our licenses back and waved us on. I willed Michael not to stall. And he didn't. Instead he threw it in reverse, and we started back toward Marfa.

The agents didn't bother hiding their laughter.

Michael said, "Shit, man."

Then he stalled. Charlie lost his balance, fell over in the bed, and gave me an aggrieved look. A few minutes later he tried to dive out of the back. I jumped from the cab and somehow caught him before he could hang himself on his leash. It felt like the temperature in his fur was two hundred degrees.

I said, "Jesus, Charlie. What are you doing?" He lifted his nose and gave me a gentle tap on the neck. I sat him between Michael and me, and took the wheel.

Charlie was a Catahoula, the state dog of Louisiana. Though his appearance frequently provoked the questions "Is that a wolf?" and "Is that a dingo?" when he was happy his eyes—deep, orange, unblinking—laughed and he opened his mouth, curled back his lips, and nodded his head up and down. He was also conversational and made a lot of noises that definitely weren't barking, growling, or anything canine. Things like: "Wroarowlwolf." "Oohwar." "Rrolf." "Aaahlh!" "Meol." "Wrrp." Going by all the distinct letters I heard him pronounce (a talent shared by Steinbeck's Charley), I was pretty sure I could have taught him to speak a few words in English.

Virtually every time Daphne or I walked him someone reacted with alarm or surprise. One time four young black men in North Face jackets and sweats stood blocking the sidewalk as their seeming leader held forth, "She got seventy million—if that's not real money, what is?" Then he noticed Charlie and pointed: "Don't that look like one of those wild dogs of Africa?"

A young Latino man with a hard face and a boxer's physique, loitering in front of the downtown New York branch of Planned Parenthood, briefly shrugged off his sadness when he saw Charlie and said, "Looks like one of them hyenas, don't it?"

Daphne once told me, "Charlie's got a special relationship with you because he thinks you're part dog." But Charlie was not a dog himself. And not just because the Catahoula is the only breed of canine whose name contains the word cat—twice (the official name is Catahoula Leopard, though Louisianans call them Catahoula Curs). Dogs are supposed to abandon manners at the first opportunity, but Charlie did not. He was courteous, decorous, even courtly. He *was* gentle. He'd've opened doors if he could have. "After *you*," Charlie always seemed to be saying. This is strange behavior for a dog but common for a wolf. They are collaborative. Interpack aggression is routine in dogs and rare in wolves, who  survive through concerted effort and subtle communication (though they are obviously dangerous to non-wolves). And, as in the case of windshield cracks, New York state law is unequivocal on their domestication: "No person may possess, release, transport, import or export…any animal, the overall appearance of which makes it difficult or impossible to distinguish it from a wolf (*Canis lupus*) or a coyote (*Canis latrans*)."

I once called St. Tammany Parish, Louisiana, to ask some questions of Don Abney, the author of *The Louisiana Catahoula Leopard Dog*. In response to my inquiry about the rampant assertion, spread by web and averred by Wikipedia, that the Catahoula was the first dog in America, Abney snorted, "Wikipedia's full of crap." Barking in the background. "The Catahoula began back in de Soto's age."

Hernando de Soto (whose name means "Bold Voyager of the Thicket" in English) was the failed leader of the first European expedition through the southern United States. "When the explorer came from Florida and bred his mastiffs and greyhounds with the native red wolf. Then the French came and bred those dogs with Beaucerons to make Catahoulas. De Soto came in the spring of 1541, and if that's the oldest dog we've got, well, it doesn't sound too old to me." Pause. "I guess this is America, though." We agreed. Then he brightened. "They grin. Like they're thinking, *you'll never get it*. I couldn't say that on a stage in front of other breeders, though. They'd laugh at me."

I'd noticed this sort of gentle mockery in Charlie, directed at me and at canines. During one hot afternoon in the Tompkins Square Park dog run, a big Rhodesian ridgeback kept starting fights, until Charlie backed up as far as he could and ran straight at the dog. At the last moment before impact he jumped *over* it—legs fully extended during the hang time, as several people shouted *"Whoa!"* The Rhodesian ridgeback lay down on the ground and caused no further trouble.

In much of America a permit is required for a wolf hybrid's ownership (let alone a wolf's), and only given for research, education, or exhibit. According to a spokesman with New York State's Department of Environmental Conservation, the same permit "also covers things like lions." Legislation in Hernando de Soto's home continent states: "Any generation of 'hybrid' with wolf in its ancestry… cannot be classified as *Canis familiaris*, theoretically *ad infinitum*." That was Charlie.

The landscape unfolded, changing only because the light was changing. It seemed that we were making no progress. Only my discomfort had progressed. The truck's bench seat had springs that poked most of the way through on the driver's side, which had collapsed over the decades into a scar tissue–like accumulation of patched fabric covered by a horse blanket. A couple hours sitting on wad and wire produced searing pain, which, prolonged over days, became near crippling. Adding to the discomfort was the fact that Charlie kept imperceptibly shoving me, until my right arm was fully extended to reach the Bakelite knob on top of the shifter, my left hip pressed hard into the door, and he was *at the wheel*.

"Charles just wants to be in charge," Michael said.

(Or, like a wolf, he wanted to contribute.)

The first European to see this part of West Texas was Hernando de Soto's countryman and contemporary, Álvar Núñez Cabeza de Vaca (Elfin Army Son-of-Grandfather Head-of-Cow). He came right past Marfa in the 1520s. Ignoring the scenery, he limited his observations to the inhabitants, whom he described as "well built" and "whiter than any we had met." He also wrote that those native Americans who acted as his guides were "great liars" who terrorized their countrymen: "wherever we arrived, the people would be robbed and plundered by those in our party."

Now Michael said, "Uh."

I said, "Yeah?"

"I found out a couple days ago that I'm one of the six finalists to design a memorial for the victims of the attack on the Pentagon."

It took me a second to realize what he was talking about.

"What? The 9/11 memorial in Washington?"

"Yeah. Right where the plane crashed."

"Wow. What's your design?"

"It's a viewing pedestal. The people who come to remember are the memorial. They're living statues. The idea is to be really small and intimate next to something that is out-of-control big—one of the few man-made objects you can see from outer space. For a memorial it seems better to be modest—it's more likely to be built if it isn't expensive. But I can't believe they picked me as a finalist."

"It's amazing."

"To be able to memorialize something on the same ground where people died is amazing. But I don't know what the victims' families are going to think about my idea. I have to meet with them next week in DC. And the New York victims' families, too. The New York families also want the New York names in DC. Of course the DC names aren't going to be in New York."

This struck me as an insult to grief.

"When do you have to meet the families?"

"Uh." Long pause. "Tuesday."

"Michael—that's in five days! It's impossible!"

"Let's just keep driving. We'll see what happens."

A situation of foregone failure, or mutual conning (a consensus to ignore doom somewhat reminiscent of our national decision-making process), had been set up, and it would pull at us for the rest of the trip. What would happen to my plans to go slow?

Signs of civilization began to appear along the road, indicating our emergence from the landscape of the Paleozoic and into twenty-first century America.

A change in acoustics that had begun in Del Rio was complete by the time we pulled into the empty lot of Triple T Mexican Restaurant in Uvalde. I could no longer hear every breath or snuffle from Michael and Charlie. Traffic was muted, too, shushing by like a river instead of a West Texas rock slide. In the empty dining room we were waited on by a pretty Mexican girl with a diamond tennis bracelet. I ordered a salad. Michael got a burrito. The waitress seemed actively disgusted that we had chosen her restaurant. In the bathroom—filthy; mud and toilet paper all over a cracked-tile enclosure that was damp like a cave—I discovered that the handles had been removed from the taps in the bathroom sink. The only water that flowed flowed constantly in the stained and sweating toilet. When I got back to the table my salad had arrived: shredded iceberg and chunks of under-ripe avocado, all soaking wet.

"My salad was dressed with water," I said.

Michael shrugged. My mind flashed between the flowing toilet and my sodden lettuce. I ate a few bites, pushed it away, and turned to a basket of chips, which were good. Nobody in West Texas had forgotten how to fry.

*   *   *

At around midnight we arrived in San Antonio and pulled up to the Menger Hotel in Alamo Plaza (next to the Alamo itself), where we were to meet Don, and asked about a room. The answer: no dogs allowed. So we drove to the outskirts of town and found a Red Roof Inn beside I-37. Michael waited in the truck with Charlie while I went to see about a vacancy.

When I entered the lobby a fat man was lecturing the female desk clerk in a drawling, deep, sarcastic tone: "I want to make sure I will not be disturbed tomorrow morning. Last night I hung out the Do Not Disturb sign and the maid knocked on my door this morning to ask me if I knew I had the Do Not Disturb sign out." Very long pause. "I had a real hard time staying polite."

This hint of menace and plans gone wrong was a fitting introduction to San Antonio: a town of failure, identity defined by a lost battle, where minor skirmishes overlaid an atmosphere of general thwartedness. A town where, visiting Geri, I once saw a woman pushing a baby carriage in a Day-Glo T-shirt that read:

FUCK

Y'ALL

I'M FROM

TEXAS

A skinny, wiry, compactly muscular man was standing off to the side in the Red Roof's lobby, smugly observing this exchange. His general affect: *you'll never get it.* He had long, flaming-red hair, a pronounced chin, and was smirking. He was also a quarter inch thick, and made of a pneumatic-hydraulic laminated cardboard. A name tag on his chest read "Red."

This was the Red Roof Inn's brief mascot, or "Director of Guest Happiness." The company's Senior Director of Marketing in Dallas told me, "He was useful till 2005 when we retired him. He didn't fit our business imagery. There's a fine line between quirky and irreverent, and he wasn't right for us, so we walked away from him. His time as an icon had passed." Our 2002 visit had corresponded with his brief reign. But soon it would be impossible to find any evidence that Red had even existed.

I noticed that there was a back entrance, over Red's shoulder. He seemed to gesture at it. And I realized that it led straight to the elevators, circumventing the desk.

A night cost fifty dollars. I paid cash. While Michael took our stuff inside I walked Charlie around the neighborhood, then through the back, catching the door before it closed behind a woman in a tight gray business suit. Charlie followed me like a gentleman. She gave him a look of withering contempt.

I later wondered if she had mistaken Charlie for an animal called Smut, another, very similar-looking, and locally notorious Texas Catahoula. This canine's notoriety stemmed from his compunction to tear through a field of motion detectors, dodge flak-jacketed Secret Servicemen, and go swimming in then-president George W. Bush's pool. His owners, Bill and LaJuana Westerfield, "chained him up some," per Mr. Westerfield, because "every time we'd turn him loose, that idiot was gone." But chaining was not effective. When Vladimir Putin came to visit, Smut slipped his collar.

From the *Dallas Morning News*:

> President Bush was giving Mr. Putin and his staff a coveted tour of the ranch, bouncing across creeks and country roads.
>
> Mrs. Westerfield noticed Smut was gone as she walked across the driveway to her art studio. In the distance, she could see and

hear her dog, barking and chasing after the president and his visitors.

"He chased those Russian dignitaries all over that place," says Mrs. Westerfield… "Poor old Smut. That's when we knew we had to get rid of him."

In the end, Mr. Westerfield even consented to castration for Smut.

"We thought that might slow him down, but it didn't," he says. "That old boy lost everything because he wouldn't stay off the president's place."

As soon as we got in the room Michael turned on the TV and hit the bathroom. A CGI Director of Red Roof Guest Happiness appeared and said, in a drawl, "Hi. I'm *Red*. I'm like *you*—I don't like to spend a lot of money. And I'm *smart*. That's why I stay," growlier, sexier now, "at the *Red Roof Inn*."

Then he just stood there looking at Charlie and me.

"The Red Roof Inn has a CGI mascot called Red," I said to Michael. "Is he a communist?"

Hmm. Silent now, Red was staring while shifting side to side, gunslinger-style, all rough and ready. I expected him to come out with something like, "Hell, trash your room and skip out on the bill. I don't give a shit. S'what I'd do." His voice was the actor John Goodman's.

"He looks like he'd rather sleep in his car than spend the fifty bucks we just spent. That's probably what we should have done."

"No! We've got to look good for Don. I want to build my first house. Maybe tomorrow we can sleep in the truck."

"We'll need blankets."

"Charles can be a blanket."

* * *

I n the morning I found a rolling meadow perfectly designed for running dogs—the landscaped on-ramp berm for I-37. It was freshly mown, with traffic hurtling by at eighty miles per hour on its high end, and Charlie kept lying on his back, rolling in the dewy grass shavings, and fetching a splintery piece of packing crate that must've fallen off a truck.

Michael and I then left an animal that required the same license as a lion behind the Do Not Disturb sign and went to eat. Red Roof had promised a free breakfast for our fifty dollars, and I had visions of a buffet. Off the lobby we found a sterile, closet-size rectangle that contained a Formica table and four folding steel chairs. On offer were plastic bins full of creamer and stirrers, hot water, and machines that dispensed orange juice and cereal. It was like visiting the cafeteria of a moon base built by a budget-strapped space program.

A pair of women in their seventies—both in pantsuits; one beige, the other brown—were sitting at the lone table, both heavily made up. We joined them.

"Where you guys from?" I asked.

"I'm Ginnie from St. Louis," the woman in beige said. She hooked a finger at her friend. "She's from Duluth."

"You travel together a lot?" I asked.

"We met on a trip to Europe"—her voice changed here—"with our *husbands*." Significant pause. "We like to take trips together. Our *husbands* can't anymore, of course." I pictured walkers, oxygen tanks. Michael shifted uncomfortably.

"What've you seen?"

"The River Walk and the IMAX."

I'd visited both of these on trips here to see Geri. The latter featured a film called *ALAMO: The Price of Freedom* (from the script: "Talkin' about freedom's a whole lot different than comin' face-to-face with a man who would take it away"), which a San Antonio city councilman had threatened to boycott because "*Tejanos* are portrayed as subservient, of loose morals and less heroic than their non-Hispanic counterparts." He pointed out that "Mexican soldiers did not parade around the room inside the Alamo with Jim Bowie's body held high and pierced by the ends of a dozen soldiers' bayonets, as shown." He most strenuously objected to, and managed to have excised, a smutty scene whererin an adult male Texan was seduced by an underage Mexican girl—in a church belfry.

I'd brought a ripe mango from Marfa and began to peel it. As the smell exploded into the tiny room a figure appeared at my side and shouted, "Is that a *mango*!?"

I startled, then leaned sideways so I could see: a dark-haired woman in her late forties, braless, in a sheer brown shirt and bright white short shorts. Bruises ran all down her legs, which ended in very clean, white tennis shoes. Red, the Director of Guest Happiness, declared: *Here at Red Roof we know how to look the other way. We understand that sometimes you do your stuff behind a shut door. Cut loose. Get your freak on. Let t'all hang out. Not a problemo. Just hang out your Do Not Disturbo…*

I said, "Uh-huh."

"You get that *here*?"

I looked around the room. A mango was about as probable as it would've been on an asteroid.

"Nope. I brought it along with me."

She responded with a drawn-out sound of pleasure, "Mmmmmmmmmmmmmmm."

I said, "Yeah. It's from Mexico."

"They're good," she said. "*I love to eat them.*"

"Yeah, me too. They're just so bright and full of flavor."

"*Yeah.*" Our eyes met. Everyone was looking at us.

Then she leaned in even closer and confessed, "*I eat the peels and everything.*"

I paused a beat. It felt as though a spell had been cast in the room.

"Isn't eating the peels supposed to make your lips itch?"

She seemed stunned, then defensive. "*Nyah*." Bracing her hand on the wall, "Ha! Ha! I've never heard of *that*."

"Yeah. Seriously. Mango mouth."

The Midwesterners looked appalled. Michael wore the expression of a man nearing his threshold for pain. But I was right. The resinous coating of a mango's skin can produce a reaction similar to that brought on by other members of the sumac family. Witness this internet forum posting:

> I just got back from a visit to a doctor who was baffled at the cause of these poison-ivy like rashes which developed under my chin and all over my "male piece." Then I explained my condition to a friend and the first thing she said was "have you eaten any mangos?" I replied, "In fact I have, 3 of them and right near the time I broke out…" She asked "Did you eat the skin, because that is what made me break into a severe allergic reaction."… I didn't have sex with the mango or my hands… didn't get any juice under my chin either. My lips are chapped too… ugh… I probably used the bathroom after handling the mango and got the oils on my manpiece.

Red shook his head and *tsk*ed.

"Not for me," the woman declared, and exited the room.

I turned back to the Midwesterners and said, "Mangoes are great," which caused my new friend to pull an immediate U and reappearer at my elbow.

"Excuse me!" she said, a bit breathless now. "Did you just say mangoes are *brain food*?! *I think the same thing!*"

Michael mumbled something about needing to get going. Ten minutes later we'd checked out of the Inn. The lobby's cardboard Red said: *You won't mind if I tag along. Red Roof, Blue Roof; hell—no roof.* *Stars over my head outside on the roadside, sleeping—nice thick diesel* *exhaust's all the blanket I need. Dew-n'-roadkill: my breakfast buffet.*

In the parking lot we loaded bags and dog food and slid sloshing gasoline drums. The woman in short shorts reappeared, unsteady on her feet despite the tennis shoes. A couple steps behind her was a middle-aged man in a rumpled gray suit.

She said, "*Oh*, so this is *your* cool truck!"

I said, "Yeah."

Then she caught sight of Charlie. "*Is that a Catahoula?!*"

I nodded. Michael and the man exchanged a look.

"What's his name?"

"Charlie."

"Ooh, Charlie!" She hugged him. Nobody *ever* hugged Charlie. I tensed in anticipation of his decision to rip or not rip out her throat. He seemed to like her.

The man smiled and said, "*Travels with Charley*."

And as we pulled out of the lot they both waved.

The lobby of the Menger Hotel was pillared, balconied, sconce-and-stained-glass-lit, Victorian. Don Harris, a middle-aged man in the midst of all this distinctiveness, was perfectly nondescript. He had a white shirt and a rounded physique that seemed to make the light fall away from him.

Michael said hello and introduced me as a writer. Formalities concluded, Don asked if he could tell us a bit about the city, then started talking, without stopping—delivering a monologue that was, to me, a coastal American with an occasional bias against our landlocked interior, a total revelation about the history, depth, and texture at the heart of the country.

He said:

"San Antonio has always seemed to me to be a city out of a Borges story, particularly one with knife fighters, political thugs, and Hispanic-Irish gangsters, like *Death and the Compass*. The past here is so intense that it's also the present, and nothing ever really disappears. The city's always existed with wild Indians, soldiers, priests, *vaqueros*, *pachucos*, socialites, aristocrats, writers, and working people, in a constant mix. Conrad's favorite writer, R.B. Cunninghame Graham, the Scottish lord—the real king of Scotland, some say— spent several years in San Antonio, attempting to become a cattle

baron, going broke, and then, out of desperation, beginning his writing career with an account of a hanging in Cotulla for the San Antonio *Express*. Stephen Crane wandered around with the Chili Queens in the same plaza where the Comanches would ride into town and receive tribute—pay or the town would be burnt and looted. Till recently it was represented by Congressman Henry B. Gonzalez, the boxer congressman—who flattened another congressman with a single punch, and tried to impeach the first Bush. This lobby is the setting for a scene from *All the Pretty Horses*. John Grady Cole spies on his mother, sitting with 'boots crossed one over the other.' (I know *El Cormac* is being reappraised here and there—but he's still bulletproof in Texas.) Eisenhower had an office in town, and he was in it on the morning he heard about Pearl Harbor. I don't even think he was a general then. The San Antonio gangster Freddie Carrasco, while in prison at Huntsville, made a suit of armor in the style of Ned Kelly and tried to shoot his way out. This is what I mean when I mention Borges."

The above was all delivered in a con artist's *you-already-know-*

what-I'm-telling-you tone. *You're-clued-in-I'm-just-recapitulating*, Harris invited us to agree. And it put me on alert. I started suspecting I would have to write about all this. And there's no surer impediment to a good time than knowing you'll have to write about it.

Waving a hand at the lobby Harris told us, "I chose the Menger because it's easy to find—you just ask someone how to get to the Alamo and everyone knows where that is. Plus, it's a beautiful place in its old age, and full of stories." He took us around an atrium, then down a staircase to the hotel bar—smoky, dark—and said, "Copy of the tap room in the House of Lords." No mention that Teddy Roosevelt mustered his Rough Riders here. Back up the stairs he pointed out a shop that sold tin soldiers. Later I visited and asked a salesman, "Do you have a model of a military jeep from World War II?"

Long pause, glare, then: "No, *sir*. We're sold out of *those*."

I glanced around, noticing some Nazis and Brits. Churchill strode along a shelf followed by a stout woman in pumps.

I said, "I see you've got Churchill. Do you have FDR?"

"The man who designs these is Scottish and he favors the Anglo side, *sir*."

"You've got *Hitler*."

"Germans sell well, *sir*." Not surprising. Road signs around San Antonio point to New Berlin, Scherz, New Braunfels, Greune, Pfeil Road—Texas is as German as America gets. An SS officer sat at mission control in Houston and made the moon launch possible. If the state flew another flag above its current six that flag would be an iron cross.

"You've got Teddy Roosevelt."

"*President* Roosevelt was *in* the Menger, *sir*," he said.

I pointed behind Churchill and asked, "Do you have any other nurses besides this one?"

They did. At the Nuremberg rally: swastikas on posterns, rapt soldiers beautifully rendered, statesmanlike Führer. A pretty blonde in a white dress with a red cross on the right breast stood tall in the back row.

I leaned down for a better look.

"She's giving a Nazi salute," I said.

"Yes, *sir*."

Other female figurines, in a non-Nazi case, were severe, border-line battle ax–ish. One appeared to be yodeling.

I was shopping for a five year-old girl.

"Any sense of when you'll get more military jeeps?"

"I really couldn't say, *sir*."

"Well, do you have any other women that aren't so *butch*?"

The word *butch* hit him like a slap. So I pointed at Churchill's attendant and said it again, "You know, she's really *butch*."

He looked so upset I laughed and told him, "I'm just trying to draw you out!"

At which point he took a step closer and the muscles in his neck tensed. Cocking his head to the side he said, "'Draw me out.' What, *exactly*, do you mean, *'Draw. Me. Out,' sir*?"

"Be friendly. Get some conversation going."

"What would you like to talk about, *sir*?"

Don Harris led us outside—snubbing the Alamo, not even *pointing* at it. A brisk couple-block walk and we were on a corner. He pointed behind us with one hand and ahead with the other. "The Menger and the Gunter—both cattle-king hotels. The latter is where Robert Johnson made his first recordings, in 1936, and rock and roll was born. The state finally put up a plaque five or six years ago. It's kind of cheesy."

Thirty years after Johnson sang (in room 414) a chambermaid ignored a Do Not Disturb sign and walked into room 636 to discover a man dismembering a female body. He looked up, held a finger to his lips, and fled with a large bundle wrapped in red sheets. The maid told police she'd noticed the Do Not Disturb, but "people forget and leave that sign out all the time." A homicide detective later said the room was "the bloodiest place I had ever seen...just sticky." The bathtub had a "red ring around it like it had been drained of blood."

(Red, of Red Roof: *Dang.*)

Harris went on, "Menger's where O. Henry lived for a bit"—O. Wilde, too—"and several of his stories take place in or just outside the place."

Brisk walk now, quick but smooth, sticking close to the sides of buildings, Don pointing and gesturing as he strode—"Aztec art deco Alameda theater. Former office of O. Henry's magazine, *Rolling Stone*, over there."

"Ha!" from me.

"I know—can you get over that?" Head shake. "There's where Eisenhower had his office—the first skyscraper of reinforced concrete west of the Mississippi." He turned to Michael. "Terra cotta, of course."

A few quick turns, and we dodged inside a bar where three gamblers blatantly played cards for money. A drunk hollered "Dammit!" and lurched at nondescript Don, who wove and kept walking toward a glimmer of sunlight at the back. It was a very long bar, terminating at a balcony overlooking the San Antonio River. We stepped out onto it and Don hooked a thumb behind us. "The Esquire Bar, *the lost state of Esquire*. Claimed to be one of the longest bars in Texas. Kind of place that people have *their* booths in. Completely democratic crowd, too, in the social sense: criminal lawyers and their clients, thugs, and socialites."

Later I looked the place up and found it reduced to the following customer reviews on *Citysearch*: "Pros: cheap drinks… Cons: staff, bathrooms, local Hispanics," and, "Only nefarious locals go here. Not recommended for northerners or passers-by."

Don showed us the courthouse, "machine gunned one morning during the early '70s amidst a ferocious drug war that came to a head with a federal judge's assassination by Woody Harrelson's dad." Then he placed San Antonio in continental context, taking us to the edge of a sleepy square and declaring: "Travis Park, in my view, is where Latin America begins. Everything north of this park, in governance and culture, is English; everything south, all the way to Cape Horn, is Spanish. It's the actual border of the two Americas."

On the way to lunch in Don's (nondescript) Nissan my thoughts turned to Charlie. Was he comfortable? How pissed off was he going to be? Snatches of monologue drifted my way. "The first full-fledged American matador, Harper Lee, fighting in the ring in Mexico in 1910 or so, ended up raising chickens here on Commerce Street in the 1920s… I used to hang out at Infinito Botanica, a storefront art space where you went to have an offhand conversation with Carlos Monsiváis, up from Mexico City, and a character in Roberto Bolaño's *Savage Detectives*… I used to live in the Paradise Valley in Montana with my literary friends Richard Ford and Thomas McGuane."

We detoured to look at two sites for the "house with no walls." Both were on the river, the first industrial and exposed, the second secluded—just cypress trees and moving water and Don's unstoppable talk. Then we went for lunch, past three, at the Liberty Bar, a slant-floored mansion with wavy glass windows through which already-low sun shone in shafts. "Tommy Lee's favorite restaurant," Don said, by which he meant the actor Tommy Lee Jones, adding, "Tommy Lee always says, 'San Antonio is a sweet old lady.'" Martinis were being served. Don's Mexican wife, who behaved with deference toward her husband, joined us with their small son.

We had been together for almost seven hours and yet I had said no more that a handful of sentences. Never had I encountered a person whose inner visions were so obliteratingly vivid that he took no notice of what was happening in the present. I mentioned that Michael was a finalist for the Pentagon memorial. Don took this in with a smile. Then he asked where we'd stayed the night before.

Perhaps due to my long period of vocal inactivity I shouted, loud enough to be heard across the restaurant, "The Red Roof Inn!" Don gave me a look of naked scorn, tempting me to disparage the place, till the Red in my head said, *Don't shit on my roof*.

After lunch Don's son asked, hopefully, "Are they coming home with us?"

We said good-bye. Charlie'd been sitting in his crate in the back of the truck for all these hours. He took a long ramble along the border of the two Americas; then we got back on the road, exhausted by information. Don wouldn't need Michael to design him a place. Don had just shown us his place. This was a man who lived at all times in a house without walls. My mind crammed full, I drove right past Geri Crumpler's grave and forgot to stop.

"Dude, who *is* he?" I asked Michael over brisket and white bread at Black's BBQ in Lockhart, seventy-two miles later.

"I don't know. He's just this guy who wrote me and said he wanted to build a house. I don't know."

I do know now. Coincidence provided a coda to our day when I met the writer Richard Ford at a wedding, and asked him about Harris.

Ford squinted and said, "Don Harris... Don Harris..." Then he raised his hands and shouted, "*Don Harris* is a fugitive from justice! He fled the country to Mexico. I was giving a reading in South

Carolina when someone said there was a friend of mine who wanted me to go outside and see him. I said, 'Tell him to come in here,' but they said he wouldn't. I asked his name and they told me 'Esteban De Jesús' and I went outside and it was Don."

He went on to describe Harris as "ceaselessly talking" and "rather charming." His final words before the wedding cake got cut were: "If he's back in the US now and using his own name he must have resolved his legal troubles. But I'll tell you this, he can't be practicing law—he was disbarred. And don't let your friend build a house for Don Harris!"

In Crockett, Texas (named for Davey, who supposedly camped there on the way to the Alamo), the next morning, we were so far behind Michael's schedule there was no way we could make the coast without blowing the engine. Our sad room in a seedy motel, still two hundred miles deep in Texas, was of the sort Steinbeck, feeling sorry for himself, described as "dirty yellow, the curtains like the underskirts of a slattern."

We'd arrived at two a.m. I paid cash and made up a plate number for the truck (to throw off the authorities in the case of an unauthorized-wolf bust). Red: *Smooth, buddy.*

In the room Michael asked, "You think the gas is OK out there now?"

I said, "Yeah. No. I don't know. I guess we don't want somebody stealing our gas." This tiny town had had two rapes, thirty-one assaults, sixty-two break-ins, and one act of arson in the prior year—relatively low crime for East Texas. Long pause. "But we don't want to be asphyxiated, sleeping with twenty gallons of gas in an unventilated room."

"C'mon, man. That's not gonna asphyxiate you."

"Can't be good."

"No."

"So, not asphyxiation, just brain damage?"

"Yeah, Jesus, you can't even open the windows in here."

I was starting to fall asleep. "Anyway, don't worry, there's a lot of light. Nobody'll mess with it."

Red started whispering as I drifted off: *Con artist, that's what Harris was. Yep.* Thoughtful pause. A little of Harris's name-dropping seemed to have rubbed off on Red. *Lemme tell you a little bedtime story, buddy, about gasoline in a hotel room. A little episode from my other life, pre–Red Roof. I was working with Joel and Ethan—Los Hermanos Coen. They wrote this little scene for me, set it in a hotel—dirtbag place; lot nicer than this, though. I was charging down a hall holding a shotgun, big ol' fire roaring down on either side a me like an honor guard.*

I was almost asleep.

Red: *It sure was pretty...*

Michael was snoring. Charlie, too.

Red: *Those boys had me bellowing: "LOOK UPON ME! I'LL SHOW YOU THE LIFE OF THE MIND! I'LL SHOW YOU THE LIFE OF THE MIND!"*

"Splendor in the Pines" was the Crockett town motto. The reality was gasoline and junk food in the pines. I walked Charlie across a leach field from the L of our hotel, over to a pawn shop (it shared a single prefab building with a feed store), where cheap, sun-bleached acoustic guitars hung in the window.

"Michael," I said when I got back. "There's a pawn shop next door. Let's buy a guitar so we can work out a routine for Nashville."

He replied, distractedly, "Okay, yeah. Cool, man."

We ate a breakfast of packaged pound cakes and Sunny Delight, then made for Louisiana, swaying along an empty road that threaded through trees, interrupted by house after house that proved America is poor. Hours later, still in Texas, we stopped in the town of Carthage, where not a single person or car was on the main street.

Michael walked into a general store and came out with a paper sack full of peanut candies. "This is what the local people eat," he declared, and devoured six.

I said, "Damn, we forgot to buy a guitar for Nashville!"

He started babbling in a fake southern accent. "We don't need a guitar. We'll just a cappella it and get booed off stage—with a lot of thigh slappin' and hooting!"

"We have to write some songs."

Michael snorted, "How about 'I Can't Drive Fifty-five'— Literally. I *can't* drive fifty-five."

"Ha, ha."

"Ha ha ha, *ha*—it's *true!*"

I said, "Maybe we can write a song about the food *and* the accent— how you can't resist either one. From a northerner's point of view."

"Yeah, I like it. What's it called?"

"'I Got the South in My Mouth'? Here, like:

Whenever I come down South

I get something funny in my mouth

Start talking like-a one-a you

An' throwin' down that greasy fried food

I got the South in my mouth!

I got the South in my mouth!

Head bobbing from Red. I kept at it:

A southern accent just sounds cool

Come down here and I want one too

I want the South in my mouth!

I want the South in my mouth!

Michael repeated, "These candies are what the local people eat."

"Are you not digging it? Maybe we need a verse about junk food?"

"Yeah," Michael said, "Something about... What are grits? Like what the hell *are* they?"

"Polenta."

"Oh."

I did a junk-food verse:

Frito Lay

I could eat you all day

Down here guys like us

Look like we're gay...

"That's good."

"Like, you know what I mean?"

"Yeah. We kind of *do*, to them. We just don't look like *men* down here."

"We are attracted to the southern girls, though," I said.

"*Yeah.*"

"I mean, really. Southern girls."

"Southern girls," Michael said. "They are badasses."

"With great asses."

This was what I'd imagined. Why I'd wanted him to come along. It was a beautiful day for a drive. Sunny. Breeze full of birds. He took the wheel. I was worn out. We both were starting to get colds. And as the day progressed we'd fill the Apache with loaded Kleenex and cough-drop wrappers: a major divergence from Steinbeck, who stocked his truck with "bourbon, scotch, gin, vermouth, vodka, a medium good brandy, aged applejack, and a case of beer."

Entering Shreveport, out of Texas at last, Michael ran just-turned-red after just-turned-red, to avoid stopping/stalling, me shouting, "Hang on to your ass, Charlie!" when we wrenched around a corner and onto a road north toward Arkansas. Surrounded by Louisiana farmland, we pulled over. This was Charlie's chance to know his native soil. He sniffed around while I poured gas into the truck. It made a gentle rinsing noise as it slid into the tank. Michael's cell phone rang. The Pentagon finalists had just been announced that morning in Washington. A panel that included victims' family members and two former secretaries of defense picked Michael and five others out of 1,126 entries from all fifty states. On the line was a reporter from the Albany *Times Union*, the paper Michael had delivered as a boy. He talked earnestly as I drove: "I literally just had an idea. It was really last-minute… I hope they feel it's appropriate."

Near Gin City, Arkansas, we stopped at a wooden gas station with a white peaked roof, like a church. A thin, beautifully sulky woman in a housedress, right out of a WPA photograph, was sweeping some concrete around the single pump. The place was not affiliated with any corporation. It just sold gas. Maybe even *local* gas. This was still oil country. My uncle Charles, in Houston, once told me how my great-grandfather made his own fuel in a still.

Inside, raw wood boards, white metal shelves, no lights, no fridges. The housedress sweeper's twin sister was at the register, talking lazily with a sexy blonde in a tube top.

"Can you recommend a healthy snack?" I asked, trying to flirt.

There was a long pause till the counter-working twin replied, in an accent of such deep Arkansan exoticness, a subtle inflection making it clear how unfascinating she found me: "How 'bout some peanut butter and *crackers*?"

As we pulled out of the station Michael said, "They were like sirens."

On the road our conversation veered around to another writer (one I'd actually read), George W.S. Trow. Michael taught a class around Trow's long essay on the dismemberment of American culture, *Within the Context of No Context*. Trow, he said, had inspired him to come on this trip. He told me earnestly, "Man, if the world we've inherited is fragmented and broken, we have to stitch it back together again one conversation at a time."

First published in 1980, Trow's *Context* describes the USA as a wounded land that operates on two networks, "the grid of two hundred million—and the tiny, tiny baby grid of you and me and baby." Only celebrities have both private, or inner, lives, *and* a life in the wider world of two hundred million. "For them, there is no distance between the two grids in American life. Of all Americans, only they are complete."

These observations had animated Michael's memorial, which would be complete only when someone—anyone—came and stood on it; when an anonymous individual was raised up on a hidden plinth, rounded and tearlike in shape, beside a vast and brutal building. (A building that, in attempting to telegraph might, instead conveyed pure fear. An emblem of our complete terror—visible from space.) For Michael the juxtaposition was an act of healing, and homage to Trow. It was his solution to the problem of incompleteness, of no context for our ongoing national tragedies.

As we talked about all this we were rolling along a levee. Michael was driving. I looked out the window and saw, at the end of a long, narrow, wood walkway, traversing a swamp, a stilt-supported shack. It was glowing with the cool light of a television, an invention Trow wrote about obsessively:

> The trivial is raised up to power in it. The powerful is lowered toward the trivial.
>
> The power behind it resembles the power of no-action, the powerful passive.
>
> It is *bewitching*.
>
> It interferes with growth, conflict, and destruction, and these forces are different in its presence.
>
> "Entertainment" is an unsatisfactory word for what it encloses or projects or makes possible.
>
> No good has come of it…
>
> Television is dangerous because it operates according to an attention span that is childish but is cold. It stimulates the warmth of a childish response but is cold…
>
> What is a cold child? A sadist. What is a child's behavior that is cold? It is sadism.

Maybe the most mind-blowing of Trow's *Context* observations is this one: "The most successful celebrities are products. Consider the real role in American life of Coca-Cola. Is any man as well loved as this soft drink is?"

Red: *Doggone.*

* * *

As we talked Trow we drove without braking straight through stoplightless Wabbaseka, Arkansas, birthplace of the state's most notorious celebrity, Eldridge Cleaver, the Black Panthers' Minister of Information, who more than once ate Geri's cooking at my parents' table, and on one occasion reminisced to them about his time as a serial rapist: "I followed a couple into a motel room and I tied the guy up and put him in a closet and did what *he* had come there to do. And it wasn't reported… There was something about the motel situation that intrigued me, pulled me. I wrote a poem about motels. To me, a motel was like an obscene institution, you know? I kept going back, every weekend, to that motel and others."

Red: *No comment.*

Pie for dinner (no lunch), after which, Michael's cell ringing with the occasional journalist, I silently drove, and drove, and drove, and drove, the strain on the engine and the torque of our incompatible needs seeming sure to cause some sort of an explosion, till, suddenly, we rounded a corner in a blank part of the map, out of cell range, off all grids that I knew, near the Mississippi border, where a strip of river and two gas stations, plus some fireworks stalls, nothing you could call a town, had nonetheless caused two groups of young men to come into proximity—one shirtless and black and drinking beer, the other shirtless and white and selling Confederate flag patches and 9/11 keepsakes. History was thick here. Don Abney, the Louisiana Catahoula authority, told me that Hernando de Soto's body had been placed nearby in the "Mississippi River, in full body armor, and has never been found." We filled the tank at a station frequented exclusively by black customers, and looked across a dirt road at a station frequented exclusively by white people. It was a mistake stopping here. The heavy noise of insects was all around, while harsh stares came from the white gas station at the gay couple and their wild dog of Africa. Everything was lush, all sounds soft, so it was especially jarring when the whites started to shout at the blacks (for selling us gas?). When the word *Fuck!* rang out we fled. No more back roads that night. We made for the interstate.

Coming out of the midnight darkness of St. Francis County, Arkansas, we took I-40 (which runs all the way from California to North Carolina) across the Mississippi—while endless trucks did the same thing. Twenty miles from the bridge we broke into a column that stretched back as far as we could see. (Turning around, Michael said, "They just keep going *forever*.") This is the one single-lane section of I-40 coast to coast. Usually it's single-lane for only a mile. But that night construction had the highway down to half capacity for more like twenty. The lane was tight, and the looseness of the Chevy's steering was magnified by the reality of driving in a trench—I slowed down to forty, thirty-five, thirty, to keep from crashing into guardrails or road workers. Soon we were holding back a flood of trucks. Space opened up in front of us. By midspan on the Hernando de Soto, the bridge that carries I-40 into Memphis, we had nothing but open pavement ahead, while in our wake so many drivers had hit their brakes that the sky was red. I looked in the rearview mirror and saw a screaming trucker. At the same moment he blew his air horn and contorted his face in rage. A wrathful *BWOOOOOOOOOOOOOOOOOOOLF*! sound filled my ears and seemed like it was coming straight out of his mouth. We wove slowly around Memphis, truck headlights lighting up the cracked windshield like a stadium, praying that the trucker didn't lose his mind and decide to run right over us.

We exited the highway in Lakeland, Tennessee, and Michael said, "That was terrifying, man. I thought we were going to die."

We had entered the interstate system, for the fist time on our journey, at perhaps its most vulnerable spot—where, per Bill

Anderson, a project planner with the US Department of Transportation, "It's a nightmare... the road's not big enough to handle the traffic." The reason for this, he explained, was a lawsuit brought by environmentalists and the Memphis zoo on behalf of an "elephant, I believe, and a number of special exotic species," which forced the abandonment of a whole section of the freeway, and the construction of a wild swing in the wrong direction, resulting in "very antiquated geometry... the way it curves up and down and left to right... the only loop like that in the coast-to-coast stretch of Route 40." (An explanation followed by the wistful observation, "Used to be, when you wanted to build a road, you could just lay one down across an open field.") According to a representative of the American Trucking Association, the trucks bottled up behind us were likely carrying "high-dollar loads, like Gap clothing" or "Army loads, like 1.1, 1.2, and 1.3 explosives" which have a $2,000- to $50,000-per-hour delay cost. The answer to the question "What does that mean, 1.1, 1.2, 1.3 explosives?": "It can mean whatever you want it to mean. The Army keeps that confidential." Dynamite (1.1), artillery shells (1.2), jet fuel (1.3), and thousands of Shaker crewneck sweaters were jammed up on the Hernando de Soto. It was a too-close encounter with American velocity—the terror of stopping all these eighteen-wheelers from hurtling along at eighty, loaded with what only Trow saw inside them: celebrities.

My father, like most sons' fathers, was a celebrity to me. Not long after Dad's death Wilsey Trucking failed. My half brother Mike, who'd taken ownership from our father, told me: "We had co-presidents running the company, but one couldn't cope with stress and quit, and the remaining one was frazzled, started fighting with the managers, one of whom quit and went into competition with us by working at a big rival and telling them everything they needed to know to compete with us. There was a gradual decline over several years, and we sold the business to this competitor in October '04 at a loss to ourselves. Problems with this kind of trucking are drivers, who drive across the country in four days, spend a night in a hotel for one, and then drive back. It's a terrible life. And they're screwy people." (*BWOOOOOOOOOOOOOOOOOOLF*) "And the business is tough. If you're late, or too early, it screws 'em up. You're often dealing with alley operations at street, not dock, height. Very demanding. Time sensitive. Railroads are starting to compete because of inherent problems in trucking. Better to send stuff on long hauls by rail if it's less time sensitive, and then day drivers deliver it at the destination."

A co-president explained: "The typical run was a Thursday departure out of Oxnard. (Trucks loaded Thursday nights and left Oxnard by two a.m. Friday morning.) This run would start dropping product in Oklahoma City and would stop in: Little Rock, Fort Smith, Memphis, Nashville, Knoxville, and finally end up in South Carolina. We planned on thirty hours from Oxnard to Oklahoma City and forty-eight hours into the Atlanta area. So we would have been passing through Memphis late Saturday night or early Sunday morning." Just when Michael and Charlie and I had passed through. One of the wrathful truckers reddening the sky behind us had likely been hauling flowers for Wilsey. Funeral flowers, no doubt. And so I, too, had contributed to the death of my late father's company.

I can even quantify this, because the US Bureau of Labor Statistics, the Federal Highway Administration, and the US Department of Transportation's Freight Management and Operations Office helped me calculate what my impact was. According to these agencies our hour-long trip on I-40 cost the country between $567,000 and $14,176,500 in wasted time, wasted gas, demurrage, environmental impact—seeming intangibles that in fact cost at least $8 billion a year and are factored into our GDP. According to Eric Andersen at the Department of Transportation in Nashville, the federal road construction budget has decreased "at least fifty percent" since our post-9/11 wars. ("I'll throw this at you real quick… The money to support a war's got to come from somewhere… I'll throw another bone at you here. One hundred percent of the infrastructure damage to our roadways comes from trucks.") Our transportation system is the war we are always fighting. There were 42,815 US highway deaths in 2002, and every year an inch of asphalt on every highway surface in America is ground to powder and blown into the air in a never-ending explosion.

Going too slow, watching truckers de- and accelerate, haul themselves into the left lane, switch back, messing up this country's dependence on nothing ever being empty or at rest, on inventory rotating out of warehouse and into showrooms just in time to be replaced, on there being no time to do anything but make time—I was not grappling with death and friendship, I was declaring a civil (Charlie: *After you…*) war. In the interest of extremity I plugged in the highest possible numbers and discovered that driving from Far West Texas to New York City could plausibly have set back the nation $29,400,000 in wasted time, delayed cargo, missed deadlines, needlessly burned fuel. Imagine instead of nineteen hitchhikers nineteen dallyers like me, driving around at the legal minimum speed limit. They'd wipe out the entire US economy and change the world. If our enemies had an original idea or two, if they weren't so wholly our creations—victims of what they've been sold—they'd forswear violence for slowness. Then they wouldn't be shot dead in their bedrooms or yanked out of holes and hung or thrown into prisons.

That would be a moving memorial to the people we've all loved and lost.

As my brother spoke I thought about the kind of people that make a real business succeed. Then I broke down in tears. Maybe it was Mike's impassivity; maybe it was the thought of all these people out there struggling in an economic drought; maybe, mostly, it was the tangibility of what I had lost. And the fact that my dad never showed or taught or gave me anything. Except for material to write about. (Thanks for that.) But mostly I cried because I love and miss him so much.

After checking into a big Super 8, overlooking the highway, I walked Charlie along something called Huff Puff Road, dropped him in the room, and went to check the truck's engine, which looked like it was sweating oil. When I returned Michael was watching TV, Charlie was drinking out of the toilet, and an ad for *Snoop Dogg's Girls Gone Wild* came on. Snoop—a complete man—screwed up his face and framed his gold-jewelry-covered chest with his forearms; teenagers on streets and beaches flashed their breasts at him. It was mesmerizing. When the ad was over a feeling of loneliness crushed us to sleep.

At eight a.m., rain coming down, Michael threw out the rules and went to McDonald's. Charlie and I drove up Huff Puff and across a parking lot to a Shell, where I parked between the pumps, out of the rain. Charlie briefly wagged his tail but hung his head when I left him behind.

Inside I thought, *Must be something edible.* But it was all pure shit. Two walls were windows and checkout. The other two were fridge: one all beer, the other all soda and water, with a bit of ice tucked in somewhere. In the aisles: chips, dips, cookies, motor oil, individual pies, Ho Hos, Twinkies, etc.—corn, wheat, sugar, oil, and air (mostly air). The remaining space: T-shirts and hats of the sort you see in all convenience stores (aka cstores): FRIENDS DON'T LET FRIENDS DRIVE FORDS; FORD EATS CHEVY, SHITS DODGE.

Turns out you can be a Shell-branded station without selling gas refined by Shell. There is no real difference between brands. But 59 percent of respondents to a Gallup poll "said they favored branded over non-branded gasoline." So…

Red: *Why not buy a Whopper at McDonald's!? Call a Red Roof Blue!?*

It's confusing. Even to those supposedly *running the show*. This is a transcription of a three-way conversation a fact checker and I had with David Sexton, the president of Shell Oil Products, US:

> CHECKER: How much real estate does Shell own?
>
> [Long pause]
>
> SEXTON: Shell owns fourteen thousand separate service stations across the country… we are moving in the direction of more wholesale options.
>
> C: How has the recent oil crisis affected Shell in particular?
>
> [Pause]
>
> S: I'm not aware of any such crisis…
>
> C: Shell is a British company, Royal Shell…
>
> S: That's correct…
>
> ME, TO C: They're Dutch. Royal *Dutch* Shell.
>
> C: I mean a Dutch company.
>
> S: Oh, umm… that's… Is that…? Well, we are British owned, I believe, but… we have received support from the Dutch since Shell was founded, yes… although I'm sure you could find more information about that on our website.

What Ben Bernanke, as chairman of the Board of Governors of the Federal Reserve System, once called the "depth and sophistication of the country's financial markets" is, really, "Would you *like* to be able to buy a Whopper at McDonald's?"

America put a man on the moon. It's no great feat to fill our minds with falsehoods so plentiful they overpower truth. As Cabeza de Vaca first pointed out, this is a land of liars and plunderers. Only now nobody even knows who they're stealing from, or what business they're in—real estate, oil, transportation, food—while the world's most profitable enterprise is just pushing history through plumbing so we can burn it in exchange for speed.

A chunky, kind-faced woman was behind the counter of this "Shell." As I walked the aisles she regarded me with sympathy. Charlie craned his neck trying to keep me in sight. I noticed a dirty basket holding a couple apples, oranges and bananas. A tiny hand-written sign said, TRY A HEALTHY SNACK. FRUIT. I picked a red apple, plus two spotty bananas. She rang them up and the total came to $1.46. I had twenty-one dollars, so I pulled out the dollar and started scrounging in my pocket for change. The cashier leaned forward and peeked into my wallet. Her face registered concern. She began rooting around in a dirty wicker change basket I hadn't noticed. (From the University of Missouri-Rolla's publication, *Convenience Stores*: "Pinhole cameras can monitor employee activities.") A man behind me in line—black and slender—also took a peek into the wallet, out at the broke-ass truck and depressed wolf, caught the cashier's eye, and then started feeling around in his pockets, too.

"We'll help you out," the woman said.

Outside Charlie looked sad as shit, with none of the menace even shit has. Michael came strolling across the pump island with a breakfast burrito and said, "Charles is all down in the Dumpster."

At Michael's insistence we spent the whole day on the interstate, needle at forty-five, occasionally fifty, steady rain falling. After an hour or so I noticed that the hood of the Apache was shimmying. We were going so slow the rainwater had pooled.

"Hey, look," I said to Michael.

"*What?* No way."

"There's a *body of water* on the hood."

"There's a *pool*," said Michael. "I've never seen anything like that."

"I guess that's what happens when you drive really slow."

"*Yeah.*"

Silence. Between Lakeland and Nashville I pulled us into a two-pump BP station. Michael looked up, pointed across the road to a twenty-pump Texaco, and said, "What are you doing, man? Go to that one. They've got a store."

I said, "There's a little store here, too." There was a rack next to the cashier with some gum and chips on it.

"That's like nothing. That's a real store over there. *C'mon*, man."

I pulled across. While Michael went shopping a blonde woman in a balsa-colored Acura approached me and said, "I'm having some car trouble. Could you help?"

Apparently I had begun to look like a man. Under the hood I spotted a green-and-white Afro of acid corrosion atop the positive terminal of her battery. When I scraped it off the connection looked good. The woman gave me her keys and I slid into the front seat. A towheaded three-year-old boy was strapped in behind me. He stared with a child's version of *Who the fuck's this guy?* on his face. In the low bucket seat, climate controls within easy reach, legs stretched out, I was more comfortable than I'd been in days. Not just more comfortable than in the Chevy—more comfortable than in the motels where we'd been crashing.

I put the key in its socket, which—ingenious!—was encircled by an illuminated plastic hoop. Red whispered, *If it starts: We. Are. Out. Of. Here. Ditch the rug rat at a Red Roof and we strip this ricer for parts.*

Then I twisted the key, got a dead cough, climbed out, and told her she'd better call Triple A. Michael returned with Diet Coke, pork rinds, a bag of Doritos, and a copy of the Nashville *Tennessean*, which said a sniper had shot seven civilians in Maryland, Virginia, and DC, where Michael was going to meet the families of 187 people who had also been murdered.

In five more hours we got to Nashville, ate, and kept going, not even mentioning our plans for an open mike. Hoping to relieve the spring-induced pain in my thigh, I let Michael drive till he crossed the painted yellow line on I-40, nearly sideswiped a truck, overcorrected within a few inches of a guardrail, braked hard. I relieved him. Torture or certain death—those were my choices. A mechanic later told me, "You were lucky. There were only two millimeters left on your brake drums. If you'd needed to stop quickly and you'd pushed hard on the brakes, they would have disintegrated. You'd have stepped and kept going." Steinbeck described the interstate as a "wide gash" where the minimum speed "was greater than any I had previously driven," and added, "You are bound to the wheel and your eyes to the car ahead and to the rear-view mirror for the car behind and the side mirror for the car or truck about to pass... When we get these thruways across the whole country... it will be possible to drive from New York to California without seeing a single thing."

By nightfall in Knoxville I was done. We exited into a deserted downtown. "This is it," I said. "I can't take any more of this. You want to get there on time, just rent a car."

"Shit, man. *No*," Michael said. We hadn't talked for hours. "We have to do this together."

"Do what together? Sit silently in terror? This thing won't go any faster. And *that* experience, all day on the highway—it was *messed up*. I'm done. I've got to stay on the back roads. Rent a car if you want to make it." Michael was silent. Unable to think of anything else to say, I came out with, "And that's such an *architect's* belt buckle."

Then I got out of the truck with Charlie and walked off.

When I got back Michael said "OK. I'll get a car. But I don't want the trip to end like this. Let's find a back road and drive as far as we can tonight. I'll get a rental tomorrow."

What followed was the best drive of the trip. Michael took the wheel, and I looked out the window: a hundred miles along an empty road that followed a low ridge line, like a levee through the woods, nothing but trees with slashes of cloud-filtered moonlight coming through their leaves, and shreds of a river visible beyond their bare trunks.

We ended up in Kingsport, improbably large for a fume-choked industrial city nobody's ever heard of, and checked into an L-shaped Econo Lodge. We unloaded our stuff into a room near the crook of the L and I went right back out with Charlie for a walk.

This was a company town. Eastman Chemical—the first to roll out the plastic soda bottle in the 1970s—occupied nine hundred urban acres. In 2002 they were working on an additive that, in the company's words, "prevents the oil-soluble ingredients and water in beverages like fruit juices, energy drinks, carbonated soft drinks, nutritional tonics, malt beverages, and new age drinks from separating during storage… to help brands achieve the natural look consumers demand." Such chemicals, now ubiquitous, are called "weighting agents," and, to paraphrase Steinbeck, they exist because we'd rather not see a single thing. Of all beverages only they are complete.

I was suddenly so weary I thought I might fall asleep standing up. I stuck close to the wall of our wing, on the dark porch between cars and rooms, till I got to the back of the lot, where it ended at a steep, shaley slope about thirty feet high. I struggled up while Charlie did it in five deft bounds. At the top I expected a blustery mountaintop but found a Kroger's parking lot. To our left, at the bottom of a crevasse, was a Sonic Burger.

The parking lot stretched away to the right, views of Eastman's plant in the distance, and a strange moaning and shuffling sound all around. I crossed a lake of tarmac—dimmed lights humming above—to another near-sheer incline. The moaning sound strengthened and localized. It was coming from above. Charlie pulled me up where we were confronted with a view of a mud-colored plain, shimmying like the puddle on the hood. I looked harder. Cows. More than I could count, surrounding a long, low shed. We stared at them for a while, Charlie now scared, the smell overpowering and half chemical. Then we walked slowly back down and found a road that led to the motel. On a median I noticed what looked like a piece of suede in some wet grass. Charlie noticed it, too. I let go of his leash so he could go and investigate. Immediately Charlie was lying on his back and twisting. He *dug in*. Legs straight up in the air, head kicked back, he shimmied side-to-side, a look of ecstasy on his smiling face, his eyes rolled into his skull and pure white. I'd never seen him so fulfilled. Here was his inner Smut. I laughed. *Oh, Charlie, he loves the dewy grass.* When he got up, I saw what had been beneath him: an oversize pork chop draped in a flap of skin beside a gray-brown rack of ribs: a dead animal that had gone flat and sunk into the earth. Then the smell hit me—*hard*. Death: *You've been pondering me. Well, hellooooo!*

Back in the room Michael took a sniff and said, "Ha! Good job, Charles!"

The next morning, air reeking, Michael called a rental car company. Then, in a light rain, he held Charlie's leash as I loaded the truck. When I returned to the motel's covered walkway for a final bag Michael gestured to Charlie and said, "He started shivering because he thought you were going to leave him."

I wished Michael luck with his memorial. He wished me luck with the rest of the trip, then leaned down to deliver a pat and call Charlie

"Charles." We stood awkwardly in the Econo Lodge parking lot till Michael said, "Good call on the belt buckle. I'm gonna get rid of it."

I carried on in what smelled like a coffin. Forty minutes later, on a brief stretch of unavoidable interstate, Michael passed me in a silver Ford and we honked/waved. Then Charlie, Red, and I disappeared into the rainy closeness of Virginia and West Virginia, following Route 460, where the two states traded places every few miles. For lunch, on the main street of an old mining town, I went to a pizza place where there were four tables. I ordered a salad, and the dark-skinned proprietor brought me fresh feta, olives, lettuce, peppers, bread—the homemade American meal I'd been wanting the whole trip. After devouring it I asked him where he was from and he told me Egypt.

We passed signs for "Bug Street" and "Country Girl Road," and we passed a woman loping along the side of the highway swinging arms so long they almost touched the ground. Families of dead deer lay on the asphalt every fifteen miles. West Virginia needed some bears. And a better name. Red: *I second that: West Virginia, may's well be Virginia Jr. S'like a fatherless child. Better name'd be Shenandoah. That's got a ring to it.* Maybe Red really was a communist. He was certainly an orphan.

I got gas and a jar of sourwood honey in a nameless town where a sign—brown with white letters—labeled a winding dirt road "Mike's Street" (with the apostrophe). My half brother's street. I parked and followed it, Charlie rooting in the underbrush, overjoyed, weaving around rain puddles, beer cans, faded cardboard from cases of Busch. The dirt street lead to a churning river, hidden from the road. Its sound was so loud the world of the road was erased. Standing there I imagined a lean, muscular, West Virginian version of Red. He'd step from the trees, come at me silently, eyes narrow, and, before he cleanly slit my throat, I'd have time to say, "You Mike?"

The next time I filled up was at a backwoods gas station, buried in a ravine, pumps coming straight out of muddy earth and wet leaves. A young hunter, lean, stubbly, Red-like, in fatigues, nodded and said, *flirtatiously*, "I like your Chevy. What you got under the hood?"

This was a new one. I'd been ready to agree with the wrong year. After a doubtful pause I said, "A four."

"Never heard of a four cylinder in a Chevy," he shot back, flirtation gone.

Since I didn't know what the hell I was talking about I decided to act completely certain of myself. "*Yep*," I said. "It's just a *little four*."

We stared at each other. Then he tensed to brush me aside and open the hood. But a second hunter's voice came out of the dark of the wooden service station.

"Hey! You got a nickel?"

My would-be assailant's hands went into his camo and then he turned away. I jumped in the cab, cranked the engine, and blew across the muddy lot to the road, slaloming down hills, downshifting to stay off the brakes, watching the mirror for pursuit. A few hours later, checking the oil, I counted the spark plugs: six.

I drove seventeen hours without a rest, crossing the Mason-Dixon line at one a.m., at the same time as an Amish buggy with

reflective bands Velcroed around its horses' ankles (Red: *This guy's up way past Amish bedtime*); a quick sleep in Harrisburg, Penn., where, beside the banks of the Susquehanna River, hoping to remove the spring that had been boring into my pelvis, I disemboweled the bench seat with a pocketknife; past the Hershey chocolate factory, over toward the Jersey border; across the deep-carved bed of the Delaware River on a gleaming steel bridge, barely wide enough for the truck; another highway gash, and finally we saw the New York skyline. My dog said: "Wroarowlwolf!"

Michael didn't win the contest to design the 9/11 memorial in Washington. He told me, "They're actually really smart at the Pentagon, and they could obviously see through my criticism of the massive war machine." His Trow-homage was killed, he told me, from "way high up" in the Bush administration: by Donald Rumsfeld himself. Michael also told me his license had been suspended during, and for two years prior to, the trip.

Don Harris read much of the above and offered his opinion: "You are blind to your surroundings, or lack the compulsion to under-stand and describe them... You were driving across one of the most charged landscapes in America, stories swarming off every hill, every turn in the road, yet your writing of the drive from Marfa to SA... reads like a likeable *Seinfeld* episode."

I told Michael Meredith about all this and he said, "Don Harris, man, I almost forgot about him. I actually can't remember what he looks like even... But that's pretty good writing, no? I mean, *Seinfeld*. Good show."

Seinfeld: a fun piece of sadism. As Trow might have put it. And whether Michael and I had failed or succeeded in accomplishing anything with this trip is impossible for me to answer. We were far too invested in our own... con. In the end it was Trow (1943–2006)—that great seer of class and status and the things we trade in to make ourselves feel significant, authoritative, alive—who had the most useful insight: "The con man does give you something. It is a sense of your own worthlessness. A good question to ask: 'Does this event exist without me?' If the answer is no, leave. You are involved in a con game."

You can't con your way to a higher place. Only a higher station. The con man does not have an eye on the long term. The long con is only *so* long. The length of life. Heaven or enlightenment or the weary soul's deserved rest: non-con-to-able destinations. Though what's life after life after life getting conned? History. The things we pump and burn. As the writer whom Don Harris referred to as El Cormac said: "I think the notion that the species can be improved in some way, that everyone could live in harmony, is a really dangerous idea. Those who are afflicted with this notion are the first ones to give up their souls, their freedom. Your desire that it be that way will enslave you and make your life vacuous."

Michael's now teaching at Princeton, and has twins and a dog of his own.

Red continued asserting himself, while I could find no evidence of him, not a single image or mention, online: *I keep my pic off the web. Don't go looking for me on the internet. Don't go looking for me, period. I just checked out of the Re—shhhh.* I began to think of myself as his custodian. The keeper of his memory.

Solitary man.
No family.
Un'tached.
Toothpick.
Hick.
Skinflint.
Wit-liver.

Ts'me.

When I hide, I hide good. The key: a good night's sleep!

Finally I contacted that Senior Director of Marketing at Red Roof in Dallas, the one who explained that Red was suppressed because he'd crossed that fine line between quirky and irreverent. I expected them to deny Red had ever existed. It had all been a dream. But they put me in touch with Rob Bagot, who thought up Red while a creative director at Hill Holiday (Bank of America, Dunkin' Donuts, Major League Baseball). He was now at McCann Erickson (IKEA, Coca-Cola, Nestlé) in my hometown of San Francisco.

"Let me see if I stored a copy of the spots… I've blocked out many memories of this period because the client made it all so very painful. 'There's a fine line between quirky and irreverent.' I will pass that on to my children." As to what he remembered about inventing Red's patter, he replied, "It was a few years ago, but he said a lot of stuff about bucket seats, long roads, cacti, and chicken."

Pa. I love you.

Bagot, like a lot of dads, was busy, and I doubted he'd find the time to dig up anything more. But I was wrong. He sent me the following:

> Ah, the story of Red.
>
> No one has ever asked. But since you did, I'll give you the short story. Red was a character we came up with for a "pitch" to Red Roof Inns. If you're not familiar with the ad business, a pitch is where agency works way too hard for free to secure the advertising business of a client. In this particular instance we won. The original Red was a kind of pasted together Ken doll with a red Mohawk—thus the name. After the pitch we did a number

of character studies... From a month development program Red emerged. He had two defining characteristics—the hair, still red, but now a mass standing on end, and an exaggerated chin. The client keyed in on the chin insisting that he looked too much like Jay Leno, so I spent Christmas Eve [2000] in the apartment of an L.A. artist slowly grinding excess chinage off our 10-inch mock-up. After final approval we shipped the prototype to China where we made 5,000 dolls for $1.72 each. Considering the work that went into each bobblehead, I see no time in the next century where we will ever match the Chinese on price. The next thing we did was assign Red a voice. The perfect choice was John Goodman, who to our surprise signed up for the gig. We recorded with John in pre-Katrina New Orleans in January of 2001. We completed 20 radio commercials, and also recorded his voice for 6 television spots. We sent the television scripts to a number of commercial film makers, and for reasons still not clear to this date, Michael Bay fresh off Pearl Harbor agreed to direct. Red had his commercial debut in March of that year. And the rest is history. Or rather Red is history. Somewhere out there, probably in some long forgotten storage shed, are 4,998 Reds. I still have two somewhere.

He sent me one. It speaks, angrily at times: *Fuck. You. Red Roof. I'm goddamn well gonna sneak back in. I know the sunnovabitch better than anybody. Get all up where you can't find me. The ghost in the machine...*

Charlie died of cancer in 2004, just a few months after the birth of Daphne's and my son. When he saw the baby he gave him one of his gentle taps; wet nose on top of bald head.

I still have the truck. It cheers up everyone who sees it in New York, especially firemen, especially when Daphne's driving.

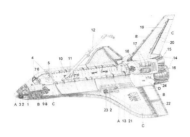

NASA REDUX

2009

ILLUMINATION.

A man steps off a ladder. This is not a setup for a joke. It is the greatest accomplishment in human history.

Forty years later, I was in a convertible. My destination: Kennedy Space Center, or KSC, in Cape Canaveral, where the first Americans had left the planet. It was the day before launch (L-1, in NASA parlance), and I was going to watch what NASA still called the Space Transportation System (STS)—and the rest of the world called the space shuttle—head for low earth orbit (LEO). (NASA is a constellation of acronyms, so many and so arcane that they take on a quasi-mystical quality—as though the administration were speaking in tongues. To quote one public-affairs officer (PAO), "We have all these wonderful acronyms... I can't remember what half of them mean.") The shuttle, flying for nearly thirty years, ideally offered very little in the way of excitement—but with the whole program slated for retirement in a few months, this mission (STS-126) was the last one scheduled to launch after dark, and I'd been told to expect drama, the sky relit by a controlled explosion of rocket fuel turning night back into day.

The road to Canaveral was like a line across a flat green mirror—trees, water, reflections of trees—till nature gave way to the asphalt and advertising of the coast. I checked into the Cocoa Beach Hilton, went swimming, and read Tom Wolfe's classic history of early cowboy-era space flight, *The Right Stuff*. Wolfe devotes some of his more scalding observations to the Cocoa Beach nightlife, full of contractors, street-racing astronauts, and German rocket scientists who "materialized as if from out of a time warp... pummeling the piano in the cocktail lounge and singing the 'Horst Wessel Song'!" (the Nazi national anthem). When Cape Canaveral became the launching site for NASA, those first astronauts had also rented convertibles and headed to Cocoa for "a little Drinking & Driving & the rest of the real pilot's life."

That sounded research worthy. So after sunset I crashed a prelaunch party on my hotel's deck, walking in with no problem, a goofy/boozy atmosphere in effect—congressmen and contractors mingling and drinking. By a buffet, I heard a woman in a trilby, chest decorated with an illuminated brooch of earth-orbiting LEDs, ask, "Are you the movie star?"

A man replied, suavely, "I was in a movie."

"What movie?"

"*Office Space*."

He then signed her ID badge: Ron Livingston. I introduced myself and asked what he was doing there.

"I'm going into space."

I thought, *Office* space? and said, "Yeah?"

"If a monkey can do it, they figure I can."

I gave this a good laugh.

He gestured to the man next to him ("This is Bert from NASA"), who invited me to a "night viewing" of the shuttle: the last public opportunity to get up close and see the thing illuminated on the launch platform before the following day's liftoff. "Come to the Residence Inn at midnight," Bert said.

I went up to my room, and when I came back down a big man in black, his arm around a young woman in a khaki shirt, was shouting to another man, "Hey—I'm *squeezin' on* yer *wife*!"

Smiling, the woman asked him something, and he replied, "Them? They've got *whores* in their room."

Delirious female laughter.

The man whose wife was being squeezed on said to another young woman, "You're such a Pollyanna."

She said, "What?"

Man: "You're such a *rule follower.* You're like, *'Schnell! Schnell!'* Pollyanna."

More laughter from squeezer and -ee.

Between my hotel and the Residence Inn was Cheaters gentlemen's club, its lot full of cars, and the Lido Cabaret, where a sign read GO ENDEAVOUR KSC LAUNCH AFTERPARTY HERE. On the bus to the viewing, I wound up in the front row with Livingston, who was studying up for his role in a TV series about international astronauts on a six-year space mission. A man with a microphone, who'd been "the 143rd person hired by NASA," stood up, pointed to his arm, and spoke into a PA: "If you were to cut a vein, rocket fuel would come out I am sure." He then told a joke about Eskimos having "the most ICBMs." (It's phonetic.) As we started to roll, Rocket Fuel said, "Young people often wonder what good the space program does. I always tell them, 'Your cell phones, your GPS—throw those out. They wouldn't exist without the space program.'"

Out the window I could see KSC's main landmark, the vehicle-assembly building (VAB), a towering white cube emblazoned with an American flag and a massive NASA logo: a blue circle full of stars bisected by a forked red velocity trail, known, mysteriously, as "the meatball." After passing through security, we marveled at KSC's time-capsule-like assemblage of midcentury buildings (like visiting the future and the 1960s simultaneously) and the juxtaposition of so much nature—white birds that looked like Egyptian ibis, reptilian marshes—and so much technology.

At the viewing site, Bert from NASA warned me, "Watch out for alligators."

"Seriously?"

"Seriously."

Most other night viewers were thronged around a jumpsuited astronaut posing for pictures. I moved away and got as close as I could to the shuttle, finally leaning on a fence beside a couple of other loners: a solidly built, slightly thick-in-the-middle older man on my left and a tall, thin man in his fifties on my right. Though flashes popped frantically behind us, it was dark, still-primeval Florida here. The three of us seemed to be in a shared trance, looking at the moon-and-xenon-lit scene: huge shuttle (which up close looked homemade, hand-painted, arts-and-craftsy), boosters, fuel tank, American flag, the words *United States* in Helvetica lettering. Rockets—flying up there in our national anthem—are as old and as American as America. Our flag has space sewn into its corner. Forty years earlier, in his book about Apollo, *Of a Fire on the Moon*, Norman Mailer described this place, pad 39-A—the actual liftoff point from which the massive Saturn V rocket had carried America's astronauts to the moon—as "a shrine... welcoming footsore travelers at dusk." In the distance, hydrogen overflow was being burned off, calling to mind a ceremonial torch.

Later, when I found Bert from NASA he was talking with Rocket Fuel about someone called Neil.

"Who's Neil?" I asked.

"Neil Armstrong," Bert said. "You were standing right near him."

Most of the world has no idea what NASA is doing. And NASA, tongue-tied by jargon, can't figure out how to tell us. But the agency is engaged in work that can be more enduring and far-reaching than anything else this country is paying for. At NASA's inception the government declared that "activities in space should be devoted to peaceful purposes for the benefit of all mankind," and this is one of the few promises in American history that have been kept.

As of this writing NASA was fifty. The moonwalk took place exactly forty years before. NASA did the unimaginable in eight years, making good on President Kennedy's assertion that "this nation should commit itself to achieving the goal, before this decade is out, of landing a man on the moon and returning him safely to the earth." It succeeded for two reasons: access to a staggering 4.4 percent of the federal budget (in 2009 it was half a percent—and dropping) and, more importantly, one might hope resurgently, a national desire to believe in ourselves—and in something *more* than ourselves. Since then, NASA, vision flickering, public imagination uncaptured, has stooped to offering belittling practical justifications for spaceflight (GPS, cell phones) that ground and practicalize the sublime, killing its poetry.

In explaining why space is worth exploring, as NASA frequently has found itself doing, there's a mistaken supposition, because—as with anything of real value—the benefits are largely unknown. Why do it if you know why you're doing it? It's a philosophical matter, almost religious in its insolubility. Why do we need to love or live at all? The answer is in wondering. And NASA is about wonder. Its last administrator, Michael Griffin, attempted to reinstill said wonder when he gave a series of soaring, sermonlike speeches, and asked, "What is the value to the United States of being involved in enterprises which lift up human hearts everywhere when we do them?" His answer: making the world unite. (Or, in flawless NASA-ese: doing "the kinds of things that make others want to work with us to do them.") A *Star Trek*–like ideal, in line with Kennedy's vision in the early '60s. But now, just a few decades into the endeavor, all is uncertainty. Obama, a Kennedy-like president who wants NASA to "inspire the world," took office; Griffin was let go. Cell-and-GPS-like utterances have been made, the herald angels of restraint, practicality, belt-tightening: enemies of art. And NASA is an arts organization disguised as a federal agency trapped within the government bureaucracy.

Nobody outside NASA knows what we're doing in space. Here are some obscure, suppressed, declassified, wonderful, and curious facts:

Apollo astronauts navigated with sextants and liked to refer to people on earth as "cats." Humans can perceive a scant 5 percent of what exists in the universe—the rest is "dark energy" or "dark matter," descriptors for things about which we know nothing at all. Laurie Anderson was NASA's first, and only, artist in residence. In 2005 she told an interviewer: "I keep thinking what it would be like to be a kid in this country. I think it would be really depressing, except for NASA."

When the shuttle stopped flying the Russians began bringing American astronauts into space. And NASA was supposed to embark on the Constellation program, an Apollo-dwarfing series of missions that entailed going to the moon, building a base, and staying there as we got set for Mars. In 2009 3,800 people were employed in building Constellation equipment (400,000 worked on Apollo), including the enormous Ares V rocket, the largest ever—designed to produce 11.8

million pounds of thrust (that of fifty 747s) and have us back to the moon by 2020. Then Obama killed it.

According to an article in *Cosmos* magazine, an astronaut was "so inebriated" at a Russian launch site that a flight surgeon "stayed in his room overnight for fear that he might choke to death in his sleep." NASA went into full denial mode, calling stories of drunken astronauts "urban legend"—though a half-empty bottle of tequila was found at another site's crew quarters. Apollo 11's lunar-module copilot, Buzz Aldrin, drank wine on the moon and, after returning to Earth, used his NASA-issue T-38 supersonic jet to fly from Houston to New York and cheat on his wife. Aldrin's NASA nickname: Dr. Rendezvous. The wine: for Communion.

One of the most popular foods in space is the tortilla. The most useful cooking implement is duct tape. (To hold the tortillas down.) Apollo 8, the first manned mission to orbit the moon, was plagued by nausea and diarrhea and other bodily intrusions. An excerpt from the flight transcript:

> FRANK BORMAN, COMMANDER: I'm going to take a leak, a little leak would feel good.
> JAMES A. LOVELL JR., COMMAND MODULE PILOT: … went floating by here.
> BORMAN: Huh?
> LOVELL: A bunch of crap just went floating by… a little piece that got away from somebody… Boy, there's some things in my pocket they don't know about.

A Mars mission will last two and a half years. Astronauts do not always get along. From Apollo 7:

> WALTER M. SCHIRRA JR., COMMANDER: Walt, you going

underneath there again? I'm dead serious, I've got to pass here!…

R. WALTER CUNNINGHAM, LUNAR MODULE PILOT:

Wally, I can't help it. I'm just—

SCHIRRA: Well, I said it and I meant it.

CUNNINGHAM: Jesus!

SCHIRRA: I ask you to—

CUNNINGHAM: Would you lock your seat down? That's what is doing it. Can I lock your feet down in the—

SCHIRRA: Yes, I've got about five minutes to get into a fixed attitude, and you're freaking around down there like you—

CUNNINGHAM: I'm not freaking around down here! I Just drifted into it. I couldn't help it. That's why I asked you—

SCHIRRA: Now I lost the damn attitude. Aggravating! And shit! It's your trouble I can't get anything done right.

A projected 520-day Mars simulation began in Moscow in 2009. During a shorter simulated confinement, two Russians got into a fistfight. Per the *Boston Globe*, they fought "so viciously that they left bloodstains on the capsule walls." (Vodka was blamed.) Then a Russian grabbed the one female participant—a French-Canadian who, fearing for the simulation's safety, had hidden all the knives—and, as she said, began "really aggressing my personal space" via a "very intrusive… kiss with the tongue." One space-psychology researcher, when asked about an eventual Mars mission, suggested that astronauts choose "expedition spouses" to serve as temporary sexual partners— they would "have an exclusive relationship… for six to nine months" and then "return to their normal lives and families."

David Baker, a NASA systems analyst on the Apollo missions, said that a lot of veterans of the US space program are "convinced that UFOs exist." When a lunar-conspiracy theorist confronted Buzz Aldrin (seventy-two at the time), saying, "You're the one who said you walked on the moon when you *didn't*... You're a coward and a liar and a—" Aldrin punched him in the face.

NASA operates like its own country and, at its best, like countries don't even exist. The International Space Station, 924,739 pounds of metal and tortillas two hundred miles above you right now, assembled by former enemies, has been described as "the greatest engineering project in the history of mankind." But much as looking at the night sky clarifies the insignificance of our lives, looking at the federal budget clarifies the insignificance of NASA. After we beat the Russians, the public lost interest in Apollo. And the interest never really came back. With Constellation's plans for some of the most astounding things we'd ever done in space, the agency thought it was on the cusp of a period of renewed health—a redux. The reality is something like extinction.

There is a lot to explain.

T he day after the night viewing I headed for the press site, a rectangular building on a rise overlooking the launchpad filled with desks that faced a tall counter, a pair of TVs, and a countdown clock. I was given the site's last desk and an excellent chair: red, swivelable, with padded arms. The area was alive with journalists, engineers, corporate spokespeople, high school students, NASA retirees, congressmen—all interviewing, glad-handing, walking to the cafeteria and back, watching NASA TV (an astronaut adhering globules of water to a mirror; cosmonauts drinking champagne), watching the clock. To my left was a teacher and students from a Kentucky high school, and to my right, a tall, serious man who said he was with the German space agency (*Deutsches Zentrum für Luft- und Raumfahrt*) who, after neatly arranging his papers, computer, two-liter plastic Coke bottle, and fluted highball glass, managed to steal my chair.

Before I could protest, I was called over to talk with Bob Bagdigian, an ursine and extremely cheerful man from Alabama's Marshall Space Flight Center (MSFC) in charge of the newest piece of tech in NASA's environmental-control and life-support system (ECLSS), a Dumpster-size machine that can reprocess wastewater, including sweat and urine, into drinking water. It is a critical piece of hardware if your goal is to create a long-term, self-sustaining human presence in space. A "big Brita in the sky" is how a friend described it—one you can pee in!

A near scale mock-up was sitting in the middle of the room.

Jennifer Morcone, a public-affairs officer from Marshall dressed entirely in purple, half-curtsied as she gave me a sample of the water. I felt like I'd been offered a refreshment in the Old South. Bob said, "Some of that's me."

I took a sip. Weird aftertaste.

Bob replied, "Antimicrobial iodine. We put it in there for storage. It'll be removed."

"There's water in solid waste, too—can you recycle that?"

"We're working on it."

"So astronauts will have to urinate first, and *then* defecate?"

Bob looked a tiny bit uncomfortable with this line of questioning but carried on: "It's a special potty. And the urinal hose system is discriminatory. It has different interfaces for different-gendered crew."

I followed up with, "So for a penis it's a hose, and for a vagina?"

"A hose with a cup attachment. I'm sure we have a technical name for that, but I'm not sure what it is."

Female urine receptacle (FUR).

When I got back to my desk, my new German neighbor, whose

name was Gerhard, looked at my name tag and said, "*GQ*, what is it?"

I explained my own acronym.*

He regarded me not so much neutrally as nihilistically. Then, after a few beats, I said, "Hey, did you know that they're giving out samples of the urine-and-sweat water?"

The availability of beverage-grade urine and sweat was transformative information for Gerhard.

"Who can get this for me?"

"Jennifer, in purple, from Alabama."

His face was illuminated. "I know exactly who you mean." He leaped up from my chair and galloped away.

When he returned with his toilet water Gerhard was made anew, as though he himself had been run through the ECLSS. Kindly, he volunteered to explain launch protocol: "There is forty-three hours' counting time, and this includes built-in holds… One at minus twenty minutes, which is about ten minutes long, and another, for forty-five minutes, at minus nine minutes. Then the control groups are polled to 'go' or 'not go.' Then the launch director proceeds." I forgave him for stealing my chair.

More people were gathering in the press area. On live NASA TV the astronauts walked through what looked like the set of *Office Space,* past clapping cubicle workers. In a parking lot they lined up beside a silver Airstream, then rolled down Kennedy Parkway trailed by a retinue of Huey helicopters. At pad 39-A suit technicians dressed them. Hatch technicians helped them into the shuttle. They lay on their backs and waited. Mission Control came on the

---

* By the way, I made that FUR one up. I asked Morcone for the technical name and she responded, "I'm on it…" But not long after, she told me, "Sorry to disappoint you, but the urine-collection hose is officially called the urine receptacle. It does not have a special name/adapter for male/female."

com: "This is Houston." Dusk arrived. Someone said, "That looks beautiful." It was true. The shuttle was in the gloaming. A hatch technician picked his nose.

Someone said, "There is a moon over the launchpad that's amazing."

I walked outside. A huge yellow orb, crossed with orange continent-like shapes, hung over 39-A. The xenon-bathed shuttle glowed in the distance. An outdoor countdown clock was illuminated. Clusters of press and VIPs had begun to gather on a sloping lawn. Multiple newscasts were in the process of filing reports.

Jennifer Morcone came up to me and said, "I should have asked you if you were allergic to iodine. Some people are. I could have killed you."

Back inside, I looked for Gerhard. The only person nearby was Jack King, known as the Voice of Apollo, whom millions heard intone, "Liftoff. We have a liftoff. Thirty-two minutes past the hour. Liftoff on Apollo 11," when we first went to the moon. I introduced myself and asked him something I'd been saving for an old-timer: "Mr. King, can you tell me why the NASA logo is called 'the meatball'?"

"Because of the roundness."

A voice said, "SRO is go."

Voice: "I do concur. Go for launch."

Voice: "Vehicle's in good shape, weather's beautiful, so on behalf of the entire launch team, good luck, Godspeed…"

I walked back outside with King. The PA said, "Legacy…quest for knowledge… Godspeed… got launch… BLT has been cleared." Two minutes on the clock. A collectively held inhalation. An accentless female voice, futuristic in its clarity, uttered the words: "Ninety seconds to launch of space shuttle *Endeavour*… auto sequence set…. ten, nine, eight, seven, six, five, four, three, two, one, booster ignition, and *liftoff* of space shuttle *Endeavour*!"

The glow of the xenon lights surrounding the pad expanded into a marshmallow, then a half circle of pure white light, inflating to a thousand feet on either side, and then leaving the earth, becoming a circle, rising up to meet the moon, with a calligraphic black trail of smoke connecting it to the ground. We were all bathed in light and silence till the circle passed the moon and the sound arrived: firecrackers everywhere.

The percussion of the shuttle's solid rocket boosters continued to amplify until the sound took on a physical quality. It felt like the sky was trying to shake some sense into me. (Apollo's Jack King: "Solid fuel pulses and burns rough. It's like a fork in your garbage disposal.") The sound was rummaging around in the trees behind the press area. I imagined all of KSC's gators hidden there, about to panic, then stampede. I turned and looked. Nothing but stillness— the effect was pure ventriloquism. When I turned back, the shuttle was at high altitude, with haloing clouds spreading out from its path. Soon it was a bright dot. Everyone applauded. A chopper landed in the parking lot.

I asked King about the halo clouds.

"Ionization, the vehicle stacking and compressing air, creating a shock wave. Never seen that before." He shook his head, paused. "Conditions were perfect."

"Out of all the launches you've seen, how'd that rank?"

"Twenty-seven. Ha. You didn't see Saturn V."

I found Gerhard, shook his hand, said, "How about that?"

He replied, "*Gut.* Perfect."

* * *

A NAZI PARTY ON MARS.

After leaving Kennedy I was scheduled to inspect infrastructure for the death-row-bound Constellation program at three other space centers: Marshall in Alabama, Stennis in Mississippi, and Johnson in Houston, where I'd been going for thirty years to visit my aunt Glendora, who lived in El Lago, a few blocks from Neil Armstrong's house. Being a Texan, and a dangerous driver, Aunt Glen favored Cadillacs and wrecked one every five years, once taking out three hundred feet of NASA fence. Her husband continued to buy them for her and name them after her, putting the word *Baby* before her name to make the car's name. Aunt Glen doted on me, as she had no babies of her own. But she did do some naming: of a local park, after Neil Armstrong. He'd told her he did not wish to have a park named after him. She pushed it through anyway. She also created an Astronaut Wall of Fame in El Lago, collecting dozens of photos from the town's spacegoing citizenry (Armstrong among them). I always felt that she expected me to be on that wall one day.

The shuttle launch left me with a desire to do the one thing no writer had done before: go into space. (Norman Mailer had wanted this but despaired: "NASA would opt for Updike!") Tom Wolfe said that to have the right stuff, a man must "have the ability to go up in a hurtling piece of machinery and put his hide on the line and... pull it back in the last yawning moment." Wolfe's astronauts in *The Right Stuff* got used to weightlessness "in the cargo holds of C-131 transports" that repeatedly climbed and dove in parabolic arcs, their contents floating. This seemed to me like the craziest possible thing I might have a chance of actually doing. So I made some inquiries and was told I *could* do it—in a hollowed-out 727, flown by a private contractor called Zero G. Only later did I discover that this aircraft was known as the Vomit Comet.

I planned my trip so that I'd have four days to visit the three space centers and then get to Washington, DC, where I'd fly fifteen parabolas. My first stop was Marshall, inside the Redstone Arsenal, a military facility where signs said NO KNIVES OR FIREARMS and LIMIT YOUR MOVEMENTS. After arriving I was met by a public-affairs rep who said he'd convey me to "the Cedar Room." I anticipated juleps and southern hospitality.

Alas, my destination was not some bower of comfort but the Collaborative Engineering and Design-Analysis Room, where I was reunited with Jennifer Morcone, who'd supplied me with the recycled urine and sweat at KSC. She introduced me to Danny Davis, in charge of building and testing the upper stage of the new Ares I rocket, which would launch Constellation astronauts into orbit. He explained the complexity of the engineering, saying, "The good Lord gave us a really tough equation to solve." I mentioned a recent *New York Times* article describing a "chorus of naysayers" who believed Ares was a terrible idea, that its controversial solid-fuel engine would vibrate dangerously, that it was being designed by autocrats convinced they could "mandate reality," that existing satellite-delivery rockets could be adapted to do the job just as well.

Davis told me simply, "We've made the right decision," and then added, "We need advocates."

This resembled something Wernher von Braun, Marshall's first director and the scientist behind the Saturn V rocket, said to Mailer: "You must help us give a *shove* to the program." There's a particular strain of PhD that has become a shorthand for anyone of giant intellectual prowess: the rocket scientist. But the original, the ur–rocket scientist, was von Braun. Born a baron, he was recruited by the German army in the 1930s when found launching jerry-rigged rockets in an abandoned ammo dump. The young baron had actually wanted to be an astronaut but became a terrorist instead—his V-2 was what Nazi Germany used to attack London during the final months of World War II.

Von Braun's *von* isn't what the *V* in V-2 stands for. It stands for *vergeltungswaffe* (vengeance weapon). Mostly it killed, and was expected to kill, civilians. At the National Air and Space Museum in Washington, there's a display on the V-2 showing an under-age-looking victim, pants blown off, lying uncovered in the street. A placard makes one of the only references to von Braun, who, in 1938, the year of *Kristallnacht*, disported himself at a costume ball thrown by German rocket engineers (theme: the first Nazi party on Mars) and—riding history as few ever have—a few decades later created a masterpiece, the Saturn V (its *V* recalling, uncomfortably, that other *V*). A public-affairs person at Marshall marveled that von Braun was perhaps the only person to have worked for both Hitler *and* Kennedy. Moreover (moreover!), his Saturn V may have had its infancy in a mythic program that remains undiscussed at both Marshall and in DC: *Projekt Amerika*, which supposedly called for a suicide-piloted two-stager to fly in half an hour from Germany to the edge of space, across the Atlantic, and then... straight into the Empire State Building!

Near the war's end von Braun engineered his own capture by the US, was never prosecuted as a war criminal, and became the presiding genius of NASA. Installed in Alabama, he not only put us on the moon but built up the agency's infrastructure to such a degree that it is now largely prepared to go to Mars. I saw much of this infrastructure, and it is astounding. Of course, if it hadn't been for the tragedy of Nazism, it all might not have been in Alabama but in Germany, and the *Deutsches Zentrum für Luft- und Raumfahrt* might be on Mars *already*. Von Braun, not Armstrong, could have been the first man on the moon. Omitting him from the history of the space program, as the Air and Space Museum largely has, is like omitting Jesus from the history of Christianity.

But von Braun is still Jesus at Marshall. Or God. As Jennifer Morcone and I drove around the center's test stands and mock-ups, we encountered his numerous progeny, objects of biblical proportion, among them the vibration-test stand, thirty-six stories high, where fully stacked rockets are put through launch simulations; a skyscraper-size engine-test stand and "flame bucket" designed to take twelve million pounds of thrust from an eventual Mars vehicle; and relics, huge Redstone and Atlas rockets, in a "rocket garden." Surveying this domain: a heroic sculpture of von Braun, decked out in a space suit and ready for the first *NASA* party on Mars.

Morcone and I kept picking up engineers, security personnel, and PhDs as we went along. At one test facility, I had a six-person entourage. An engine had recently been fired, and we looked at the scorch marks where the flames had hit. Someone explained that the material was an ablative heat absorber: "Ablatives take energy out of heat."

This reminded me of Neil Armstrong. If von Braun is the fiery, egomaniacal archetype of space exploration, Armstrong is the opposite. And successful rocketry, a science of combustibles and supercoolants, is all about the creation of velocity through the proximity of opposites. Mailer thought Armstrong had a personality of "unequalled banality," as compared with von Braun's "obvious funds of charisma." When we launched the moon rocket, the German issued this statement: "I think it is equal in importance to that moment in evolution when aquatic life came crawling up on land." Armstrong, when explaining what had inspired his immortal and off-the-cuff line ("That's one small step for [a] man, one giant leap for mankind"), said, "I thought, well, when I step off I'm... It's just gonna be a little step. Gonna be a step from there down to there. But then I thought about all those four hundred thousand people that had given me the

opportunity to make that step. I thought, It's gonna be a big something for all those folks… So it was a kind of a simple correlation of
thoughts." The first man on the moon was an ablative taking out all
the hype and bringing the endeavor back to Earth.

Space is not about ego. It's about all of us. One of NASA's most
noble qualities is humbleness. You shouldn't overstate, or claim to
possess, the sublime. You should share it, as Armstrong did, even
by Mailer's definition—"banal" meaning trite, trivial, petty, but
also something communal (a "banal oven" was where medieval
towns collectively baked their bread). I like to think of the man—
who didn't even want my aunt to name a small park after him (but
wouldn't presume to stop her)—as democratizing the sublime.

But it also took the German's ego to ensure our success.

Von Braun's long dead. Armstrong, now, too. But in his seventies
he was asked if he'd like to go to Mars with Constellation.

He replied, "I don't want to say I'm not available."

CONSTELLATION.

The next morning, in Houston, I woke up early and headed for
Johnson, where I met a public-affairs officer who'd asked me
on the phone, "Do you want to talk to any women or just guys?"
Confused, I'd told her I definitely wanted to talk with both genders.
Now I inquired, "Am I going to meet some women today?"

She replied, "You're not gonna see *any* women. I told everyone
GQ was coming and the guys are just clamoring."

So, masculine conversation, in which the following was disclosed:
Orion, the Constellation crew capsule that was scheduled to replace
the shuttle, was meant to splash down in the ocean but could also
land on land. (The project manager told me, "I'm not saying it'll be

fun—but they'll survive.") Constellation was to launch two rockets almost simultaneously—the new Ares V would go up with 157,000 pounds of cargo for building the moon base, and once Mission Control had verified that all systems were go, then its companion, the Ares I, would follow with the crewed *Orion* capsule on top. Logos for Constellation were commissioned from a *Star Trek: The Next Generation* designer.

Then lunch at a conference table in a corner office with the top men on Constellation: Jeff Hanley, an elegant, self-contained midwesterner, and Doug Cooke, a ruddy, near-silent Texan. It was a Last Supper of sorts. After our meeting, Hanley and Cooke were attending Constellation's budget-development meeting (at which the allocation/withholding of $6.9 billion would be discussed). They were not looking forward to it.

I began by saying, "The public at large has no idea what the Constellation program is or, really, that it even exists." This brought on strong cringing, after which both men's faces sank into resigned sadness. They nodded beleagueredly at each other.

I asked if the Ares rockets weren't maybe a mistake.

Hanley, the midwesterner, cool and restrained, in an off-white suit jacket: "The Ares V's the biggest rocket anybody will have ever built. This gets lost in discussions of performance. To redesign and human-rate"—i.e., make it safe for humans to sit on it—"an existing launch vehicle would cost a lot of time. There's a lot of momentum behind Ares. It'll improve crew safety by a factor of ten. Airlines have a one-in-ten-thousand fatality rate. The shuttle has a one-in-sixty... as safe as getting in your car... We're shooting for one in a thousand."

Cooke, in a blazer, drawled from behind his lunch: "Preliminary design review went very well."

Hanley: "We're opening up all locations on the moon for

exploration. Apollo only went to the near side and the equatorial regions."

I asked about getting to Mars and, once there, how we would get back.

Hanley: "We can make fuel from the Martian atmosphere—that's simple chemistry."

Cooke: "There's an opportunity to send something to Mars every twenty-six months. It'll take six Ares V rockets to do a Mars mission. But first we've got to close the life-support-system loop." Hence the moon base, where lunar soil—regolith—will be converted to oxygen, water, and fuel, and where options for growing food will be explored.

"What about leaving the solar system?"

Hanley: "Barring some breakthrough... A hundred years ago, nobody would've guessed we'd go to the moon. Visiting other planet bodies—that's why I'm here." Then, wistfully, "Seems like it's taking a long time."

In six missions, Apollo astronauts spent only eighty hours on the moon. Constellation was to take us back long-term, maybe permanently. What were we to do when we got there?

That afternoon, outside a gray building marked HANGAR X, I was given some answers. My informant was Robert Howard, an African-American man in his mid-thirties with a Vandyke and a crew cut, who was in charge of "human factors" for the new lunar lander, called *Altair*. In the background loomed a hulking steel two-story mock-up of the spacecraft, which was to separate, Apollo-style, from a large command module and descend to the lunar surface. Howard's colleague, Clinton Dorris, the deputy project manager, said, "We brought Armstrong and the others to see this and they said, 'Holy smokes—it's huge!' It has three times the mass of *Apollo*'s lander."

The three of us climbed through an air lock (airplane-lavatory size) and into the crew module (twice as big). Howard said, "We're a couple of generations out of phase from knowing how to get to the moon." Translation: We've forgotten how to get there. "So you think, What's going to kill the crew? Then you think comfort. You need hammocks. Jungle or rigid? Four people will be in here. So we figured three hammocks and one on the floor. But when we brought the astronauts in, nobody wanted to sleep on the floor."

I said, "I'd want to sleep on the floor."

Dorris said, "Yeah. Hammocks aren't that comfortable. But they're a lot more comfortable than some of the places I've slept." I gave him a where-have-you-slept look. "Before coming to NASA, I did covert ops. I lived in a hole in the desert with three guys for a month... I also flew Apache helicopters."

We talked aviation for a minute, and I said I was going on the Vomit Comet.

"You guys ever been on?"

Howard said, "I went on the Zero G one. About thirty percent of people throw up. It's always the people that don't take meds. Are you taking meds?"

"I'm not sure."

"You should take meds. Those who don't lose it. Two on my flight did. They didn't get to their bags on time, either. They have a bag zipped into your jumpsuit right here"—he pointed to his left shoulder—"but nobody ever gets to it in time. They call that 'a kill,' when you throw up on the Vomit Comet."

"Big mess?" I asked.

A wry smile: "It *floats*."

I started to feel claustrophobic. Three of us filled the entirety of the crew module, yet there was supposed to be another astronaut and a ton of gear in the same volume when it was on the moon.

I said, "Maybe let's get out of here."

Dorris, Howard, and I drove over to another hangar to see the new lunar electric rover (LER), a long-range vehicle that was designed to make wide swaths of the surface available to exploration. I'd imagined a buggy but found what looked like a party van mounted on a swiveling twelve-wheeled chassis. We got in. A tall, rangy astronaut in a blue jumpsuit followed. This was Mike Gernhardt, head of the rover project, the man who'd piloted it in Obama's inaugural parade. He stood up straight, so his head touched the roof.

As we shook hands someone said, "We made it one Gernhardt tall—ninety-fifth-percentile white American male."

Meanwhile, Howard was reconfiguring the back of the rover to create a private stateroom. He drew a curtain, apparently made out of some proprietary NASA material, that instantly canceled all noise and light. Then he opened it to say, "There's a misting hose for sponge baths." He reclined the gray leatherette seats into beds and loungers.

It was not just a party van; it was a make-out van!

Gernhardt said, "With a nonpressurized rover, you could only make short trips. But this one can go out for weeks. And I'll spend most of my time in shirtsleeves with a cup of coffee." He opened a medicine-cabinet-size air lock at the rear and accessed a surface suit hanging off the rover. "I can step straight into it"—he grabbed a bar and half swung through—"close this air lock, depressurize, and then walk outside. I did the first spacewalk from the space station. It took me six hours to get out the door. Here I'll be able to do it in twenty minutes." He got in the driver's seat and said, "We had Humvees chasing us in the field, and they could not keep up because of the terrain-crossing ability."

The rover is operated with fighter-pilot-style control sticks. Every wheel can turn a full 360 degrees. It also has huge blind spots. Gernhardt pushed his stick forward. We glided smoothly out of the hangar—until we felt an impact and a voice over the radio said, "Mike, you hit a box."

Gernhardt mumbled, "I didn't see that."

An older man, jumpsuit matching Gernhardt's, sauntered in to observe our predicament. After my close encounter with Armstrong, I thought he might also be an Apollo veteran—maybe Gene Cernan, who reputedly uttered the last words spoken on the moon ("Let's get this mutha outta here!").

I asked Gernhardt.

A wry smile. "He's the Space Center Houston tram driver." Then, cleared to proceed, he added, "We would have won, and the box would have lost."

From the back: "So far we've never had any automobile accidents in this."

Gernhardt switched on the AC (which slowly began to leak on him) and said, "We're going to do excursions up to a thousand kilometers long." We were crabbing on a smooth diagonal across a vast expanse of sunny lawn beside the hangar—the moon to us. "If I find a vein that a geologist wants to follow, we can move sideways right alongside, the geologist down on the floor"—he pointed to a round bubble at the bottom of the rover's front canopy—"inches away."

He spun straight ahead and floored it for a drainage ditch, where the shocks absorbed the impact and translated it into a smooth curve, then said, "You want to drive?"

"*Yeah.*"

I tried diagonals, laterals, and hitting the irrigation ditch.

I asked if Gernhardt had been on the Vomit Comet.

Gernhardt: "I flew fifty or sixty parabolas this morning."

I lowered the rover, nose to lawn, like a grazing animal. The air-conditioning was leaking hard now. Dorris, the Apache pilot, asked to take over driving, and I moved back. Gernhardt requested towels: "I'm getting showered."

Howard started opening up ingenious storage compartments. I felt a strong desire to have NASA organize my apartment. Dorris hooked and sliced, Apache-style.

"Wanna race the tram?" Gernhardt called back to me.

I did not. Suddenly I was in danger of throwing up and being the first "kill" for the LER—if I couldn't handle this, I was doomed when it came to parabolas.

Gernhardt was a deep-sea diver who repaired oil platforms before joining NASA. He had the look of someone who'd spent a lot of time in salt water—like a surfer with a PhD in bioengineering. He was wearing combat boots that came up to midcalf and were wrapped, for reasons I couldn't figure out, in leather cord. Having flown four shuttle missions, he's one of the most experienced astronauts at NASA. We talked a bit back at the hangar. I asked him, "How much sleep do you actually get in space?"

"You're so excited to be there. You're working your tail off. Six hours. Sometimes two. Post-mission I'm shot." He thought the moon would be a much different environment, work-and-stress-wise. "With the new suit we'll go out for pleasure—just to take a walk. Picture the games you can play. Lunar basketball; the high jump. We tried powering the rover with an ergometer, which is good exercise—you pedal in Fred Flintstone mode—and it worked. But we didn't get going very fast."

Then he mentioned that he liked to write. Fiction. So I asked him to send me some stories.

Prose-wise, his stuff was straight out of the Richard Ford and Thomas McGuane school. He was living in the golden age of straight-ahead American fiction, if not the golden age of space flight. My favorite story described the world of oil-rig diving, and opened in a Mexican bar where a man carried a hand-cranked electric generator attached to a pair of exposed electrodes from table to table.

> He was charging people money to get shocked. A big dial on the front showed how much current he was cranking. All the men were competing to see who could hold on the longest. There was this one big guy who was shooting tequila and carrying on with a nice looking whorishly dressed girl. They seemed to be having a great time. Then she slapped him and said, "*Pendejo*!" He tried to slap her back, but she ducked and started walking out. He stood up knocking over his chair and took a few steps toward her, yelling obscenities... Then he sat down, called the twelve-volt man over, flipped him some money, took a shot of tequila, and grabbed the electrodes. Twelve-volt cranked away and as the dial was about to peg the generator short-circuited or something and the big guy went flying across the room. He had this shocked look on his face and then stood up slowly shaking his head, like he didn't know where he was.

One more reason to admire Gernhardt: the guy could write a sentence. Another story described what it felt like to go into orbit:

> I remember when I first looked out the window at earth. It took my breath away. The jewel blue earth suspended in black space, swirling white clouds, vast empty oceans, continents, countries without borders, everyone you know covered by your raised thumb. For a fleeting moment, things made sense. Then back to

work, details, and checklist after checklist for hours, then days on end… Everything a blur, not quite real, almost like you weren't really there, like you were watching yourself from a dream or some other place… One reason I got in this business was to recognize I was alive, to feel it, to know it. Sure, the ride up made you feel alive because you were so close to death, but with your mind focused on your job, it seemed like it was over in an instant.

Contemporary NASA—billions spent launching people to a location where they can maximize human intimacy with stress and paperwork. I suppose a Muslim agency would spend its time up there befuddled by how to face Mecca. A Catholic one would degravitize guilt. Ah, for a secular Spanish space program.

"You know who I don't like but is in the *New Yorker* all the time?" Gernhardt asked.

"T.C. Boyle?"

"No. John Updike."

In the novel *Rabbit Redux,* Updike described astronauts as "pretty boys in the sky."

"He just died," I said.

Brief pause.

Gernhardt said, "I still don't like the way he puts things."

That evening I found myself walking around my hotel room saying, "It really does stupefy me how great this agency is and how little the country appreciates it. When people think the best thing we've ever done as a nation—put a man on the moon—is a con, or a waste, and not a wonder, that is when we know we are truly lost. Anything that creates that much wonder, gets that many people working in concert, and trivializes things that truly *need* to be trivial-ized is to be valued above all else!" Gernhardt's coolness, his obvious funds of right stuff, had pushed me over the edge: the man could fly into space at seventeen thousand miles per hour *and* denigrate John Updike! I wanted to be like him. (I could only do the latter.) And this feeling only deepened when, the next morning, I found myself in an air lock with Carlton C. Allen, a white-haired man in his sixties who runs Johnson's Astromaterials Acquisition and Curation Office—the keeper and distributor of every artifact NASA has collected from space. (He described his office as a "ghetto of geologists.")

A sign designated the room beyond the airlock in which we were standing a "Bunny Suit Area," and, accordingly, we were dressed completely in white—jumpsuits, gloves, caps, booties. Prior to entering the air lock Allen handed me "one of the oldest and least-changed" objects humankind has ever encountered—a rubblelike asteroid that was 4.5 billion years old. He contextualized: "Fourteen billion years ago was the big bang. This rock is one third that age. That is the oldest thing you will ever touch. And you'll probably never touch anything from further away."

Then he explained the origins of life: "Early Earth was a very, very hot place. We think that the whole outer crust was completely melted. And melting rocks takes you up to about two thousand degrees—so hot that any organic compounds are completely destroyed. So the early Earth was sterile. But we *have* complicated organic compounds all over the Earth. We're part of them. That's what life is all about.

"One of the things that modern astronomy and planetary science has come to understand is that there is a natural way of delivering complicated organics to the planets. As they were forming. We think that a lot of the organic chemistry that we see in life on earth was delivered by meteorites." Pointing to the oldest object on earth he clarified, "That's not saying there's anything alive in here."

"No," I said. "I understand."

"But the basic chemical compounds that came together in the early earth and started up as life came from space."

"That's mind-blowing."

"Yes. Yes. *Yes*."

Laughter.

Rocks change on earth. You can't pick up a rock that is unchanged and primordial. The only timeless rocks, like Allen's meteorite, come from space. And a tiny fraction of unchanged rocks from space contain microscopic crystals that, as Allen put it, "we understand to be stuff blasted across billions of miles of space from other stars." So we were wearing bunny suits to avoid bringing any rogue information into the study of these rocks. Allen: "You see pictures of Pigpen? We're all like that. Little clouds of debris."

I asked if there was a market rate for moon rocks or asteroids. He replied, "A tiny little bit of an asteroid or planet is worth thousands of dollars. But the government owns these so they don't have a street value."

From the air lock we entered a bright fluorescent rectangle full of positively pressurized stainless chambers accessed by glove boxes. The glove boxes were covered with white caps because uncapped gloves used to occasionally flutter and set off motion detectors. "Serious people come around if you get an alarm in this lab." At the far end of the room was a Federal Reserve bank vault, and, inside it, "the only lunar rocks in the world. We keep them as if it took a thirty billion-dollar program to get them and we're not going to get any more." The vault was closed with two dials. No one person knows both combinations: "Like the two-man rule for nuclear launch. We do the same thing here."

We walked through the room in our white suits, looking at these captured chunks of the moon. Allen, whose capacity for wonder seemed wholly intact, said, "I see a bunny when I look at the moon."

The majority of the lunar samples were gray, but one was pure white, and powdery, like cocaine, with little metal instruments beside it. A fist-size rock had been riven with hundreds of tiny pinpricks. Allen said, "Dust-sized particles make shooting stars on earth. On the moon dust particles make pin-sized pits in rocks." These pinpricks were ancient, as "most impacts and all eruptions are over. The moon is a place where nothing happens. An end member in the planets— what a small body without atmosphere becomes."

Many rocks had a pumicelike quality—"think of freshly broken crystals." And the moon may as well be covered in teeth. That's how sharp these broken crystals are. Also, carrying on with the oral metaphor, the moon is thirsty. If an astronaut were to disrobe on the moon, a NASA website explained, "the water would get sucked out of the astronaut's unsuited body in an effort to even out the water-vapor pressure… very quickly and completely, leaving behind dry dust."

I imagined Gernhardt and Allen up there, the former propelling the rover with his own effort, the latter in the observation bubble, inches away from the surface.

Gut. Perfect.

CONFLAGRATION.

From Houston I flew to New Orleans, where that night I went to see a trumpeter called Kermit Ruffins, who had a regular gig in the Ninth Ward. Ruffins played a short set, then announced it was time for a "cannabis break." While he fired up, I took a beer outside and talked with a Canadian woman in her sixties named Nancy, who was wearing a yellow Bourbon Street T-shirt and a flowing skirt. She said she'd ridden a motorcycle across America, and asked what I was doing. I explained about NASA.

She asked, "With NASA what's your aspect?"

I had no idea what she meant. "Aspect? Do you mean what's my angle?"

"Yeah, angle. What's your angle on NASA?"

"Just to try and understand what they're doing."

She thought about that for a minute, then asked, seriously, "Can I come with you?"

Just across the Mississippi border, at the Stennis Space Center (SSC), I was met by Paul Foerman, fiftyish, with a boyish face, my guide. Foerman and I took a government van for a "windshield tour." Our driver, who looked like she had recently been a high school soccer player, was Stennis's visitor-relations specialist, or VRS (Foerman: "Yeah, we're big into acronyms"). The place was enormous, surrounded by an "acoustical buffer zone"—411 square miles of forest, swamp, and five ex-towns the government took over and turned to ghosts, naming it all after the state's most powerful senator. During one von Braun test at Stennis, involving 7.5 million pounds of Saturn V thrust, the reverberation was felt more than a hundred miles away, in Baton Rouge, and broke the bank windows in the town of Picayune. Now shuttle and satellite-delivery engines are tested there. It will be a huge proving ground for Constellation.

I recounted the prior night's outing. Foerman translated "cannabis break" for the VRS: "Smokin' some dope."

She cried, "Mr. Paul!"

We turned off Trent Lott Parkway and came round a corner, and I got a look at a structure more than twice as big as the biggest engine-test stand in Huntsville, a steel-and-concrete monolith with double flame buckets and a red control tower emblazoned with a huge meatball, like the burning-blue-and-bloodshot eye of a cyclops. I asked, "What's *that?*"

Foerman: "B stand."

Forty-three years ago, when NASA hadn't yet launched an Apollo spacecraft, von Braun built this monster to hold in twelve million pounds of thrust, almost twice the capacity of the Saturn V. (He had even bigger plans in mind.) Pratt & Whitney was leasing it for the long term. "It's on the plate for Ares V tests."

I asked if we could tour it, and Foerman said that was up to the lessee. So we found the company's strategic-planning manager, who agreed to show us around. They were setting up to hoist an engine into position.

I said, "I'd love to get a photo of that."

Negative from Strategic Planning: "Lotta tech on that engine that we don't want other countries getting hold of."

We all took an elevator to the top of the stand—warm on the ground, but 340 feet up we'd punctured another atmosphere. Out through some blast doors and the view carried on across Mississippi and deep into Louisiana—trees and water as far as the eye could see. Someone pointed out a site where NASA was building another stand for the Ares engine tests. Called A-3, it was to be the first large-scale test facility since Apollo. A test engineer who'd joined our group matched his stride with mine and said, "You can't write about how you feel when you see something you worked on go to space. I used to tell my mother it was like kissing a pretty girl. The same loss of memory… You ever feel that?" He said poetry did a good job explaining. "I've got an 1860s book in my truck, poetry from Hansboro, where my daddy was the postmaster."

On to an engine plant. As we entered a room full of rocketry,

Foerman shouted, "Shut off your phone!"

The plant manager explained: "There are shunts on the pyrotechnics that are installed in our hot-gas drive assembly, and if the shunts should fail, then it would... uh... it would go off. It's pyrotechnic. And that would not be good."

Cafeteria lunch. A can of something called Tony Chachere's Creole Seasoning had a high-profile spot on the counter. Foerman and I joined Lonnie Dutreix, project manager for A-3, and a group of rowdy test engineers.

"Do you guys like blowing things up?" I asked. "What challenges you as test engineers?"

The choral response: "Biggest challenge? Keeping management away from us!"

"I'm worried about nozzle hoop strength."

"I like fires. Blowing stuff up."

"*Expensive* things."

"Biggest challenge? *Yeah*, keeping management away from us! I con*coah* with that."

"When NASA wants smart people, they always look out of state."

"Uh, I'm from Mississippi."

"Well, yeah."

"We're *friggin'* cool down *heah*—stuffed shirts every*wheah* else!"

"I'm seriously worried about the nozzle."

Finally, a quick windshield tour of A-3 in the shirtsleeve environment of Dutreix's SUV. Mostly steel girders, the stand resembled a bridge mistakenly built vertical. Dutreix: "I don't want to be the project manager who builds this facility and it doesn't work—got a big bungee-jumping stand here." If it works, it'll create a vacuum simulating atmospheric conditions at one hundred thousand feet, the altitude at which the second stage of the Ares I was expected to start. This huge new thing, being built by a Native American contractor, called to mind the construction of Stennis itself—a Soviet-looking endeavor involving thousands of workers (and more mosquitoes). Of the workers back then, Dutreix said, "A lot of 'em just quit. They couldn't take it."

I got back to New Orleans in time to stop at a bar called Cooter Brown's for a pint, a dozen oysters, and some cheese fries. A long-haired guy next to me in a black concert shirt was having Jäger shots. He turned out to be a space enthusiast. When I told him I was to fly on the Vomit Comet in the morning, he said, "And you're eating *that* shit?!"

At the airport my plane had mechanical problems, so I cabbed it back to New Orleans, wolfed down a big African stew with spicy peanut sauce, Creole tomatoes, and more beer, then left four hours later for another flight, hungover and sleep deprived.

From the website for Zero G: "We recommend you to be well rested for the flight day, and avoid alcohol the night before…"

FEET DOWN!

I arrived in DC the next morning, just in time to meet my plane— *G-Force One*—on the tarmac at Dulles. A Zero G representative gave me a jumpsuit, then briefed me on safety. I'd already released them and NASA from liability by signing a waiver that stated, "Inherent risks include… personal injury or illness (minor or serious) and/or death… resulting from weightlessness."

I boarded the aircraft with a couple of dozen other passengers, all quiet, except for a boisterous group of Mexicans. We entered by a staircase at the rear, through a military-green snarl of cables, wires, hydraulics. The interior was completely covered in padding.

Ropes ran up and down the cabin, stopping at the back third, which was filled with seats. Everything was stowed, stripped bare, tied down. My seatmates were a neurologist and a Defense Department employee. The Mexicans, salesmen who'd sold harder than any of their salesman countrymen, and so won this trip, sang. Everyone was seemingly on major meds. Many had not eaten dinner the night before. I contemplated my beer, oysters, stew, lack of even Dramamine. I had wanted an unfiltered experience.

We all lay down on the floor, feet forward. I had brought along a yellow skateboarding helmet and put it on. Someone explained that at the end of each parabola we'd hear a shout, "Feet down, coming out!" our cue to right ourselves if we were upside-down and lie on our backs for a period of intensified 1.8 gs.

The plane climbed steeply, then went over the top. Martian gravity. I weighed sixty-five pounds! I was an eight-year-old with the strength of a man! The Mexicans did rapid-fire push-ups across from me! "Feet down!" I weighed over three hundred pounds! Now lunar! More feats of strength from Mexico! "Feet down!" Zero! Levitation! A kick in the head from someone. "Feet down!" Skateboarding moves I'd been trying my whole life—now effort-less! Aerials! A perfect stalled handplant! "Feet down!" Zero G unleashed some toys! A blowfish-like blue orb, a dog toy, whizzed by, and I caught it, then hurled it at Jorge from Guerrero, who booted it back! I flew up toward the ceiling, somersaulted, and lost track of which way was up—complete detachment of meaning from direction. Everyone was screaming and laughing. (Except one young woman, who was so sick she had to go strap herself in for the rest of the weightlessness.)

I softly sailed up and over to one of *G-Force One*'s two windows, in the emergency exits. Direction doesn't matter when you're weightless. Up and down are no longer markers. I suddenly

understood how in space there is only everywhere. And this revelation was accompanied by the fleeting physical knowledge of what
it was to leave the earth. I could move in any direction. All was
calm and effortless. And to an astonishing degree—astonishing
largely because the understanding was so matter-of-fact, as though
I'd begun to internalize my own understated Neil Armstrong—this
sort of comfort with wonder felt like the goal of both science and
religion. Here I was with a bunch of Mexican salesmen, on the Vomit
Comet, doing the kinds of things that make others want to either
throw up or, in NASA-ese, "work with us to do them," and lo, it was
good. I looked outside and saw that we were canted violently toward
the ocean, like a bombing run or a suicide mission—like *Projekt
Amerika*, DC-bound, coming in. A wave of vertigo… "Feet down!"

Later a woman told me the sensation of weightlessness was
"familiar—I have flying dreams all the time." She was, in fact, like
Neil Armstrong, who once described the following recurring dream:
"I could, by holding my breath, hover over the ground. Nothing much
happened. I neither flew nor fell in those dreams; I just hovered."

I had passed my own test. I'd flown the Vomit Comet on no
sleep, hungover, full of oysters and stew, hung my hide out over the
yawning abyss, and come back. Strapped in again, my neurologist
neighbor said, "You must have an iron stomach. And I'm glad to see
you wore a helmet. There's a lot of potential for injury here." Aunt
Glen would have been proud.

As we flew, the Mexican salesmen all sang together:

> *Ay, ay, ay, ay*
> *Canta y no llores*
> *Porque cantando se alegran*
> *Cielito lindo, los corazones*

Sing, and don't cry
Because singing makes you happy
Beautiful little sky, the hearts. ˙

ALDRIN'S WATCH

2009

B uzz Aldrin may have been only the second man to walk on the moon, but he was the first to wear a watch on its surface. In 1962 NASA visited a jewelry shop in Houston, bought some chronometers, and subjected them to what agency historians describe as "exhaustive tests aimed at determining performance reliability in the conditions likely to be experienced during EVA." That acronym stands for "extravehicular activity," which means moon walking, which means temperatures ranging from -250 to +250°F. The agency also exposed the watches to "accelerations of 12gs" and the violent shaking of a "vibration table." The only one to survive was the Omega Speedmaster. Despite congressional pressure to buy American, NASA went Swiss, and ordered one for every astronaut.

Neil Armstrong left his in the lunar module as a replacement for the ship's timer (American made), which had malfunctioned. Aldrin wore his strapped to the outside of his surface suit, because, as he said recently, he wanted it to do "more than just sit inside the spacecraft." A few years later, back on earth, he lost it. But on a warm Wednesday evening in June, at an event to celebrate the fortieth anniversary of the first moon landing, he could be found at the Omega store on Fifth Avenue, looking at replacements. Aldrin, in marked contrast to the rest of his Apollo crew, is a regular on the promotional circuit, and was contemporaneously featured in a Louis Vuitton campaign. (The web search "'buzz aldrin' 'media whore'" returns over 1,800 results.)

White coated men with monocles hustled about. Aldrin, in a blue bespoke pinstripe suit, answered questions about time, Mars, and *Magnificent Desolation*, his recent memoir (the title a reference both to what the astronaut saw on the lunar surface and to his terrestrial struggles with alcoholism). During the Apollo program, Aldrin and my aunt Glendora were neighbors. Thanks in part to Aunt Glen's enthusiasm, I had been reading his book. I told him I was enjoying it and had "just got to the point where you crash your Saab Sonnet."

The astronaut responded with a jerk of the head and a disbelieving look. "That was a really *bad* time for me! Don't talk about that!"

Then he reached down (those onlookers who were aware of the fact that Aldrin had punched a man just a few years back for badgering him about complicity in the supposed faking of the lunar landing could be forgiven for flinching), fished around in his pocket, and pulled out an AA medallion, which he held up a bit too close to my face.

"Twelve years," he said.

The medallion was gold and inlaid with red and blue stones. He repocketed it.

NASA had spent the last few years designing and testing a new series of spacecraft to return to the moon and continue on to Mars. Aldrin, like many of his Apollo program colleagues, was dismayed by the slowness of the project. The Obama administration had just convened a panel to review the whole thing and determined that there was not nearly enough money to make it happen.

I asked about the new lunar rover. A bystander and amateur lunar historian pointed out that Aldrin had never driven the original rover, and could not, therefore, be expected to have an opinion on the new one. There was a brief, tense pause, till Aldrin released the built-up pressure with a one-liner: "Beats walking."

A woman with red red lips and white white hair walked past. She appeared to be a regular denizen of Fifth Avenue boutiques, and caught Aldrin's eye. After saying hello he asked: "Where do you live?"

"New York," she replied. "But I see you in Monte Carlo all the time!"

He nodded.

"See you there soon!" she said.

The evening ended behind a pair of ebony pocket doors, where white-coated men and the Swiss president of Omega presented Aldrin with a diamond-encrusted Speedmaster. The diamonds were starlike—and looked valuable enough, in the right hands, to go some way toward getting us back up there.

ALWAYS BE CLEANING

2011

I once shared a kitchen with a friend who left a trail of vegetable trimmings, uncapped olive oil, soy sauce and vinegar bottles, dirty bowls and rejected greens across every surface whenever she made a salad. It was a great salad. But it made me smug. It ought, I told this friend, ungratefully, while eating her salad and looking at the demolished kitchen from which it had come, to be physically impossible to cook and not clean. Cook and clean shouldn't just be mentioned in tandem, but bound together with bonds unsunderable, fused into a single utterance. Sharing a kitchen with her was like flying with a copilot who could get a plane into the air but did not know how to land. I believed I knew how to land. I prepared complicated, multicourse meals that hit the table with nothing to be washed but cutlery, glasses, and plates.

I thought all of this up to the moment I became a father.

* * *

My wife, Daphne, and I split the work in our house. Since I am a show-off, and have amnesia, and allergies, I often prepare four different dishes, plus sides, at each meal.

Our five-year-old, Owen, grouchy on less than ten hours' sleep, can best be restored to himself by pancakes. I make them often (on Sundays with a side of bacon), employing one mixing bowl, one skillet, a whisk, and a measuring cup, plus a knife, fork, and plate. Let's say this is a Sunday and throw in a second skillet, a pair of tongs, and a plate covered in paper towels for the bacon. Sometimes I get a chance to wash the whisk right after I've used it, but not if Owen's two-year-old sister, Mira, is up. The sound of clomping feet precedes her arrival. When she gets to the kitchen she stops and throws her lilac-and-gray blanket over her head.

Owen says, "Dad, ghost. At breakfast."

I say, "Haunted breakfast."

Mira nods.

I put her in the seat we have clamped to our counter, and ask, "Do you want an egg?"

"Mnh-hnh."

My daughter, lover of soft-boiled eggs, seems to get eczema from egg whites, so I try to cook precisely, making the yolk soft and the rest discouragingly (but not unappetizingly) inflexible. For the same reason Mira drinks goat milk, which she likes to have warmed for twenty seconds in a pan. Add to the dirty list one pot, one pan, a slotted spoon, a knife, an egg cup (votive holders work well here), and a spoon.

At this point some dialogue:

Mira: "I want go-go!"

Me: "Sure, you can have some yogurt. How would you ask if you wanted me to give it to you?"

"CANIHAVESOMEYOGURT*PLEASE*!"

I give her some plain yogurt (Owen: "Goatgurt.") and turn around to get some honey, which we buy at the Union Square Greenmarket in half-gallon glass jars that weigh ten pounds each. Mira wants to eat an entire one of these for breakfast. I wrestle a jar down from a cabinet, stick in a spoon, prepare to drizzle.

Mira says, "I can do it!"

"OK," I say. "You can do it." I give her the spoon, full of honey. Suddenly it's in her mouth.

"Mmmm." She removes it slowly, then reaches for a second dip.

"Wait, don't *re*dip!" I get another spoon. "Last time, OK?"

She dips and drizzles with total focus, allowing me to secret the honey into an invisible zone on the floor. I then try to get some conversation going so the disappearance goes unnoticed. My strategy: talk off the top of my head, fast, and with enthusiasm. Circling police helicopters in lower Manhattan, a background annoyance and source of background anxiety (is something *happening?*) since 9/11, can be helpful.

"Hear that helicopter? Maybe more than one helicopter. A *group* of helicopters. Is there a word for that? A group of birds is called a flock. Unless they're crows. A group of crows is called a murder."

Owen: "Murder."

Mira: "Where's the honey?"

"Do you know they use helicopters to fight fires? Firefighting helicopters haul a big bucket full of water and dump it on the flames."

"WHERE'S THE *HONEY*?!?!?"

"Wouldn't that be cool if we had a remote-control helicopter that could carry a bucket full of maple syrup and dump it on your pancakes?"

"WHERE'STHE*HONEY* DADDY*THEHONEY*?!?!?"

"Honey's gone, sweathart," I say in a neutral voice.

"*Not* gone."

"It's gone."

"But I don't *want* it to be gone!"

"You've got a lot there." I point to her yogurt.

"*Not* a lot."

"Uh."

"You're trying to trick me, Daddy." (I am proud of her for noticing.) "We have a lot."

Owen comes in. "She's right, Dad, we have a lot of honey." He cranes over. "She doesn't have too much."

Mira: "Thank you, Owen."

Owen: "You're welcome, Mira."

Mira: "Can I have the honey, *please?*"

I cannot resist a "please." If one of my children were to say, "May I have some weapons-grade PU-239, please?" I would be helpless to refuse. I put Mira's honey back on the counter and we go through another three spoons.

More cleaning time spent not cleaning. Mira and I get sticky and Mira asks for a wet washcloth (without saying please).

Owen says, "Dad, that was an interesting idea about a remote-control helicopter that could pour maple syrup on our pancakes. Maybe we could get a little jar, fill it with maple syrup, and tape it to the bottom of a remote-control helicopter. Really, we could do that, Dad."

"We could. Though I was thinking you'd maybe use wire and screws and make a sort of harness."

"What's a harness?"

"A series of straps and buckles designed to hold people or things safely when they're hanging in the air."

Owen: "Harness."

Pause.

"Would you use a harness to hang from a mountain?"

"Yes. Or a bridge, or any other tall thing. Like a building."

Mira mixes a lot of the honey into her goatgurt, and the mixture into her hair. I peel her an apple, then wash some blueberries and give them to Owen in a bowl, racking up two more spoons, a plate, a bowl, and a peeler. Plus cups for milk or juice and/or water for each child (if they don't want *tea*). There's so much stuff on the counter that I'm running out of space. I am out of my depth.

New vocabulary words learned while not cleaning any of this up: *murder*; *harness*.

Things needing to washed up midway through breakfast: thirty-one.

In the fall of 2001, long before I became a parent, the air in our neighborhood smelled like melted plastic and nobody knew what to do. There was a police checkpoint at the end of our block. A man shouted at me on a crowded subway car because I was opening my mail, which he was afraid contained anthrax. I felt generally insecure, but specifically very good about one thing: my cooking/cleaning skills. So Daphne and I started inviting friends and acquaintances over for regular Sunday-night dinners that served as improvised comfort and family for people who had neither.

I made a series of dishes that I now almost never make (Owen: "That's just not my taste, Dad." Mira: both hands clamped over her mouth): seafood risotto with peas; gnocchi Bolognese with pork, beef, and San Marzano tomatoes (from Di Palo's Fine Foods down the street); porcini mushroom tagliatelle (fresh from Raffetto's around the corner); spaghetti with white wine and clams. Standing in the same spot from which I now ration honey I would have conversations with friends in the immaculate kitchen. Everything was flavorful, everything was comforting and grounding and under control, and the next morning I would wake up and not even think about pancakes (which I've never much liked).

The assumption in describing the morning above is that it is the one time a week (maybe month), Daphne gets to sleep late (eight fifteen), and I'm flying solo. By the time breakfast winds down the whole kitchen is completely trashed, and, because I almost always stay up till midnight or one, and get six hours' sleep, I'm trashed, too.

But everything changes faster than I can complain about it. Mira just ate some peas without requesting honey. Both kids' palates have broadened to include soy sauce. After dinner the other night Owen put his plate in the sink and instead of running off he got a wet cloth and wiped up the floor under his seat. I almost cried.

Ten years ago, on the beautiful fall day that provided lower Manhattan with its flocks of police helicopters, as executives came streaming up my block, the first thing I did was boil a pot of pasta. I made ravioli at ten thirty in the morning, grated cheese, sat down with a friend stranded on his way to midtown, and began to grasp what was happening. Fatherhood, at times, has also been a bewildering state of emergency. Cooking was, and remains, my response.

And then it is time to clean up.

DANNY MEYER BIT HIS TONGUE

2011

The most successful restaurateur in the world scaled the subway stairs two at a time, emerged on Lexington and Seventy-seventh, lengthened his stride, and called over his shoulder: "Have I told you about the Meyer Street-Crossing Method? Meyscrom." He scanned traffic. "Cut off every possible angle without being killed."

A car whipped by. Another stopped. He severed the end of Seventy-fifth Street ("That was a baby jay") and reached the Whitney museum, home of his newest restaurant, in two minutes.

Danny Meyer—fifty-three, trim, salt-and-pepper hair—had greeted me an hour earlier in his Union Square office. It was March, and the branches outside his windows were just beginning to blur green. He stood up from behind a desk, backed by a wall of books (sample title: *The Power of Nice*), took my hand, and applied the ideal amount of pressure for the ideal amount of time: a better handshake than any I could recall. It was nine a.m., and he was reviewing final edits for *Eleven Madison Park: The Cookbook*, a collection of recipes from his four-star restaurant. In the hall, his assistant, Haley Carroll, examined lunch reservations on a computer.

"I'm looking for notable people," she said. Meyer would spend from eleven thirty a.m. to two p.m. visiting their tables. A prominent book publisher would be eating at Union Square Cafe. "He's made 878 reservations and always sits at Table 38." Onscreen a note said to give him 38 unless someone named Peggy wanted it.

"Does Danny do dinner visits?" I asked.

"He will, depending on where." She called out, "Danny, how often do you do dinner drop-ins?"

"Three times a week for Maialino"—the Roman-style trattoria across from his apartment—"two times a week somewhere else."

Carroll told me: "If there's a school play at seven thirty"—Meyer is a father of four—"he can stop by the bar at six forty-five and say hello. It's all about schedule."

Carroll handed a printout to Meyer. He pointed to a name and asked, "Doesn't she write us notes?"

"Danny caught one that I missed."

After going over the cookbook manuscript ("They're trying to get me out of the present... I don't want to be in the conditional"), and lamenting a mishap that had occurred at dinner the night before ("I bit the crap out of my tongue") Meyer made his way to the Whitney for a ten a.m. meeting with his staff. The scheduled opening of the restaurant, named Untitled, was a week away. Meyer devotes unlimited time to his new ventures, tasting every item on the menu multiple times, suggesting alterations to such minutiae as the size of a sous chef's dice, and constantly consulting with the manager. I heard him instruct Untitled's chef to alter a BLT so the bacon would stick out on either side. "That's called turning up the 'home' dial," he explained.

In the museum's basement, Untitled's chef, manager, and three dozen waiters, waitresses, busboys, runners, and line cooks sat on uncomfortable chairs. Meyer greeted them and went into a speech— one of three he would give that day—calibrated to inspire. (His mother, Roxanne Frank, told me of his public persona: "That's something that has evolved as he matured. He was a little bit shy growing up.") "When an artist can't decide a name it's untitled," he told the group. "When the name is Untitled, it's underlined. We are underlining it… I thought it would be refreshing—make of it what you want. Put it on yourself. 'I'm <u>Untitled</u>.' Put it on a coffee. Every coffee has a big brand on it. Wouldn't it be great if you could just serve really good food and make people happy?" He segued into the decline of the Upper East Side coffee shop, the ascent of big-brand-owned boutiques, the economics behind corporate entities that can afford to pay almost any rent for exposure at a particular location. "We thought, Let's do New York's first farm-to-table coffee shop. Why is it that coffee shops aren't that good with coffee?… When was the last time you went to a coffee shop that cured and smoked its own bacon? Right here at <u>Untitled</u>. We're here for you and what you want to be."

We left and walked up to the Upper East Side branch of Shake Shack, one of Meyer's five Manhattan hamburger stands. On Park Avenue he was recognized by a pedestrian and briefly stopped to talk. "Occasionally they'll see me up here, and I'm like that doorman they can't place," he told me.

When we reached Eighty-sixth Street, Meyer asked, "Smell it?" I did. Shake Shack makes its first impressions olfactorily. He breathed deeply, stepped inside, stood atop a flight of stairs leading down to the cash registers and slowly scanned the scene. "My favorite thing is watching people enjoy our food," he'd told me earlier. "I get sort of an insane amount of pleasure out of that."

After a quick walk-through—Meyer spotted and comped a

customer he referred to as "New York's first celebrity woman chef"—we stepped back outside to ponder logistics. Could we hit the Upper West Side Shake Shack, and then the Modern, his restaurant at the Museum of Modern Art, and still make Eleven Madison Park, where he was expected to address a private party, by two p.m.? It was eleven fifty a.m. Into a cab. Through the park. Out in front of the Shack, on Seventy-seventh and Columbus, where Meyer was recognized by a slender woman pushing a stroller. The baby seemed to recognize him, too. He greeted her without breaking eye contact, then, as she walked off, turned to me and pointed out a damaged chair through the Shack's window ("See that slat?") that he'd somehow noticed without averting his gaze from the stroller pusher. He went inside, had a brief word with the manager, and descended a staircase to "the scrum"—a basement dining room with a flat-screen TV, packed full of kids and nannies.

Meyer told me: "One of my greatest moments was right here. A bunch of sixth or seventh graders were carrying their trays down. One said, 'Yeah, I guess I'm glad we're here—I couldn't bear one more day of Chipotle.'"

He decided to add the theater-district Shack to our itinerary. After grabbing another cab, we stopped at Forty-fourth and Eighth Avenue. "Former Chipotle manager here," Meyer said with satisfaction. We entered into the Smell. Now that Meyer had pointed it out, I was struck by its tactile qualities—the presence of more airborne grease than even the most advanced exhaust systems can dissipate. In the manager's office, pictures of a multi-branch Shack outing on a booze cruise covered a bulletin board. Meyer smiled and said, "That's what I want to see—people goofing around and having fun." As we exited, the staff waved, and Meyer told me, "This is management by walking around."

To make it to MoMA he opted against a cab—we'd Meyscrom through parking lots and breezeways, cheating the Manhattan grid.

Midblock in a hotel atrium, he stopped, shook his head, and said: "If you can get joy out of this, life isn't so bad."

At the Modern, Meyer pulled a silk tie out of his jacket pocket, knotted it on, and made for a grand cru Chablis tasting in the private dining room. He approached a young man in a thick-napped brown suit: Romain Collet, of the Jean Collet wine dynasty. Meyer introduced himself and began detailing, in French, the long relationship between his restaurants and the family's vineyard. Collet surprised me by *responding* in French.

Next, dining room visits: with a former neighbor from his home town, St. Louis; the chairman of the Sotheby's board (which Meyer had just joined); and a gray-blonde, very attractive businesswoman who, refusing the half hug Meyer offered while she was seated, exclaimed, "That's not enough; I need a full-body hug," stood up, and got it.

We took a cab to Twenty-sixth and Madison, Meyer on a call all the way downtown. Then he hopped out and skirted around the park, still talking into his phone while pointing out the first flowers of spring (yellow), crossed the avenue, and stepped through the revolving doors of Eleven Madison Park. We walked to the back of the restaurant, passed through an upstairs kitchen where penny-size petit fours were being arranged, then into a room where a group of Tammanyesque men, the Country Club Chefs of Connecticut, had just pushed back their chairs. One stood and introduced Meyer: "He's a man with a lot of ambition."

Meyer delivered an effortless postprandial speech, insidery for the industry crowd, dropping the surprise that he was planning a Shake Shack for Connecticut. Huge applause.

After jaywalking across Twenty-third Street, dodging a clip-board-bearing solicitor—"Watch out for the shmegegge" (Yiddish for buffoon)—and making Union Square in six minutes, Meyer told me: "This is what I do. I couldn't sit in a chair in an office all day."

* * *

New York is a city of rooms. Most of them are tiny, dark, lonely, and the wrong temperature. A few—Central Park (no roof, but still a room), Grand Central Terminal—are better than any other city's, if impossible to reserve. Meyer makes rooms that are exquisite—overlooking, in the case of the Modern, work by the greatest sculptors of the twentieth century—and intimate. You feel at home. His goal, he told me, is for customers to make his restaurants their clubhouses.

Meyer's track record is near perfect: one closing (Tabla, a 283-seat Indian place that lasted for twelve years), twenty-five openings and counting. And for most of his career, he has expanded without repeating himself. He has created new restaurants as though they were each his first and only—the singularity of a place always as important as the food. His looseness and precision are qualities more reminiscent of an athlete or an artist. Whatever Meyerness he's engaged in—jaywalking, French speaking, grease inhaling—receives his complete attention. Anyone who's ever opened or wanted to open a restaurant wishes they were him.

Some of this is hereditary. Meyer's father, Morton, owned hotels in St. Louis and had a gift for hospitality. As Meyer told me, "My dad gave me the gene to enjoy cooking, and to enjoy consuming good food and wine."

After college, with his father's help, Meyer apprenticed in European kitchens. He worked as a successful salesman (of plastic shoplifting-prevention tags) in New York and saved up. He became an assistant manager at a Manhattan seafood restaurant, got to know chefs and critics and one of his future partners, and met the woman who would become his wife, Audrey Heffernan, an actress who was working as a waitress. In 1985, he withdrew his savings and opened Union Square Cafe. Anticipating that the *New York Times* was going to review the place, he came down with Bell's palsy. The left half of his face was paralyzed, and the left half of his tongue lost its sense of taste. Symptoms abated after two weeks. The review was a rave. And Union Square Cafe went on to critical and popular acclaim. The natural next step was to try to repeat his success at another restaurant. But Meyer had seen his father overextend and fail. Morton Meyer was in the travel-tour business before jumping into more hotels—in Rome and Milan—and spending much of his life on an airplane. Unable to balance ambition and finances, the elder Meyer went bankrupt at forty-two, destroyed his marriage, went bankrupt again, and died at fifty-nine, when Danny was thirty-two. Meyer told me his father's notions of hospitality were always "right on the money," but his weakness was "business disciplines" and "team building."

The son has managed every aspect of his career to avoid repeating the mistakes of the father. It would be nine years before his second restaurant, Gramercy Tavern, opened. Other restaurants followed, approximately one every four years, each requiring vast investments of time to meet his standards. It has taken Meyer twenty-six years to go from the owner-manager of a single place to CEO of a company—Union Square Hospitality Group—that employs 2,200 people and oversees the operations of all his restaurants. His mother calls the company "his business family." Its core is a tight-knit group of five general partners whom Meyer has known for an aggregate of 102 years. One afternoon I sat down with all but one of them in the private dining room at three-star Gramercy Tavern. They had gathered to sample the (pastry-centric) menu for Untitled. Everyone dug in hard while, due to a gluten allergy, I watched. Pressed for details on this allergy, I explained that I got a rash. Then a particularly well-baked plate of biscuits hit the table. Meyer grabbed one, took a bite, gave an "Mmm!" and shoved the rest in my mouth, saying, "You gotta *live a little*! Little rash, c'mon—*I'll* scratch it for you!"

This struck me as a Morton Meyer sort of moment. As Danny put it, "He loved to entertain others, but more so loved to consume." And provoke.

Meyer and his partners oversee three places that are in the Zagat Guide's Top 5 (Gramercy Tavern, Eleven Madison Park, Union Square Cafe), plus the Modern, Maialino, Blue Smoke (BBQ), the two cafés at the Museum of Modern Art, the newly opened restaurant at the Whitney, a jazz club, a handful of seasonal stands including one at Citi Field, and a catering and events company. Meyer is on the board of Open Table, the internet restaurant-reservations service that not only allows him to materialize midlunch for a full-body hug but also tracks the eating habits of his 3,500 or so fine-dining customers each day. (Shake Shack feeds more than twelve thousand daily.) This has all taken decades. And Meyer might have remained an incrementalist were it not for Shake Shack, which began as a hot-dog cart that he told the staff of Eleven Madison to set up in its namesake park in 2001. The cart was such a sensation that he expanded the menu to include burgers and milkshakes and opened the current four-hundred-square-foot shack in 2004. Eleven Madison owned Shake Shack from 2004 to 2009, when it became its own company—but the mobbed burger stand provided the capital required to hire the Swiss chef Daniel Humm away from a restaurant in San Francisco, reduce the seats in Eleven Madison's dining room, double the staff, and establish a venue so elevated in its pursuits that it's less a restaurant than a graduate program in taste. Four stars from the *Times* ultimately followed.

Shake Shack began spreading throughout Manhattan in 2008, along the Eastern Seaboard in 2010 and 2011 (Miami and Washington), and now overseas, with branches newly opened in Dubai and Kuwait City. The total number of Shake Shacks now stands at thirteen—in three years, Meyer has doubled his restaurant holdings.

In *Setting the Table*, his memoir-cum-manifesto on hospitality, published just after Shake Shack opened, Meyer describes his mood upon opening restaurant number two, Gramercy Tavern: "I had the sense of being close to a dangerous outcome. Was I now treading down the same path my father had taken—expansion to bankruptcy?"

These fears have been definitively put to rest. Meyer has embraced what he described to me as "the profitability edge" of Shake Shack—an edge that is sharpened by volume and expansion, in marked contrast to the world of white tablecloths. According to the National Restaurant Association, profit margins in "full service" restaurants, with an average check of twenty-five dollars or more per person, range from -2 percent to 6.8 percent, with a median of 1.8 percent. That means that Meyer, having perfected fine dining, may only just be beating thirty-year Treasurys. Shake Shack changes that, with margins in its category, "limited service," as high as 13 percent. Of course, odds are that Meyer is dramatically beating all these markers. He would not tell me. But for the first time in his career, Meyer finds it impossible to visit all his restaurants in a single day. Ubiquity and hands-on attention—essential to his success—are incompatible with expansion.

Union Square Hospitality Group has begun to produce some Shake Shack ingredients in a Louisiana factory (instead of in an auxiliary kitchen at Eleven Madison Park). In the walk-in fridge of one branch, I handled a gigantic plastic pillow of cheese sauce: designed to travel. A day earlier, I wondered about a sticker on a bag Meyer was carrying: MSY, the New Orleans airport code. I imagined him flying in, sniffing the cheese vat, recalibrating machinery. It was a reassuring vision. But I had to wonder if the man—without being present to indulge customers, tweak recipes, and notice every broken chair—can perpetuate the dining experience that is expected of him. Later I walked past Union Square Cafe and saw that it had been given a Health Department grade of "B," indicating fourteen to twenty-seven sanitary violation points. How could Union Square Cafe and his other restaurants preserve their essence without constant infusions of Meyerness?

I met my friend Charles Bock, who grew up in the back of a pawnshop in Las Vegas, for lunch at Eleven Madison Park. I tried to get a noon reservation but they said it was impossible. So we ate at the bar (though the dining room was empty). Charles had never eaten in such a formal setting. He wore his only suit jacket. His wife, Diana, diagnosed with leukemia a few months before, was receiving her second bone-marrow transplant. He'd been living in a hospital for weeks.

Now he looked around, ill at ease, and said, "There's an indulgence to it."

A lobster-and-crab pasta arrived. He took a bite, another bite, and his face changed. He declared, "I could make an argument that this pasta and crab is art. Because it's pretty good." Pause. "Insanely good." Pause. "This is literally the best pasta I've ever eaten in my life." Pause. "I cannot think of anything I've had that I've enjoyed as much as when I have a good bite of the pasta and crab together. I really can't. I wish Diana was here eating this with us."

We looked at the dining room—deco moldings, thirty-five-foot ceilings, tree-filled windows, ubiquitous sunlight. (Eleven Madison Park is arguably the most beautiful restaurant in New York City. In fact, shortly after writing that sentence I read a review in the *Wall Street Journal* that opened with this line: "Eleven Madison Park is perhaps most [*sic*] beautiful restaurant in New York.") Charles went on, "It creates its own vacuum. That's part of the beauty of it." Meyer made a similar observation when he told me that "hours evaporated" in the restaurant. Three tables in the dining room were now occupied. We agreed that our fellow diners looked like people who were rarely distracted by anything but their own desires. (Empathy, for example.)

Refinement is a form of corruption. Sharpening of the palate may well correspond to deadening of deeper feelings. Human organs of sense and experience, cut free from anything but their own pleasure, catered to so scrupulously—how can it end in anything other than a spoiled, infantilized, ever-more-demanding state?

Charles asked, "But why doesn't that SOB—why aren't there more Shake Shacks at Shea Stadium? Why do I have to stand in line for an hour and a half to get a burger."

Me, mouth full: "I mmgree."

"Wouldn't it be better if you could get those burgers at a couple different places in the stadium instead of missing three innings of your game?"

"Have you indeed missed three innings of your game for one of those burgers?"

"You're goddamn right I have."

We each took bites of pasta, paused, and together said, "Beautiful."

"New York is becoming something else, and this is part of it," he said.

Was that so bad? It was clear that we were thoroughly insulated from all the dangers and discomforts for which New York had once been infamous.

"Yeah," I said, "nothing bad's gonna happen here. I'm not afraid for my life."

He replied, "Just my soul."

I looked out at the diners in the still-empty dining room, plutocrats, I supposed, perhaps leading lives that guaranteed they would go to hell, but renting a piece of heaven. The evaporation of time provided by the restaurant called to mind the afterlife. Maybe "eternal life" doesn't mean time goes on forever, but time no longer exists. Somehow that seems easier to grasp. We ate some more. Bock said, "I hate scenesters. I hate professionally cool people. I just recoil from them. And then, the flip, is that you move to New York to have conversations like the one we're having right now."

Vigorous nodding from me. I hated New York when I first got here. But I had moved here in search of success, sex, and conversation. And where would these things take place? In a room.

Charles: "I wanted my life not to be holed up in a room writing— which is really what it is most of the time. But what I really wished it would have been is those three in the mornings in a booth with a bunch of people that I really liked talking about whatever and being *engaged* and some beautiful woman across the room that you thought you might have something with—that's all I really wanted from my life.

The waiter came and asked, "Would you like to see the desserts?" We said we would.

Charles was on a roll: "New York's thing is that it's everything. It is money, it is power, it is fashion, and it is glamour. That was one of the things abut the eighties that people loved and that I remember being fascinated by was those *Spy* magazine or *Interview* magazine photos where you had these businessmen at Limelight next to freaks, like complete, utter *freaks*... the worlds connect and overlap and combine. It's not *just* like 'LA is entertainment.' It's *everything*, the writer, the intelligencia... the academic people, the financial people, the fashion people, the food people, where are you going to, where else, I mean after you've lived here where are you going to go?"

Nobody beyond professionally cool people can tell you who actually owned the Limelight or Max's Kansas City or CBGB's. Everyone knows Danny Meyer.

The waiter returned. Charles, completely at ease, having left his whole life outside this room, speaking in a casual and contented voice I'd never before heard him use, inquired, "What would our fine guide for the afternoon suggest?"

"The coconut meringue is quite nice… tropical fruits with a little coconut meringue, it's refreshing."

After a taste Charles said, "Oh my God!" Then he remembered that he was missing a doctor's appointment and had to run out of the restaurant.

I stayed behind for the rest of the afternoon. The tables we'd been told were unavailable never filled up.

The next day, in Miami, Meyer participated in a mass grill-off called Burger Bash. Shake Shack, past winner of the event's People's Choice award, was a returning champion. Meyer opened a Miami Shack in 2010, and he wanted to use this trip to scout for a second location— with a management group in place, he needed to give it more to do. He told me that if I was interested in Shake Shack I should come along.

As I waited to board Delta flight 2579 to Miami Anthony Bourdain and his wife, Ottavia, breezed past. In my boarding group a very tan woman with hair the color of canned pineapple shouted, "I *need* a *boat dress*! I should have bought that *gold dress*! It would look so good on me in the wind."

I slid into row eleven and the boat dresser glided past. She wore skintight pants and a tiny, doll-size tank top that revealed over a foot of bare, tan, flat belly and ribs. I pictured her in a strong wind. Then another woman asked: "Is that Danny?" I looked up and spotted Meyer's close-cut hair, a row behind the Bourdains.

Our flight was equipped with in-flight internet, and, after takeoff, we were invited to buy some time on the web. Ottavia Bourdain posted on Twitter:

"Danny Meyer on my flight. Trying to contain my enthusiasm."
Two of her followers replied:
"Squeal like a teenager! Haa haa"
"You might sit next to him! I am verklempt."

In Miami, Meyer was waiting at the end of the jetway. We shook
hands. His handshake was better than I remembered—possessed,
it seemed to me, of a slightly addictive quality. I wanted the shake
again immediately after it had ended. He ran through the schedule
and warned me, disarmingly, "You're about to see so much bullshit.
So much reverence for nonsense."

With that, we headed for the beach. Chefs towered above the city
on a highwayside billboard. There for the weekend were Bobby Flay,
Rachael Ray, Emeril Lagasse, Martha Stewart, Giada De Laurentiis—
the gods and demigods of an industry that generates an estimated
$1.7 trillion.

The cab pulled up in front of the W, Meyer's hotel, and we agreed
to meet in half an hour. Unfortunately, only Meyer was staying there.
My hotel, the Days Inn, was next door. I walked across the shared
parking lot, and, as I drew closer, realized something was wrong.
Plastic banners saying "The Seagull" were draped over the still-
visible Days Inn sign. An announcement in movable type beneath
the banners read NEW BED S.

The place had no record of my reservation, but after some
discussion I was given a room with pry marks around the door from
past attempts at forced entry. There was orange mold in the dark
carpeting. I thought twice about declining the offer of a safe for an
extra two dollars.

Surveying all this, I got a call from Meyer: "Can you meet down-
stairs, now? I couldn't check in."

In the elevator was a seedy stoner girl in cutoffs, a bare-chested weightlifter, and a security guard in a uniform three sizes too big. Outside Meyer shook my hand—*Ah!*—and I said, "My hotel is like a hotel in a pacified Beirut, filled with frat boys."

He froze. "I can see it, that *blue* carpeting, and the thin bar of Camay soap."

But the W was equally antithetical to Meyer's idea of hospitality: "You know what the guy behind the desk told me when I asked for an estimate of when my room might be ready? 'We're not allowed to do that, sir.'

"I said, 'I'm not going to hold you to it. I'd just like an estimate because I want to use my time effectively.'

"'But what if I don't hit it? I just can't do that, sir.'"

He threw up his hands. We stepped onto the sand. Under a huge oceanside tent, American celebrity chefery was prepping to sear hecatombs of flesh. Shake Shack would produce a few thousand burgers and chorizo cheese fries. As we dodged front-end loaders and harried interns, Meyer took a call and said, "I'm walking the grounds of Burger Bash the way they take a racehorse to the paddock before the race."

Shake Shack competes with "better burger" chains—Five Guys, In-N-Out, etc. But the scale and execution are different. Those chains have hundreds of locations and exponential expansion plans. In-N-Out operates two meat-processing plants. And they have no aspirations beyond growth and consistency. With Shake Shack, as Meyer told me, the vast majority of management "began their careers with us in our fine-dining restaurants," which gives them a vested interest in creating an atmosphere. And the meat comes from Pat LaFrieda, a third-generation butcher popular with chefs for his willingness to do the onerous paperwork required to supply meat from outside the corporate slaughterhouse system. For Shake Shack

SEAN WILSEY

La Freida produces a blend of sirloin, chuck, and brisket designed by Richard Coraine, former general manager of Wolfgang Puck's Postrio in San Francisco, and now one of Meyer's general partners in Union Square Hospitality. As Meyer put it: "There are a zillion variables to a hamburger. What part of the animal went into it. What coarseness. What temperature." Coraine told me he spent months "tasting and modifying the blend to hit the right chord." He unpacked the details like this: "You can also factor a few other elements… the amount of butter brushed on the bun before griddling it (there is fat in butter, so the brisket was taken down a level) the composition and amount of 'Shack Sauce' (flavor in there as well) and the type and 'slice width' of the American cheese. This may sound a bit neurotic and finicky but it was the way I did it." He once said that he "approached it like a winemaker, like I'm making a Bordeaux blend… The through line is cabernet sauvignon, and that's the sirloin. It's a big flavor, it gives it a structure and it defines the taste. Next is chuck. It's like malbec: It's bold, but it's one-dimensional. It gives body and weight, but it doesn't have a lot of nuances. Brisket is like cabernet franc. By itself it's not going to make a great hamburger, or a great wine, but it gives a beautiful, round flavor. You add twenty-five or thirty percent brisket to soften it, and make it delicious."

The critic Oliver Strand told me—hyperbole be damned—that the meat was "every bit as excellent as what you'll find in Peter Luger's or Keens's." The top NYC steak houses. Beyond the exalted flesh, the Shake Shack aesthetic is unintimidatingly midcentury, the marketing is pointed (if you want cucumber, tomato, and relish on your hot dog, the kitchen will "drag it through the garden"), and each branch supports a local charity.

At the Shake Shack booth I was introduced to another one of Meyer's partners, David Swinghamer, a straw-haired Wisconsinite

264

so tall he stooped. Swinghamer fed me a Shack burger: cooked through, barely a suggestion of pink at the center, as they are in every Shack. Then I sneaked off to Umami Burger, a five-unit Southern California chain planning to open soon in Miami. The competition. Umami's meat was capped with a mushroom, but it was raw on the inside. I got a sample for Meyer. He and Swinghamer devoured it, communally—ripping it apart with their hands.

Meyer, mouth full, declared, "It's not cooked, but the beef is mighty good."

Swinghamer: "I like the shiitake."

Me: "Maybe I should tell them the meat's not cooked."

Meyer, solemnly: "Napoleon said, 'Part of brilliance is winning and part is leaving your opponent alone when he's losing.'" (From blogger Ethan Shapiro's account of the event: "[M]any of the burgers were very rare or barely cooked at all… [T]hree of the six of us got sick last night. I'm wondering how many others had similar stomach problems and if someone needs to look into this for next year. Regardless, this burger fan had a blast!")

This was the VIP part of Burger Bash. And the VIPs were numerous. While thousands of non-VIPs strained against crowd-control barriers, dressed up and held back. The scene called to mind a refugee camp combined with a prom. Homer's *Iliad*, too—the Greek army's always setting fire to thousands of pounds of beef in the sand before Troy.

I stood behind the Shack's counter listening as a young woman in a gray canvas dress confided to Meyer, "I was a vegetarian till October. But Bobby"—Flay, for whom she did PR—"cooked for the staff one day." She opened her mouth wide in amazement: "*Burgers* are *good!*"

Meyer: "*Yeah!*"

Anthony Bourdain strode past and waved. Swinghamer said, "Rachael Ray is about to stop by—it's heating up!"

With that eight men with shaved heads, wearing nothing but black—shoes, pants, jackets, shirts, ties—descended upon us. One of them took me by the shoulders and danced me back, ten feet from the counter.

I said, "I'm a friend of Danny."

He replied, "Fine, but you gotta keep your distance."

"Who are you guys?" I asked.

"Who are *you*?"

"The *New York Times*."

"Hmm."

"*You?*"

"Rachael Ray's Security Detail."

It was obvious which one held more sway.

I watched an exchange of inaudible pleasantries. When Ray left Swinghamer said, "Those guys are completely serious. I couldn't break through."

And then the walls fell. People streamed in. I saw Ray's Myrmidons form a phalanx as she retreated.

Meyer sighed and said, as much to himself as to me, "Twenty-five years in the fine-dining business and it's all coming down to cheeseburgers."

The Bash was on. I got a beer as skinny women in sandals, short shorts, flowing dresses, a pregnant woman in a shift and a gold Rolex knockoff, men in muscle shirts, skintight polo shirts, designer eyewear, linen jackets, formed a line for what it all came down to. The ravenous and scantily clad surged around me. I wrote in my notebook, "Grease laden air... Tray after tray of fake breasts." Meyer stood on the Shack battlements smiling and serving chorizo cheese fries. A young woman in a trilby sidled up close to him and said, breathily, "My husband gave me a twenty-five-dollar Shake Shack gift certificate for Christmas." Explosions of flash bulbs. Every tenth person wanted a photo with him. I had never seen so many people with their mouths full of meat.

A Frenchman jostled through the crowd to say, "Hi Dannì. You look great."

Meyer said, "Laurent. You left Chicago. You got your Michelin stars and…" He pantomimed a wave. "You look great, too."

"Yeah, I *do*! I'm well rested!"

Meyer handed him a burger. The Frenchman devoured it and was off. I asked, "Who was that?"

"Laurent Gras. Incredible chef. Three Michelin stars."

The band got louder. A video projection of a fiery grill, a pair of back-to-back Bs endlessly licked by electric flames, flickered like hell behind the stage. A man hollered at Meyer, "I e-mailed you! We met a couple years ago!" Then he was swallowed up by the crowd.

An attractive blonde woman leaned flirtatiously across the counter to tell Meyer she was also from St. Louis. This earned a fist bump and the proffering of custard.

But—"My ass says no, Danny!"—she demurred.

"Tonight's gonna be a good night!" said the band.

Meyer served, shook, occasionally Purelled his hands. Rachael Ray took the stage to commend the South Beach Wine and Food Festival for how it had managed to "bring out all that talent and put it between a bun."

I took a walk.

"Tiffany crystal Heinz ketchup bottle!" someone shouted.

A heavily made-up woman with those ubiquitous meaty teeth wondered aloud, "Does that guy have a TV show?"

There was an end-times vibe. *The end times, they could be good times*, I thought.

The wind was coming up. Boat-dress weather? Party balloons blew past a dirty-dancing woman in her sixties. Masaharu Morimoto (TV star) was slapping sunny-side-up egg after sunny-side-up egg on top of his burgers—indefatigably. His sternness seemed to be only augmented by his ceaseless smiling. Michael Symon (ibid.)—bald, with a soul patch—layered salami on top of beef while a man on his line hypnotically stroked the back of a woman's miniskirt. Palm trees thrashed. Bobby Flay stood in a cloud of smoke surrounded by girls in GET CRUNCHIFIED tees, all screaming to INXS's "What You Need," while fans' flash bulbs lit up billowing explosions from the grill. I got a burger and walked it back to Shake Shack.

Meyer grabbed Swinghamer, and we all withdrew to a stainless prep table.

Regarding the offering, Meyer said, "This is Bobby Flay."

A dissection ensued. He removed the top bun. Something white jiggled to the bass line.

"Is that an egg?" Swinghamer asked.

"Goat cheese," Meyer said.

He broke it up and began to eat.

"It's good," he conceded.

Then, with a vulnerable gleam in his eye, Meyer asked, "How long is their line compared to ours?"

At the end of the night, Meyer left the tent and sat down, wearily, on the boardwalk. In a few minutes we were expected at a pulled-pork dinner.

He asked, "How many animals had to die for this event, and what kind of lives did they lead?"

We thought on that.

"There were some slimy people there," he said. "Just picking at me. Pick, pick, pick!... 'I e-mailed you.' What kind of greeting is that?" He continued: "I can't believe how many people tried to get me to sign a lease in Las Vegas. We're the only ones who haven't gone into Vegas yet."

Most of these people want to re-create one of Meyer's marquee restaurants in a casino. Meyer provided three highly credible reasons why this won't happen:

1) "I... cannot imagine spending my life in an airplane for the purpose of visiting a fine-dining restaurant... Saw my dad try that... and saw a very unhappy family outcome."

2) The impossibility of bonding with customers in a city "built upon so much transiency."

3) Chemical sensitivity: "I actually have a bad reaction to... the synthetic deodorizers they pump through to eliminate smoke. Really, those smells almost sicken me."

But he'll leave the door open for Shake Shack: "We never know who's eating there day-to-day anyway... There's no reservation sheet to scour; no dining room to host." As he told *Business Insider*: "Think about a business where each one does not have a chef, or a pastry chef, or a dining-room manager, or a maître d', or a florist, or a linen company, and you start to notice that a lot of the cost structure that goes into a fine-dining restaurant is missing... From a cost-structure standpoint, it's a good way to go."

Now he pulled out his BlackBerry and showed me a goat's head he'd been served a few nights before. It stared at us from the screen. "I couldn't eat the eyeball," he admitted.

A voice boomed, "You look like a couple of bums! *Sitting down*?!"

Swinghamer. The least-tan man in Miami. He sat down and looked at the glowing goat's head. In his Wisconsin accent he told us, "I ate goat-eyeball tacos in Santa Barbara."

I began to laugh till tears ran down my face. Everyone's guard dropped.

Danny sighed. "I need a martini."

Swinghamer began speaking in soothing tones: "We can do that. Let's go into my hotel. The Shore Club. Right here."

The Shore Club is wider than most of the other old South Beach hotels, with a vast expanse of chaise-dotted garden. We walked in along the pool. Two young women in shimmery dresses, reclining on a barge of pillows, watched us. One's lips matched the other's dress—red and more red. The red-lipped one smiled at us. Meyer said what I was thinking: "Sirens."

A garden bar appeared among the trees. A young woman with a waterfall of blonde hair alighted on an ottoman.

Meyer said, "There's a Breck ad over there."

We all ordered martinis. A relaxed Midwestern vibe took hold. Sips all around.

"This is nice." Meyer looked around. "This is like a park… Let's not go to this pig-pick thing. It'll just be more picking. Pick, pick. Let's sit down somewhere."

I told Meyer about my lunch at Eleven Madison and asked him why we weren't given a table when there were so many unclaimed.

He said, "I don't know."

Swinghamer suggested we join the general manager of the Miami Shake Shack for drinks at a "Japanese gastropub" he'd discovered.

On the way out Meyer was intercepted by a young female fan. He shook her hand, talked politely, and gave her a second handshake to indicate he had to get going. She happily walked off, and I thought to myself, *Genius, the shake-off.*

Over nigori sake—"Not for your everyday *shmegegge*."—scallops escargot-style, bi bim bap, Danny asked his GM, "What was tonight, six in sales?"

"Nine, almost nine."

A $9,000 dinner rush. Everyone drank to that.

The next morning, on the way down to breakfast, the Seagull's elevator stopped at a low floor and a middle-aged Latina woman tumbled in. She smelled overpoweringly of beer.

I smiled and said, "*Cerveza*."

She replied, "*¡Hehheheheheh!*"

Meyer and Swinghamer were out front. Meyer said, "I want to go in and smell your hotel." He bounded across the street and inside, then came back wearing an expression of horror and delight.

"That bad bacon smell! The really thin, cheap stuff! Reminds me of my seventh-grade trip to DC!"

We drove to Shake Shack, which is in a Herzog and de Meuron-designed building, just off a pedestrian mall (Meyer sniffed and said, sadly, "It smells different before it opens"), then on to south Miami to scout for a new location. As we crossed Biscayne Bay, Meyer admired the palm-covered islands, with their 1920s architecture. But as the traffic got thicker and the buildings blander, he said: "This strip is so antiseptic. Needs to be cool. " Then, "This whole area just gets me nervous."

Of the thirteen Shake Shacks, a majority are in parks or areas with lots of pedestrian traffic. Such locations create a boutique quality Meyer calls "Shackness."

Credit here goes to Swinghamer, who Meyer told me has a "sixth sense" for real estate. "The ideal doesn't just come up for rent," Swinghamer said. "You need to have inside knowledge. People on the ground."

A few weeks later Meyer and I would find ourselves discussing another island, Mill Rock, in the East River, off Ninety-sixth Street.

It was abandoned, and I asked if it could become a restaurant. By way of an answer he forwarded me this e-mail exchange with Adrian Benepe, Commissioner of the New York City Parks Department.

> Adrian,
> What do you know about Mill Rock Island? Notice in the website blurb that it served in the 1800's as a waterway restaurant for passing boats. Imagine it tomorrow as a self-sustaining, hydro-powered garden, restaurant, and symbol of the best of NYC—served by a little boat launch off Manhattan or LIC. Just saying.........
> Danny

Two hours and two minutes later came this reply:

> Danny:
> Interesting idea, but there are impediments. The island is difficult to get to and overrun with rats. It is in the middle of the treacherous Hell Gate...where tides and currents turn the area into a 24-hour blender for small craft. Even powerful tugs have problems navigating that stretch. I would imagine the cost of building a restaurant there and getting regular deliveries might present difficulties. That said, if you think there might be interest, we could issue an RFP [Request For Proposals—the first legal step in developing city property]. We do, however, have many other locations that would be easier to create a waterfront restaurant or café, or perhaps even a great, Cape-Cod-style clam shack...
> Best wishes,
> Adrian

Now, in Miami, as we drove, Swinghamer told me, "We have inside information about the place we're going." He added, "It's not on the market yet, so nobody else really knows about it."

Meyer asked, "It's still occupied?"

"Yes."

Passing beneath a festival billboard (Rachael Ray, Bobby Flay, and Giada De Laurentiis), Meyer looked up and said: "The *shmegegges* are following us."

Then down the coast, alongside the commuter rail line, boxed in by strip malls. As we passed a corner Chipotle, Swinghamer said, "Reliable sources say they do $2.7 million there." Pause. "We do a lot more business than a typical Chipotle." He looked hard at the corner. "Gotta do a lot… and be in a place that expresses Shackness."

Meyer was only getting more nervous. Financial upsides aside, he seemed unable to tune out the surroundings. "It's a sea of dreck," he said, and began reading the names of businesses: "Puritan Cleaners. Hookah Lounge."

"Meyer Mortgage," I pointed out.

"Saw that—I'm looking for signs."

We arrived at the place they'd been tipped to: a barbecue joint with good parking, straddling the highway and a bland residential district, within walking distance of the University of Miami.

"Can this be a Shack?" Meyer asked.

Contemplative silence.

"I see something looking back real far to the iconic hamburger/hot-dog stands," Swinghamer said. "We'll put our modern twist to it."

"Modern retro," Meyer said.

They began refining a concept. Every Shake Shack is nominally tailored to its presumptive clientele: the TV room for kids and nannies on Manhattan's Upper West Side, communal seating for tourists in the theater district, site-specific "concretes" (frozen custards with various mix-ins), like the vanilla, fudge sauce, peanut, and shattered-sugar-cone "Nut-Thing but Amazin'" for Mets fans at Citi Field.

Here the clientele would be undergrads. "Should have a lot of TVs, and ultracool music so the students come over," Swinghamer said. "This is an alternative to going to a bar."

"You'd want some neon that said something about ice-cold beer," Meyer said.

"Yeah," Swinghamer said. "A touch of a roadhouse. That would work for college."

"I like the tree," said Meyer, indicating a banyan up against the building. We pulled alongside, and Swinghamer lowered the windows.

Meyer mused, "We could name a concrete after it."

For years the question of how to expand had been something Meyer struggled with. Then he met Susan Reilly Salgado, a doctoral candidate in business at New York University. She'd been eating at the bar at Union Square Cafe, getting to know the staff, listening to waiters say things like, "When I found this job, I felt like I'd come home." In 1998 she saw Meyer "working the room" on the opening night at Tabla, introduced herself, and said she wanted to do her dissertation on his restaurants. He agreed, provided she work as a hostess for six months.

Five years later she informed Meyer that his company was too dependent on him. "There's no system for opening restaurants without you," she said, "and the more you open, the more diluted your impact becomes." Salgado proposed forming a curriculum "to make explicit everything that Danny... intuitively knew." Practically speaking, this would allow for succession (part of avoiding his father's mistakes is ensuring the business can continue without him) and, in the shorter term, for the company to open new restaurants not just in Miami but anywhere in the world.

Meyer has often been approached with the idea of franchising Shake Shack in the United States, which he has never wanted to do—"How can you franchise hospitality?" But in 2008, after Shake Shack opened its second branch, an international franchiser, Alshaya, approached him. They operated Starbucks, Estée Lauder, Dean & DeLuca, Pinkberry, and H&M outlets in the Middle East. Meyer, flattered by the interest, went to Dubai and noted that Alshaya's Starbucks were "as well run if not better than the ones on Union Square." He told *Business Insider* he decided to "get a master's degree in replication... but so far away that our audience wouldn't watch us doing it, and at the same time give us a chance to grow." Shake Shacks in Dubai and Kuwait would be the first phase.

Salgado now leads a new company, incorporated under the name Hospitality Quotient (HQ), that franchises not food but Meyer's style—that franchises, in effect, his eye contact, handshaking, infectious capacity for pleasure. As Meyer put it, hospitality is "the degree to which it makes you feel good to make other people feel good."

Salgado told me of Meyer's cloneability: "We decided the model was sustainable, the concepts transferable." And many were the companies that could benefit.

The acronym comes from Meyer. As he put it, an IQ is native and can't be taught; so, too, is an HQ. "But it can be identified.... Someone with a high HQ is at their best when providing happiness to someone else." And with HQ, "we're working with companies that... want to be the best in the world at how people feel." To this end they've trained staff at Beth Israel ("A hospital should be hospitable," the head of orthopedics told Meyer), a Broadway theater company, and a supermarket chain.

Alshaya's management teams for Dubai and Kuwait came to New York for a sort of kindness boot camp, months before opening. Then

Meyer sent a group of his high-HQ staff members to Dubai and Kuwait for on-site training.

And the businesses that Alshaya franchises are the exact sorts HQ hopes to work with. Should all proceed as planned, the profitability edge will be unbluntable.

Can kindness be corporatized? Is kindness still kindness after it's sold at a profit? Isn't the very essence of kindness purity of origin? The way it wells up unbidden? Selflessness? Spontaneity. It's the surprise of the way people make you feel in a Meyer restaurant that makes the experience of eating there so addictive.

I don't know if such things can be propagated. But Miami's W Hotel and erstwhile Days Inn could only be improved by the attempt. As Charles Bock put it during our lunch at Eleven Madison Park, "Who doesn't want to feel taken care of?"

Floyd Cardoz, the chef of Tabla, which closed last year, was waiting in Meyer's office on a clear March afternoon. The decision to shutter Tabla was, Meyer told me, "excruciatingly hard." He resisted for years, losing money, laying people off for the first time in his career.

"I always genuinely believed we could turn Tabla's fortunes around," he told me in an e-mail. "I was hanging on to the false pride of being able to say we had never closed a restaurant in our first quarter-century of doing business." He continued, "But I was ultimately convinced by my partners that—counterintuitively—the cruelest thing we could do for people's careers was to keep it going."

Now Meyer and Cardoz embraced. A new tenant had just taken over the Tabla lease, and the chef said, slowly, "I have a lump in my throat... I handed my keys over today." Tears were in his eyes. Meyer's too. "It was a very good twelve years," Cardoz said. "I learned a lot about myself. I don't know what the outcome was."

"It was good, Floyd," Meyer said. "You'd like to think that a restaurant will go on forever, like you think your life will go on forever."

Soon they began to leaf through a stack of menus from the '20s and '30s (Meyer has a collection), looking for ideas for a new Battery Park City restaurant that USHG had just announced. It would serve seafood and grow its own vegetables. Cardoz would be in the kitchen.

Meyer mentioned that the shrimp at Blue Hill, where he bit his tongue on his birthday the night before, were cooked on hibachis, with charcoal made from the bones of animals raised on an upstate farm affiliated with the restaurant.

"That's a gimmick kind of thing—it's not going to flavor the food," Cardoz said.

Meyer countered that it was smart recycling and good marketing.

Cardoz: "Lot of carbon emissions making charcoal. Not that green."

Meyer ended the argument by pointing out that the farm used the emissions to heat its greenhouse. (Though he turned out to be wrong; the farm used the heat generated by composting.)

They started debating what they'd serve at the new place. Cardoz had been to the Oyster Bar at Grand Central: "Bad food for high prices, paper cups for sauce and full of people."

Meyer leafed through his menus.

Cardoz: "A whole section on eggs."

Meyer: "Anchovies on toast. How long ago was this? Broiled lobster, $2.50." He pointed—1939.

"Vegetables are an important part of this restaurant," Meyer continued. "What if vegetables were the main course? Not just to keep vegetarians happy, but to make the restaurant a destination."

Cardoz was jotting down menu categories. "Lose 'sides' and call it 'vegetables,'" he said.

They moved on to seafood.

Meyer said: "It's become totally cliché to have a big platter of raw stuff... At the Oyster Bar, how many oysters were there, twenty?"

"And the waiter didn't even know what they were," Cardoz said.

"I want to have the best oyster you can have in New York today, opened perfectly."

Half an hour later Cardoz got up to go.

Meyer said, "Peace be with you, baby." It was time for dinner.

THE OBJECTS OF MY OBSESSION

2013

The film *Six Degrees of Separation* ends in a conversation between a matronly uptown art dealer (Stockard Channing) and a street-kid grifter (Will Smith). He's robbed, conned, and tricked her. She vows to give him a job—under the condition that he turn himself in to the police and serve a few months in jail. She'll find him an apartment, and persuade her husband to lend a hand, too.

"I have no furniture."

"We'll help you out."

"I made a list of things I liked at the museum. Philadelphia Chippendale."

"Believe it or not, we have two Philadelphia Chippendale chairs."

"I'd rather have one nice piece than a room full of junk. Quality always."

"You'll have all that."

"Philadelphia Chippendale! And all I have to do is go to the police."

* * *

I have a quasi-erotic attraction to well-built and beautiful objects. Furniture, fixtures, appliances—it is an across-the-board phenomenon, with unpredictable, contradictory-seeming implications. I'm smitten by everything from fabric patterns to the pennant-shaped washers beneath the chromed lug nuts of one in every ten thousand eighteen-wheelers. My head turns, my attention is captured, I am almost wounded (definitely smitten in the beaten-or-struck sense of the word), when the right object hits my eye in the right way. As a friend once put it: "I have a terrible defect. I like to see beauty."

Recently I have aggressively indulged this weakness in the realm of high-end domestic appurtenances—namely appliances and fixtures. Such items are overwhelmingly engineered by Germans (Bosch, Duravit, Dornbracht, Miele, which sounds Italian but 100 percent isn't), often by bona fide Italians (Alessi, XO, and Bertazzoni, which was originally La Germania, natch), occasionally by Americans (Viking, Sub-Zero), and in one case by New Zealanders (Fisher & Paykel). But to the same degree that I lust after what's produced under these brand names—with exceptions: Viking fridges are junk—I am offended by how much they cost, and how divorced from manufacturing reality, let alone ethics, the pricing seems to be.

Why am I thinking about all of this? I bought a three-story, wood-frame, two-family dwelling in the Bedford-Stuyvesant section of Brooklyn, and am preparing it for tenants. Bedford-Stuyvesant, until recently, was, in the words of one of my neighbors, "the ghetto of America" (slogan "Bed-Stuy, do or die"), but is now branded as Clinton Hill, which is branded as Fort Greene, which is branded as "Brownstone Brooklyn." On two-block Claver Place the smell of ganja wafts most evenings. To the frustration of recent gentrifiers a Guyanese reggae club (Slogan: "Jah is living") had been operating illegally, packing eight hundred people at twenty dollars a head into a backyard, with a cut, according to another neighbor, going to blind-eye-turning cops. It was here that I found my house and its large detached garage, on a 25-foot-by-127.5-foot lot. As the owner of a pickup truck and a small motorcycle I've always lusted after a garage in New York.

I bought the parcel for $710,000 with the help of a 2.25 percent line of credit with Wells Fargo, and began renovations with the intention of cash-out refinancing in six months, after upgrading the interiors and facade. The mortgage and rental numbers suggested I could have my garage for free. I would need to do some serious upgrading to make this happen. The initial appraiser's report described a bathroom vanity "at the end of its economic life" and was kind in calling the kitchens' appointments "economy grade." I visited an appliance store a friend described as having "great prices" but left feeling lied to and gouged. Still, I needed to do something. I wanted the post-renovation apartments to be low maintenance, high quality, and beautiful, because, Jah knows, when things are beautiful they are loved and taken care of. But the more I shopped for the beautiful the more outraged I became.

On the web I began searching for the best fixture producer I had ever heard of, Dornbracht, which claims to make "100% of its products in Germany," with "the highest quality of manufacturing." Its website, no doubt 100 percent translated from the German (adding to the appeal), contained the sort of bold assertions that deeply reassure the maintenance-concerned landlord/aesthetician:

> Although Dornbracht fittings… have been copied many times, nothing has ever achieved such creative and functional durability. The products, fittings, accessories, and systems… are unique and irreplaceable… As Matthias Dornbracht, the Managing Director responsible for Production, Logistics and Purchasing puts it, "Not a single millimeter, not a single radius is changed for the sake of

increasing the number of items manufactured per unit of time."
Production takes second place to design.

I soon found their single-lever lavatory mixer for sale on
homeperfect.com, the original price struck through—"~~Was $1,283.00~~"—
and replaced in red, bold, with a new one: "$898.10." On the same
site a twenty-four-inch towel bar in polished nickel that originally
had cost $587.00 was now a mere $257.94.

This was a galvanizing experience. I am often reminded of my
own ignorance, but I do know that the moment one decides that
it might be OK to spend $257.94 on a towel bar is the moment
that one becomes party to, at the very least, corruption, and quite
possibly some deeper cultural wrong. And all the high-end stuff on
AJMadison.com (the go-to, volume seller of new, warrantied appliances) to which I was drawn was priced this way: Viking thirty-inch
range: $4,979. Bosch Axxis condensation dryer: $1,074.60. Bosch
Axxis front-loading washer: $1,254.60. Bertazzoni thirty-six-inch
copper element/sealed-burner range: $3,799. Miele G7856 "profes-
sional" dishwasher: $5,449. (Did the moniker "professional" mean
that all others were "amateur"? The answer lies in the fact that it can
do a load in six minutes.)

The pricing was so venal that it seemed to be part of a conspiracy.
And the low-end manufacturers were complicit, or possibly even
coconspirators, in making their stuff noisy, ugly, cheap. I needed a
thirty-inch "counter depth" (sub-thirty-inch) fridge in order to fit
the limited kitchen space I had in the garden apartment. The only
decent-looking thirty-inch refrigerator offered by Madison was the
German-made Liebherr CS161. Cost: $4,000. Of course, as my friend
Mike put it, the handles had sexy "hydraulic action" that compelled
one to open the doors over and over again. (The power bill would go
to the tenants.) But how could it be that this was the least expensive

of the five brands of high-quality fridge that would fit a thirty-inch space? It seemed like holding design hostage from those who could not pay.

All of the above were manufactured in the first world, in ethical/ living-wage-making settings. My naïve idea of an ethical price for a good-looking stainless-steel fridge, with one of those in-door alcoves for ice and water (and maybe a digital readout of the weather?), made in conscionable conditions, was $500. What could I actually get for that? Danby Appliances' ten-cubic-foot freestanding, top-freezer refrigerator with two adjustable glass shelves, made in the People's Republic of China. A.J. Madison said it had ten "features," among them "interior light." I looked at it, looked at it, looked at it, looked at it… and realized that if I were a renter forced to share a lit interior with Danby's pointless curves and pebbled-nigh-pustulous surfaces—good or great skin, human or machine, correlates to expenditure—I'd be plotting my departure the moment I moved in. I wanted renters with longevity. My conclusion: it's a moral failing to buy retail, and it's spiritually debasing to live with crap. Paradox? No. There was a solution.

The fact that all the manufacturers I liked had managed to enshroud themselves in a rarefied air was made laughable by the fact that I could find their products where they did not want me to look. Deflation of rarefication could be accomplished by a single powerful word, with which I would replace Will Smith's "the police" in my own version of his above-quoted paean to quality: Craigslist.

Craigslist!

The *truly* open market.

My first two purchases were fixtures. I decided to search for "Dornbracht" and see if anything came up. Two hits. The first led to a twentieth-floor loft on Seventeenth Street in Manhattan, where Maria, a woman around my age (early forties), held out a white box containing a heavy silver object in a white plush bag. A gooseneck faucet. I asked why she was selling it. "It doesn't have hot."

Two braided-steel water supply lines protruded from the base, one marked with red tape.

"Uhhh." I could've lied. "It definitely is designed for both hot and cold."

"But it only has one handle."

"You swivel it to change temperature."

Awkward silence.

"Anyway, I've bought a replacement and don't need this one."

"Will you take one hundred dollars?"

"I paid over five hundred."

I shrugged, said I was sorry, and turned to go. At which point she said, "Oh, fine!" and, in the end, took $120.

This was addictive. A perfect thing for near 80 percent off. I'd give it to a tenant. It would engender a relationship of mutual respect—and, if I were to believe Matthias Dornbracht, it would never break. The other Dornbracht listing led to an executive at Vornado Real Estate Trust—the ubiquitous and ruthless-seeming owner-managers of more than one hundred million square feet of commercial space. Her name was Amelia and she was selling a dozen bathroom faucets a company architect had ordered for one of its buildings' lavatories by mistake. "We needed a hands-free sensor, but he got these, with handles," she told me, "for some reason, and we can't return them." I asked how firm she was on her price and she replied, "Considering they go for 900+ each and are new in the box I'm not going to accept a lowball offer." OK. But then why sell on Craigslist at all? If Vornado didn't have the pull to demand a waiver on a restock fee then who did? She offered to meet me either at the company offices in Midtown Manhattan or her home, a walk-up in Brooklyn. I opted for the latter and found the fixtures were so perfectly made, nestled in molded-foam caverns, that they seemed to have been pulled fully formed from deep in the earth.

I gasped when I saw them.

And then I offered $500—for three.

Deal. Plus a free Eddie Bauer duffel bag to carry them in.

This was a misleading initiation. Both of these sellers understood the rudiments of civility, and, not being avaricious, were mostly interested in avoiding protracted negotiations. I would later make the mistake of dealing with a man who changed his price repeatedly and told me, "I know you've got a lot of money!" Another oscillated between sycophancy and aggression. When I wanted to come see the freezer/fridge he was selling he replied that I had a "good heart." Then I commenced haggling and he exploded: "This piece cost 4900. You not care my money brand new."

A psychoanalyst in Jersey City was curious as to why a scruffy not-so-young man in an old truck was purchasing her used Duravit toilet. She delivered a doubtful stare when I said I needed it for a rental bathroom with outdated fixtures. She gave the toilet a farewell glance, looked back to me, back to the fixture, to me, to the fixture, to me, and asked, "What do *you do*?"

Another seller texted me a poem:

> Sorry about the toilet
> .Cant longer sell it no more
> Cuz we cracked it in half wen we 're
> Carrying it outside…

And a plumber with extra inventory told me I was wise to avoid "Home Depot shit," explaining that his Toto toilet's bowl had extra value because it was treated with SanaGloss, which "reduces the bacteria dramatically. People in Montclair love that."

But how, perils aside, was I was going to stop after such an auspicious beginning? Clearly an untapped surfeit of both waste and impatience was out there waiting to be exploited.

The word *brand* first appeared in print a thousand years ago, in *Beowulf*—which, after a few hours' shopping on the web, sounds less like an immortal work of Dark Ages lit than a corporate consolidation. *Bang & Olufsen Beosound and Wolf Gourmet Stoves have united to provide high performance grilling and lossless digital audio!*

In the eleventh century the word described "an act, means, or result of burning." From *Beowulf*: "*Hý hine ne móston bronde forbærnan*," which translates as "They could not consume him with fire." Consume!

My friend Mike, admirer of hydraulic handle action, told me, when I announced my intention to write about branding, quality, and the bonanza of Craigslist, "Careful not to blow the lid off it man! If *everybody* knows what a *gold mine* it is here…" He shook his head. He'd recently renovated his place, a few blocks from mine. "Dude, we did it for a song, and Craigslist was the highway to making that happen. It was like, check it out—I'm super scrappy, and I'm the hardest working person I know. And I'm gonna take those two things and I'm gonna turn a house that's been abandoned for ten years into the asset that it always could be."

This was my goal, too. I picked up a few other fixtures, and then I moved out of the realm of the easily portable. I needed two stoves, two fridges, two dishwashers, two toilets. I had one undeniable asset:

my 1960 Chevrolet Apache pickup truck. This would allow me to move fast on deals, and access Westchester and North Jersey, where a preponderance of new or near-new high-end brands were located. It was no surprise that such proximate-but-not-there places, with hefty tax bases but none of the lifestyle benefits of, say, Marin County, would foster a culture of compulsive expenditure (aka churning discontent). I began to think of New York's perimeter as a horde, protected by the dragons of speed traps, insensitive signage, and an almost-visible smog of ennui. Having a pickup truck with which to go after this neglected bounty—yea, a faithful steed—was almost on a par with having a magical power.

I was on a mythic quest to rescue enslaved appliances from people and places that had cast them out. There was a sense of redemption, a sort of knight-errant feeling to seizing these items from their suburban exiles and bringing them to my castle to begin anew. Inherent in the process was an almost chthonic reprisal of various archetypal roles of masculinity: hunter-gatherer, explorer, liberator, wheeler-dealer, con artist.

Consumerism and the ease it promises *is* pagan. The purchaser becomes a sort of emperor. The Viking that serves him is a willing slave. Sub-Zero has merged with Wolf (neutralizing the possibility of the joke above), making a neither-nor company that, as the website spins it, "just made sense, this marriage of ice and fire, cold and hot." Sub-Zero/Wolf sums up its brands' co-ethos as "the steadfast refusal to compromise." To live as a god. A powerful illusion. The idea of a brand is still freighted with ancient concepts of nobility and deity— the ingredients… yea… of *Beowulf*…

Anthony was a contractor in Rye who'd ripped a Viking out of a kitchen for a woman he described, unchivalrously, as "a food snob" who "never cooked." The range retailed for $4,979. He was asking $1,800. Assuming he'd gotten it for free, I offered $800 and said I'd drive up to Westchester immediately. Three days and twelve e-mails later, we settled on $1,187.50 (the price point for Frigidaire, Samsung, and GE).

When I pulled into the driveway of a house on a gentle hill a man with thick black hair walked out of the garage, looked me hard in the face, and asked, "Are you passing counterfeit bills?"

I stifled a laugh and deadpanned, "*Nope*."

Still looking dubious he said, "I'm going to take a photo of your driver's license just to be sure."

I asked for the same. We exchanged pictures—his was better— and I handed over fifty-nine twenties, a five, two ones, and two quarters. The stove was immaculate, though the letterpress markings specifying which knobs activated which burners had been rubbed into half illegibility.

"She was a clean freak," Anthony explained. "She made her maid clean the shit out of that thing."

The perfectly clean Viking weighed five hundred pounds. Anthony and I were barely able to heave it into my steed's bed. Then he threw in a Viking exhaust hood for free. When I got back to Brooklyn I needed two friends and a neighbor to unload the stuff.

Inherent in most mercantile transactions is the question of who's conning who. Perhaps that's most painfully true with fixed prices. The knowledge that you are cornered. Trapped by a series of compacts designed to benefit those more powerful than you. Power is certainly in the foreground of that scene from *Six Degrees*. As is sex. Quality and beauty being both erotic and substitutional, the refuge of those whose lusts cannot be gratified. We displace our desire onto objects.

While we have lust to thank for the scarcity of lust-worthy objects. Over the course of the last century the explosion of population begat mass production begat ubiquitous shit design. Objects worthy of our admiration are ever more rare. If Chippendale were still around it would be embossing its name in eighteen-gauge stainless steel.

Having acquired a cut-rate Viking I got curious about Bertazzoni. The 131-year-old Italian company's stoves had teardrop-shaped cast-aluminum knobs that felt even better in my hand than the Bakelite top of my Chevy's shifter. They rarely came up for sale in New York. But suddenly one appeared on the Washington, DC, Craigslist: "36" PRO Series Free Standing SS Gas Range - $2500 (Ocean Pines)." This was on the north shore of Maryland, just across Delaware Bay from Cape May, New Jersey. Partially out of a desire to escape New York in February, I decided to go for it, offering $1,000 and attempting to charm the seller into accepting such an egregious lowball by saying that I'd be driving down from Brooklyn.

A reply came back two days later from a man called Ed: "doubbly sorry guy you cant buy a piece of shit stove for 1k 2000.00 will take it"

Time to haggle, Craigslist-style—which requires patience, insistence, charm, genuine apology, denigration of Craigslist, and establishing oneself as a responsible person.

> Hey Ed, thanks for the candid reply. Maybe laugh out loud. If you go down to 1,300, I'm your man. But I just bought a perfect Viking for less than 1200. So I got to stay close to my budget. All best, Sean

> R U SURE THE 1300 WAS NOT A TYPO AND SHOULD READ 1800 THE 3 SHOULD BE CLOSED TO LOOK LIKE AN 8

That was no typo! And I am offering cash in denominations of
your choosing…
Why are you selling, btw?

WHAT THE HELL IS BTW AND THE DENOMINATIONS
ARE 18 100S

Btw: by the way.
 I would offer more, and I appreciate the communication
(Craigslist can be such a hassle), but I've got to drive down from
NYC, which is half a day at best, and $100 in gas for my truck.
$1,400 is the best I can do.

DRIVE SOMETHING THATS NOT A PIG AND GET THE
18 BIG ONES AND GET YOUR ASS MOVIVG

Maybe it was the bleak winter, or some deeper sadness, but
I found myself investing outsize amounts of hope in this small relationship. I now genuinely wanted to meet Ed. I wanted his stove.
I wanted to meet the tenant who would want the stove. I sent Ed a
picture of the truck (with the Viking in the back) under the subject
heading "Don't call it a pig!"
 And that did it. Exchanges entered a different register:

 truck looks great nothing a good paint job paint job cant fix a
 friend in boston has one completely restored. the viking looks like
 what i just purchased

I said I still wanted his Bertazzoni. The reply: "1800 and thats
not cuervo."
 I reoffered $1,400, saying my fingers were crossed.

sean boy were getting closer, are you sure that 4 is not a 9, come on my beer fund is low. if see it more my way i will be in md from tonite thru mid next week. dig a bit deeper. forget crossing fingers, pull out da wallet

I suggested we meet in the middle at $1,600 and the deal was done: "we are good to go glad you woke up." And so: four a.m. actual wakeup, two tanks of gas, thirty dollars in tolls, a thirty-dollar ferry ticket, a day on the road with my eight-year-old son, Owen. (I let him do the shifting: "It was exciting!" he'd proclaim later. "We got to meet new people, and we got to go on the ferry.") Ed turned out to be a strapping man with a kind face and a bad back who'd retired from the restaurant business. He lived in a gated seaside community that was so inviting when viewed against February New York City that Owen asked, with total seriousness, "Dad, can we move here?" It was easy to get some friendly people to help load the stove, wrap it in protective plastic, carefully tie it down.

I bought an XO Ventilation fan to hang above the Bertazzoni. It needed an Italian sidekick, and XO described itself, with unconventional punctuation, as "putting into practice our vision of becoming the most innovative; customer oriented Appliance Company in the world. Designed and manufactured by the leading ventilation manufacturer in Italy." John, the seller, was unloading a $725 model for $400. I offered $300. He agreed and gave me directions to a parking lot in West New York (New Jersey) where he'd be waiting "under the home depot sign thats held up by a black pole."

At the center of a blighted landscape I found an earnest-faced boy with round tortoiseshell glasses, just out of his teens. I handed over the cash and asked why he was selling it, in a voice that must have suggested my confusion about how he'd even come to own it.

"*I'm* a *chef.*"

"Oh!"

"In a public school." A sheepish look. "I bought this so I could experiment on my own in my basement." I pictured laundry, a single bed, video games, nary a nonmaternal female. "But the ceiling's too low and I can't use it. So I've got to sell."

I then spent an hour stuck in the Lincoln Tunnel and vowed never to return to Jersey by light of day. That way, even if I got stuck in traffic, I wouldn't have to look at it.

I had my fire. Now it was time for the ice. I'd been conducting desultory searches under "stainless steel" plus "refrigerator" for weeks and failing to find anything that worked, just a collection of too-wide, wrongly hinged, ugly-paneled flotsam. It was impossible to wade through it all. When I'd narrowed the search to Sub-Zero—the high-end industry leader—I'd still gotten the length of my arm in hits. Mine were also complicated parameters: a thirty-incher in one spot, with left-hand hinges (the majority of what I found was hinged the other way) and a thirty-six-incher in another. The latter had to have French doors. Both had to be "counter depth" (sub-thirty-inch).

Logistical difficulties were compounded by the fact that no friend so much as wanted to leave their apartment, let alone haul a used refrigerator out of someone's far-flung suburban kitchen in the middle of an unrelenting cold snap. I'd have to coordinate at least four guys (all, increasingly, suffering from various midlife injuries and stiffnesses) to drive to Jersey and manhandle a seven-foot-tall, five-hundred-pound rectangle. Nearly defeated, I was poised to go retail for dimensional precision and curbside delivery. Then I happened onto this: "Liebherr CS 1611 free standing 30" fridge - $1199 (Scarsdale, NY)." I'd heard rumors that Sub-Zero is so threatened by this neophyte brand that its employees were encouraged to clandestinely denigrate it on product forums, and that sales reps had told retailers they'd have to choose between Sub-Zero's products and Liebherr's. ("We would never condone or encourage voicing negative sentiment toward a competitor on the phone, online, or otherwise from our employees or distributors," says Michele Bedard, Sub-Zero's VP of marketing.) A picture showed left-hand hinges. And Scarsdale was a name out of an epic poem of battle if ever there was one! Adding to the delusions of heroism that had adhered to my quest, I pictured fog, dried blood, wounds, moss on old stones. I e-mailed this message:

> Dear Seller,
> I'm interested [in] the fridge and wanted to ask, with apologies, if you would take $700 for it. Sorry to turn craigslist into an open air market—but here's hoping!
> All best,
> Sean Wilsey

Fourteen minutes later, this response:

> I would take $750 for it.
> ♥ Carolyn

I hit the road the next day. Clear weather, light traffic. Off the Hutchinson River Parkway was the mythically named Dale of Scars, where a serpentine road was aflow with silver SUVs. The road was bordered by an old fieldstone wall. Rolling lawns stretched into the distance. I imagined golf, battle. Owen, were he along, would have wanted to live here, too. Around the corner from a middle school where police cruisers were guarding the parking lot, I found a huge frame house under renovation.

Carolyn—a blade-thin woman with wavy blonde hair, in a fitted, quilted, black coat, leggings, big sunglasses—got out of a black Mercedes SUV. She rounded up five Spanish-speaking men who loaded the fridge. One gave me a thumbs-up on the truck.

I asked, "What's with the cops at the school?"

Carolyn said, "That's since Newtown. All parents have to get fingerprint-scanned for admittance."

She asked if the fridge was for me or if I was a reseller, saying she was curious because it had been one of a pair, and she'd sold the other to somebody who'd driven down from New England and intended to make a profit on the resale "in an urban market." I sensed a kindred spirit. I told her what I was doing and described the brands I'd bought on the cheap for my rentals. Miffed, she exhaled a visible puff in the cold air, gave a little hip jut, and pronounced, "That's the stuff that *I* have."

"Well, my Bed-Stuy rental will be like your house."

She gave a tight smile. But then, before I left, she got up in the truck bed and let me take her picture with the fridge.

Back on the lawn-fringed road, I felt a Robin Hood–level sense of satisfaction. And after the fridge was salted away in my ganja-wreathed garage, the feeling increased. It had a function called "SuperCool" that would bring a beer from shelf to drinking temperature in ten minutes. Perfect for Bed-Stuy. Maybe Robin Hood really was the right comparison. I felt like a repossessor, a subversive, a saboteur. Coming by these things via Craigslist was a form of protest. And a successful campaign left me filled with the tingle of battlefield victory over an oppressor. A hegemon. I was setting things right. I would love these appliances as I could never have loved them if I'd paid retail.

I went on spring vacation in a warm climate the next day. Every time I had a quiet moment by the pool, drifting off into sunscreen-scented reverie, I found myself thinking of the fridge. As Jude Law put it in *The Talented Mr. Ripley*, referring to his own seaside love affair with an appliance, "I could fuck this icebox I love it so much."

But dramatic failure was borne out of this success. A guy named Nazareth had a Liebherr, in Cliffside Park, N.J.—"brand new in box." Carolyn's Liebherr had come with a faint odor of wilted vegetables.

New in box.

I wanted it.

But Nazareth attempted to forestall all bartering by writing, "I am sacrificing a lot. I have a funeral in the family... Be nice.... Sean name a biblical name." His price: "product is $4000.00...$3600.00 ok"

I said no.

He said, "3000 today."

"Sorry."

"2500 today right."

"Sorry."

"2000 today cash Only right now. Later no deal."

"I can't spend that much."

"When you have 2000 cash in hand call me only for you."

I let two weeks go by and wrote: "Hi Naz, it's Sean.... Thought maybe we could make a deal."

He replied, "I am lost sacrificing my own children moneys."

I stuck fast at $1,500. He countered at $1,700, then dropped to $1,600 and gave me the name and address of his "brother," Dave, who had the fridge in his garage. I left for Jersey immediately, greedy for "new in box" at 60 percent off. I called this brother en route. Dave explained that he ran a trucking company, and Nazareth was his third cousin. Dave seemed sane—and was only expecting $1,400!

Who was conning who here? I kept driving. *New*, I thought. *In box.* It took over an hour to slog through downtown Brooklyn, midtown Manhattan, the Lincoln Tunnel, suburban sprawl. I edged along the margin of Jersey, toward the Palisades, Google's map app guiding me. At the moment my phone's screen told me I was 450 feet from my destination, I got a call from Dave.

"Sean, I didn't even take a shower. I just ran out of my house. I'm on my way to the turnpike—my driver he rolled over a tractor-trailer and they're taking him to the Newark Hospital. I'm so sorry Sean. I give you a discount. I call you Saturday."

But Dave wouldn't answer my calls the next day. And Nazareth said he had another buyer.

"Oh, Naz," I said. "We had a deal. I came out there."

"No deal," he said. "You always cry."

A dishwasher brought about the redemptive experience of my Craigslisting career. I'd come close to buying an old model Bosch for seventy-five dollars on the way back from Maryland, but the deal fell through because Owen and I were too exhausted to make the detour. Early in the quest I'd seen an ad for a pair of Miele professional models that listed for $5,000 apiece. If I wanted something maintenance-free, this was the grail. There'd been no asking price. The ad had just said to make an offer. My casual lowball ($400!) for one had been met with silence. Now I tried again, for both.

> Dear Seller,
> I wrote a couple weeks ago with a (pretty measly) offer on one of
> your dishwashers—which you understandabl[y] ignored. But now
> I need two and wanted to find out what you would consider taking
> for both. If you could please let me know I would be grateful!

All very best,
Sean Wilsey

The seller replied: "They have never been used. These are on long island… If you really want both, make me a great counter offer."

"If you'd take 1,500k cash for both I'll come get tomorrow afternoon!"

"How about 1600? Cash would be good… Please send me your contact info for verification. Can't take too many chances w craig's list."

The seller's name was Anita and when we spoke on the phone she said her husband, whom I'll call Naresh, was a general contractor for "a number of very particular clients in the Hamptons." After he had installed these two dishwashers (in a single kitchen) this particular client reconsidered and had them taken right back out.

Anita said, "I wanted to put them in our place but it would have been too hard."

She gave me a set of manuals and told me that if I had any problems I should let her know. It seemed like she was about to offer me a warranty. After Naresh and I had loaded them in the truck, and the couple had posed for a picture, I asked about the Mieles' former owner.

"Was it Martha Stewart?"

After a brief pause. "I can't say who it was."

The question—"Will they work?"—hanging over all the time and effort I put into assembling my appliance collection was about to be answered.

I put one of Anita's dishwashers in my house. This required the assistance of an electrician (six-minute wash cycles don't happen at 110 volts) and a day of work. When we flipped the 220 breaker the

Miele's console lit up… and then died. It was like being jilted by a lover; until I realized the door's locking mechanism had not properly seated.

A small adjustment.

The lights came on and stayed on. Then a load. The dishes emerged not so much clean as rebirthed—as though they'd just come straight from the kiln. I loaded it up after dinner that night and sat on the floor, watching, listening, feeling a childish pride that human beings could make something that worked so well. It was like attending a NASA rocket launch in the 1960s—in my kitchen. Then I had a dinner party, and all the male guests voluntarily gathered around the Miele to do dishes.

I now look at other dishwashers and think, *Amateurs.*

All the stuff in the rental has worked as-new… so far. But will these objects ever, truly, be mine? No. They're less possessions than physical refutations of all the snooty slogans under which they're sold in the retail world; totems of their previous owners, the time spent acquiring them a sacrifice to the hope of finding tenants I'll love. More paganism there.

But imagine for a moment that I haven't taken you through all of the above.

What would you say if I told you I could get you top-of-the-line appliances for as much as 85 percent off. Would you call me a con man? Would you rent my apartments? You should at least come see them. I'll be having an open house. Just search for the following combination of keywords: Miele, Bertazzoni, Viking, Liebherr, Dornbracht, and— 🐝 —Bed-Stuy.

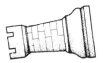

MARFA, REVISITED

2000-2014

A fter writing the long piece about Marfa that opens this book I lived in the town for several months, in 2000. An e-mail I sent to Dave Eggers about life in Far West Texas was published in *McSweeney's* 6, in the winter of 2001:

A CONTINUATION *of* "THE REPUBLIC OF MARFA," *which was* A HISTORY *of the* SMALL TEXAS TOWN *of* MARFA, POP. 2,424, FOUND IN MCSWEENEY'S NO. 2, HERE FURTHER ELABORATED, *in an anecdotal fashion*, NOT AT ALL IN KEEPING WITH THE GRANDIOSE TONE OF THIS SUB-HEAD, *and with particular attention to* DOGS, COMMUNISM, RATTLERS, PARADES AND CHILDREN WHO CURSE, *rather than* PICNICS, SHOOT-OUTS, *and the* LATE DONALD JUDD, WHO OPENED THE TOWN UP TO ALL SORTS OF ARTISTS AND ARCHITECTS—*but with additional material relating to the* UNEXPLAINED OPTICAL PHENOMENA THAT SURROUND THIS PLACE (CALLED THE "MARFA LIGHTS") AND FIGURED LARGELY IN THE FIRST INSTALLMENT. THE REASON FOR THE

SEAN WILSEY

AUTHOR'S PRESENCE IN THIS REMOTE PLACE—ALONG WITH THE
PRESENCE OF HIS WIFE, DAPHNE (BEAL), ALSO A WRITER *(this
can be difficult at times, but is mostly rewarding)*—BEING THAT
THE LANNAN FOUNDATION, AN ORGANIZATION THAT BESTOWS
VARIOUS CORRUPTING FREEBIES ON WRITERS, BOUGHT A COUPLE
OF HOUSES THERE, HAD NO ONE TO FILL THEM FOR THE SUMMER,
DUE TO THE MISAPPREHENSION THAT IT IS UNBEARABLY HOT
THEN—*it is not, since Marfa is at an elevation of 5,000 feet*—
AND SO LET US STAY THERE, WHICH WAS GREAT, *though sort of
intimidating*, PARTICULARLY DURING THE BRIEF PERIODS WHEN
OTHER WRITERS WERE ALSO THERE, AND SEEMED TO BE MUCH
MORE PRODUCTIVE, MAKING US FEEL LIKE WE SHOULD HAVE
BEEN LESS FOCUSED ON THE FOLLOWING:

We needed to get our bikes fixed. Daphne met the janitor at the elementary school who said he could do it if we came by his house in the afternoon.

So we did. As we walked into a yard full of boulders and cacti and rusting bicycles, passed a sun-bleached and gnawed-on doghouse, and saw that the front door to a low little adobe was wide open, Daphne whispered: "Get ready for a Marfa moment." She then shouted a few hellos and out came a sleepy-looking guy with a lot of decayed or missing front teeth, a blue T-shirt, and no pants. There was a lot of awkward "Oh, well, excuse us, we can come back," etc. But he said this was a good time for him. I tried to check and see if maybe he was wearing some brief underwear that were hidden by the T-shirt, but I could only identify increasingly pale and tender skin, and a tan line.

He told us to come back in an hour and when we did the bikes were beautifully fixed and he refused to take any money.

*   *   *

The Lannan Foundation's gardener, Rip Winkle, was young and buff and waxed, with piercing blue eyes and a bushy mustache—and he moved with great self-consciousness, ripping out dandelions and crabgrass as though auditioning for a nude scene. One day he was working shirtless when Daphne approached to ask him a question about watering. He interrupted her, pointed to his chest, and said, "Does this offend you?"

I looked up from my desk and saw a stubbly, heavyset, bandanaed man—like a bandit—running back and forth, just outside my window, where a fieldstone wall cut off the lower three feet of my view: a lone, cathedral-like mountain, a volcano or two, the Godbold feed plant. The bandit was shouting. I stopped writing. He seemed to be shouting... *encouragement*—to something hidden from sight. I stood up and saw that he was in the company of a pair of exuberant golden retriever puppies. So I went outside to say hello. He introduced himself as my neighbor, the writer David Foster Wallace, and told me the dogs belonged to a local rancher. He was dog-sitting. Or, it became clear as I watched him, dog training. After talking about culinary Marfa for a bit—and agreeing that the monotony of West Texas food (Dairy Queen; refried beans fried in lard) was getting us down—I told him I was planning to blow off a morning's work to drive fifty miles through the desert and buy fish at a supermarket called Furrs.

"*Furrs*," he said, drawing out the name. "You'd better give that the old sniff test."

An "ice-cream social" took place at the local Episcopalian church. It was presided over by the white female pastor, who had invited the local Catholic priest (male; Mexican) to come over with some of his friends and play the bongos.

I'd seen this same Catholic priest play at a honky-tonk in Alpine, the next town east, a week before, and it had not been evident that he was a man of the cloth. This was at the invitation of Michael Meredith, a young architect who was doing a residency with the Chinati Foundation (Donald Judd's museum; Marfa's cultural institution). His residency involved designing a residence: for Marianne Stockebrand, the museum's German director (and Judd's former lover). Meredith was a multidisciplinarian, also building furniture, painting, and producing theme songs for locals and newcomers. In Alpine the priest-in-mufti got everyone out on the floor for his rendition of "Oye Como Va." His church does a musical service called "the brass mass."

A bookstore/wine bar has opened on the otherwise-deserted main street. Patronizing it was a fidgety unshaven dude around nineteen, who kept up a patter of asinine questions along the lines of "What do y'all do for fun around here?" with the resolutely polite girl behind the counter. I sat next to him and did a decent job ignoring it all, but I looked up when he asked her, "What shampoo is that?"

She kept washing some glasses, and eventually said, shyly, and a bit caustically, "Can you *smell* it?"

"Yeah," he replied.

Then he turned to me and said, "I've been out in the woods for a year, so I can smell real good."

Daphne and I organized a trip to the nearby border town of Ojinaga (aka OJ), Mexico. We took the Chinati Foundation's capacious

Chevy Blazer, available thanks to Rob Weiner, Chinati's second in command, who came along and brought Michael Meredith, the architect/composer, Margrét Blöndal, an Icelandic sculptor, also in residence at Chinati, and Margrét's seraphic eight-year-old son, Sölvi, who had become Michael's sidekick in Marfa.

Our neighbor, Wallace, came too. In concert with Weiner, he spent the whole car ride teaching Sölvi show tunes (mostly from *The Pajama Game*), which they sang at top volume: "My love's meteoric!/ It's merely historic!/A whirlwind!/A cyclone on wheeeeeeels!/It rocks my whole solar plexus!/It's bigger than Texas!/I just can't tell you how it feeeeeels!" We were all giddy by the time we arrived in the blasted-out town of Presidio, Texas, the official border crossing. Our plan was to have fish at El Bucañero—The Buccaneer—a seafood restaurant just over the border.

El Bucañero was supposed to have very fresh fish because it was patronized by men whose lives in narcotics trafficking had obliged them to relocate from the coast. They flew in seafood to assuage their homesickness and consumed it in a dining room lined with alcoves containing relics from 1983's *Scarface*. A handgun. Ammo. A cigar. A roll of US currency. Al Pacino reclining in a bubble bath above a brass plaque that read, I WORKED HARD FOR THIS, I NEED NOBODY. Pacino leveling an M-16A1 machine gun—his "little friend"—at patrons eating (reportedly excellent) ceviche. It was a shrine to crime.

The most notorious of Ojinaga's traffickers had been the Lord of the Skies (*El Señor de Los Cielos*), who reportedly flew in Colombian cocaine using a fleet of retired-from-commercial-service Boeing 727s. The Lord came to OJ to study with a local known as the Fox of the Ojinaga Desert (*El Zorro de Desierto de Ojinaga*). The Fox had an effective system for getting contraband out of Chihuahua state and into Presidio County, which he imparted to the Lord. Then he was killed in a shoot-out, possibly organized by his former pupil (who, with his lieutenants, then took over). Though maybe not every secret got disseminated. Shortly thereafter Rob Weiner came upon a duffel bag full of drugs discarded on Chinati property. He called the police.

During the hours when OJ's criminals weren't feasting on nostalgic seafood they were lashing informers to fences and shocking them with exposed electrodes. A few years later (2008) a victim of such shock-induced cardiac arrest was taken to a ranch, soaked in diesel, and set alight. This went on for much of the decade following our visit, until it was reported in the Mexican newspaper *Reforma*, which also detailed behavior almost comical in its debauchery: "a reign of terror in which illegal detentions and searches, kidnapping, torture, extrajudicial executions, sale of drugs, and extortion were encouraged and planned in meetings on military installations, while alcoholic beverages were consumed in the company of prostitutes."

Unfortunately, El Bucañero was closed. So we went to a place where the kitchen incinerated all our food in a deep fat fryer. Everyone but Sölvi (Coke) and Wallace (Diet Coke) ordered Mexican beer. The novelist and I were seated at opposite ends of a long table. Everyone fell silent when he asked me, from ten feet away, whether I was working on a book about Marfa.

"I liked 'The Republic of Marfa,'" he said. "Is *that* going to be a book?"

"I don't think so."

"It should be."

My "Thanks!" echoed around the tiled dining room. Then I asked, "What are you working on?"

All heads swiveled in his direction—and we found ourselves confronted by a man wild-eyed before hot electrodes. This was a topic he desperately wanted to avoid.

But, being a Midwesterner, he was honor-bound to answer. He slowly parted his lips to tell us. As he did so there was a rustling/shuffling sound: a group of mariachis suddenly appeared in the empty dining room, arranged themselves around our table, and all blew their trumpets, a sound that appeared to be coming straight out of Wallace's mouth. After ten minutes of "*Ay, ay, ay, ay/Canta y no llores*" and "*La cucaracha la cucaracha/ya no puedo caminar*"—Sölvi *delighted*—I thought of Wallace's answer as music.

After dinner we walked to the town square, got ice cream, ordered warm club sodas from a kiosk, and sat on benches for an hour watching Sölvi play soccer with some local kids. Wallace sequestered himself with Margrét, who later told me, "Something that he called a 'melancholic expression' in my passport photo caught his attention." When it was time to go Wallace carried Sölvi off, as Margrét put it, "like a potato bag."

Leaving OJ I drove the Chinati Blazer down a wide, unpaved back street. In the distance ahead I saw a car ease slowly through a lakelike puddle.

I said, "Hey, Sölvi, there's a *puddle* up ahead!"

"Go faster!" he shouted.

I floored it, and, like an SUV ad, sent water spraying in every direction.

This water turned out to be raw sewage.

At the border an INS agent didn't even look at our passports or ask us a single question—he just shouted "Woah!" and waved us through in a near panic. The smell clung to the Blazer all the way back to Marfa. With the windows open Wallace taught Sölvi more show tunes—"Tsssssssteam heat!"—and we shouted them over a rushing current of warm desert air.

* * *

One of the most frequent customers at the new wine bar was Mr. Cross, the extremely cheerful former druggist, now retired, who sat on a couch with a large unlit cigar in his mouth and his silver diver's tank of pure oxygen on a dolly at his side.

Late one night, driving the Lannan Foundation's car, I saw a bright light in the road ahead. Immediately I dimmed my high beams. When I got closer I realized that it was a single pulsing point. I stared, slowing, until, when collision was imminent, it winked out. A Marfa light!

I stopped the car. Nothingness all around. Warmth in the air.

I stuck my head out the window and said, "Hello."

Sölvi, in his role as sidekick to Michael Meredith, caught on to the following English phrases, which he liked to shout:

"I'm dead sexy!" (Then he'd lick his finger and touch one of his nipples.)

"Fuck me in the butt!" (He seemed to have found this one on his own. Or possibly at *Scary Movie*, playing in Alpine, to large audiences of children.)

He taught me the following Icelandic ones:

Cuker-az: Poop butt

Hoar-hois: Boogerhead

Nu er komith ad flankingunni: It is time for your spanking.

* * *

I wandered into the Thunderbird Motel's gift shop, browsed a display case full of Bowie knives for fifteen minutes, and left without ever waking the snoring proprietor.

Daphne and I signed up for singing lessons with Jerry "Jabo" Grigadean, a former professor at UT Austin who used to teach the history of rock and roll. He was in Marfa for the summer visiting his friend Lineaus Lorette, an avowed communist who made leather medicine balls and was restoring an old grocery store called the New Star.

I arrived for my first lesson to find five large-to-mid-size dogs in front of Jabo's adobe house, which was next to the New Star. They were: a small solid white one given to unsettling eye contact; a huge shaggy black one, impressively not panting; a thin, black, midsize one with beautiful eyes; a wiggling friendly black-and-gray one with swollen teats dragging on the ground; and a little dirty yellow-white one.

Jabo was in his early sixties, tall and thin, with middle-of-the-back-length gray hair, a gray beard, spectacles, and a seemingly inexhaustible supply of tie-dyes. He had a slight drawl, and was enthusiastic.

I said, "Jabo, you've got a lot of dogs out here."

He said, "These are Lineaus's dogs!"

"You mean these are all his dogs?"

"No." Big smile. "These aren't all his dogs. These are just the traveling crew—his socially acceptable dogs. They represent about a fifth of Lineaus's dogs. And since Lineaus is a revolutionary, he names all his dogs after revolutionaries." He pointed to the shaggy one. "This is Zhu De—who was one of Mao's generals. Here's James Chaney"—white, unafraid of eye contact; murdered civil rights worker—"El Lissitzky"—thin, black, midsize; artist and member of the Russian avant garde—"Ethel Rosenberg"—dirty yellow-white; communist spy—"and Teresita"—swollen teats; medicine woman, Mexican suffragist—"here just had a litter of puppies, and they'll almost certainly be named after revolutionaries, too."

I hadn't met Lineaus at this point, but I met him a few days later. He was a big, tanned man who wore the same (clean) shirt at all times, a large red star on a white background with a silhouetted *campesino* (Sandino, founder of the Sandinistas) below it, and liked to mock Chinati—which he referred to as "Chinazi"—for its to-him fascist devotion to the late Donald Judd's rigorous aesthetic sensibility. His dream was to open a communist summer camp in Marfa. He played the tuba and Jabo accompanied on the trombone. They did this on his back porch surrounded by dogs, seven of them puppies.

Daphne was jogging down a road to Mexico when her foot landed eight inches from what appeared to be a snake. She stopped, turned, and saw that it was a snake, about three feet long and just lying there. She thought, *It looks dead, but it looks too plump to be dead.* So she walked back a couple steps to check it out. As she got close it suddenly coiled, hissed, and began to rattle. She took off fast.

The next time she had a lesson with Jabo she told him this story. He smiled, rubbed his chin, and said, "I wonder if that was my friend the rattlesnake?"

Jabo had walked outside of his house barefoot to look at the stars. Walking back inside he noticed that he had been standing and stargazing about six inches from a small rattlesnake.

He told us, "I was shaking, but I grabbed a shovel, talked to the snake, saying, 'We're friends,' gently scooped him into a bucket and put a screen over it. The next morning I strapped the bucket to the back of my bicycle, rode out on the ranch road, and released him."

The place where Jabo released his snake was right where Daphne ran into her snake.

I tried to feed a horse in the field across the street. It wouldn't come over, so I waved around a carrot and called to it until it looked up, bared its teeth, and galloped away. Mr. Cross, the retired druggist, told Daphne, "I saw your husband messing around with that horse."

From "Dostoyevsky and the Big Bend," by Thomas Wilson, published in nearby Sul Ross State University's *Journal of Big Bend Studies*:

> The first Marfa to appear in a Dostoyevsky novel is in *The Village of Stepanchikovo* (1859). The next Marfa appears in *Crime and Punishment*. A character named Marfa would appear in his next works, *The Idiot*, *The Gambler*, *The Possessed* and finally in *The Brothers Karamazov*…
>
> When you look along the route of the railroad track from Marfa… you see… the name Feodora. Feodora is Dostoyevsky's first name with an "a" on the end of it. Why is the "a" important? Unlike English, the Russian author of a novel is written in the genitive case. Genitive is also used for possessive. Therefore, the title page of Dostoyevsky's novel reads, "Feodora," or, translated, "Feodor's novel."
>
> Feodora means "Feodor's place." It seems to indicate that the person on the train, naming these stops along the route, was reading one of Dostoyevsky's novels, not someone else's. The use of Feodora means that the novel she was reading was in Russian, because no English translation would have used the "a." It also bolsters the case for *The Brothers Karamazov*, because the novel,

published in its original Russian, could easily have been in the hands of anyone in the world 13 months after publication....

The railroad was in control of the naming conventions. The track right-of-way, by order of the Texas Legislature, belonged to the Galveston, Harrisburg and San Antonio Railway Company (GHS&A), which subcontracted the work to the Southern Pacific proceeding from California. The names occasionally changed later, but only the superintendent of railroad construction could bestow the original name. We know who that was. Between Sierra Blanca and the Pecos River, we also know he gave the job to his wife.

While the construction of the trans-continental railroad is well documented, the record of the Southern Pacific is sketchy. The headquarters building of the Southern Pacific in San Francisco was destroyed by fire, and all of its records, in the earthquake of 1906.

However, we do know that the team that built the trans-continental railroad in 1869 came out of retirement to build the Southern Pacific: One of them was the husband and wife team of James Harvey Strobridge and Hanna Maria Strobridge... Strobridge took his entire family with him during the construction, in a special rail car that served as their home. However, when the Southern Pacific was built, his children were grown and he was now 51 years old... It is not known for a certainty if Hanna Maria Strobridge was on the train when it first saw what is now Marfa, Feodora and Marathon. What we do know is that her husband, James, had given her the right to name the different stops in the region, which she did.

The only Hanna Maria I've ever known was Finnish. If this one was, too, it made her a likely Russian speaker—and maybe even a translator herself. Translation, essentially piecework, fell within a nineteenth-century woman's purview. Surviving Southern Pacific records show that she lived outside of San Francisco, within sight of the twin summits of Russian Hill, where I grew up. She may even have had a servant of her own named Marfa.

She needed the help. Hanna Maria Strobridge and her husband adopted six children. And they had only three eyes to watch them: James Harvey Strobridge—"forceful, very profane," per a contemporary—wore a patch over his right eye, because, according to this same contemporary, he'd gone "into a cut before all the blast charges had gone off and a delayed explosion destroyed an eye." The Marfa in Dostoyevsky's novel might have had a particular appeal to this couple for the fact that she and her husband, Grigory, had adopted Pavel Fyodorovich—the illegitimate son of the Karamazov family's feckless patriarch, Fyodor…

But here's another theory: Marfa's name was taken from a character in Jules Verne's novel *Michael Strogoff Or, The Courier of the Czar*, which had already been published in English, and adapted into a play. The supporting evidence: a description of nearby Fort Davis in the county-by-county miscellany column—"TEXAN NEWS ITEMS"—of the December 17, 1882, *Galveston Daily News*:

> A Fort Davis letter says: Fort Davis is 500 miles from San Antonio and ninety miles from Presidio del Norte, the nearest point on the Rio Grande. It is located in the Wild Rose pass of Olympia canyon, on the old overland route, and at the foot of the Apache mountains, a spur of the Guadalupe range. It is 5,073 feet above the sea level, and is the highest elevation occupied by a fort in Texas. It is a ten-company post and was built by Robert E. Lee in about 1852 and named for Jefferson Davis. It was then the most remote military post on the frontier. Lee, who was then lieutenant-colonel of the Eighth Infantry, located the post. Now two railroads

pass through the country. The fort is twenty-two miles north of the Southern Pacific railroad. The nearest station is at Marfa, so named after one of the characters in the play of Michael Strogoff, and two or three other stations derive their names from Jules Verne's story. The fort is sixty miles south of the Texas and Pacific railroad, the nearest station being at Toyah. About sixty miles south of Fort Davis is the Chinati mountain, with a good deal of low grade silver ore, and parties are now prospecting there.

Which I find semi-compelling, seeing as it's a letter, not a piece of reportage.

And there are no other stations on either of these lines (as listed on a late-nineteenth-century Texas Railroad Commissioner's map) that connect to the Verne story. But here's some Strogoff dialogue:

> Marfa: Ah, wretch, you've become at once and the same time, an unnatural son and a traitor to the country.
> (Heavy explosions outside. A shell falls near Marfa, the wick burning.)
> Strogoff: (stepping forward) Take care, Marfa.
> Marfa: May this shell kill me, since my son is a coward!
> Strogoff: A coward! Me? See if I am afraid! (he takes the shell and hurls it out the window) Goodbye...! (he rushes out the back)
> Marfa: Ah, I said so indeed. He's my son. He's Michael Strogoff, the Courier of the Czar.

Wallace and I were standing in the street between our houses, sprinklers going on each of our lawns.

He asked, "Why did they plant grass that needs so much water?"

"Gotta talk to Rip Winkle about it."

"*Who?*"

"The gardener."

"*That's* his *name?*"

"Yeah. Or *handle.*"

"It's not really up to *Rip Winkle.*"

I laughed.

He shook his head.

"It's stupid," I agreed. "But what I really think about is the fact that there are a number of creatures living in our houses, over which we have no control, that could *kill us.* Aren't you worried about all the brown recluse spiders? You know a woman died from recluse bites back in '96?"

"No. They'll just make your flesh necrotize wherever they bite you, but they won't kill you. It's the widows that'll kill you."

The next day I was browsing the Lannan bookcase when I spotted a widow above Günter Grass's *Dog Years.* I went to the kitchen and grabbed an eight-inch Wüsthof Classic chef knife and slowly inserted the blade between the shelves till I was right below the spider. It froze, shifted footing, then attacked. Fangs latched onto knife for a full five seconds. I saw venom run down the blade. Then the spider looked side to side, seemingly confused, which gave me the opportunity to slice it neatly in half.

This flyer was up all over town:

Photo: A bearded Mexican-looking dude wearing serape, sombrero, bandoliers, brandishing a gun, and leering before a backdrop of sun-dappled buttes.

WANTED!

Models

Needed: Hispanic males between 21 and 45.

Job: Advertising photo shoot. Must be willing to be cast as a
"Pancho Villa" type character.

Contact: Bill Putman (713) 824-1600 (leave message) or at Three
Palms hotel in Presidio.

Plusses: Beards, mustaches, etc.

Pay: Outstanding

Margrét and Sölvi went back to Iceland. Michael Meredith, side-kickless now, took a hiking trip with Wallace: "When we got to Big Bend National Park there was this beautiful view. We stood looking at it. I said it reminded me of *Land of the Lost*, and he said, 'You just ruined it for me. I can't even look at it anymore.'"

Jabo convinced Daphne and me to be in the Marfa Lights Parade. So we rode on the back of a flatbed trailer, along with the Marfa Community Band, of which we were suddenly members. TMCB, in its parade manifestation, consisted of Jabo on trombone, Linaeus on tuba, Mrs. Baldridge, the elementary school music teacher, on keyboards, Art Spragg (a PE teacher at the high school, much liked for allowing the kids to bring in chips and cards and play poker), who was just looking cool, and us.

Lineaus gave us a drum and a couple contorted hunks of cast iron to bang together triangle style, and we rolled through town before a brigade of equestrian border patrol. We performed "The Washington Post March," a Name Unknown blues number, and "The Marfa Lights Rap," a surreal number in which Mrs. Baldridge—who looks every inch an elementary school music teacher—and Jabo (lyricist) rapped in front of a tie-dye bedspread that was draped over the front of our float. Art Spragg held up a sign with the words on it—"On highway 90/Look to the right/And you're gonna see/The Marfa Lights!"—while I banged on the triangle and Daphne hit the bongo.

"Wallace brought a friend on the trip to Big Bend. She had long, dark hair, and a deck of cards, and was from Vegas. She was like a hippie from Vegas. And she seemed like trouble. They met though what she called 'meaningful coincidences.' I just thought, *How can he not see that she's crazy?* But he had this weird spiritual thing with her. He was just a guy who fell for these obviously problem situations. But he liked her a lot."

On Jabo's last day in Marfa all of his students gave a recital. It culminated in the performance of "The People's Polka," by the People's Chorus: Jabo, singing and on trombone; Lineaus, on tuba; Beto Halpern, a twelve year-old, who played trumpet; Daphne and me, singing.

This is how it goes (lyrics: Jabo):

> Ban-ker says, "Will you work with me?"
> Far-mer says, "Yes, in-com-mu-ni-ty."
> Gar-bage man says, "Do I get my share?"
> The an-swer is, "Yes, you'll re-ceive what is fair."
> We va-lue the la-bor of ev'-ry-one! We're e-ga-li-ta-ri-an!
> We can learn to live with each o-ther, care for plants and animals, too.
> We can live like sis-ters and bro-thers, you re-spect me and I re-spect you.

Daphne also performed a blues song—"Sugar Blues"—for which she received a long ovation.

I did a piece Jabo and I'd worked up called "Crossing into Ojinaga." It was hummed rather than sung—very little breathing required.

I said to Michael, speaking of Wallace's Vegas hippie friend, "She must have been pretty."

"She was not pretty *at all*. She was motherly. *Earth* motherly. They were building a relationship *off coincidence*. Something had happened so many times they knew they were destined to know each other. Which is baloney! But he was attracted to stuff like that. 'Spiritual magic.' He needed that. He was really depressed."

"I guess so," I said.

"Remember how he drank those two-liter Diet Cokes? For a while there I used to think people who were really interesting drank Diet Coke."

"Those were big Cokes."

"He was a lonely guy. He used to come by my studio and talk to me. Remember those theme songs? I had one that was so depressing and sad, like slowed down bagpipe music. Wallace said, 'I'll take *that* one.'"

Jabo left town. Wallace left town. Our Lannan residency was soon up. But we decided to stay in Marfa. Lineaus gave us Jabo's house. We just needed a car. And then I was smitten by a silhouette in front of the post office: a 1960 Chevy Apache 10 pickup, hard used but rust-free and well loved, gorgeous, really: boxy, with a side-mounted spare tire, like a shrugged shoulder, up high behind the driver, and covered in sky-blue house paint. The whole vehicle was metal, wood, fabric, straw, and glass. Outside of fan belts, fuel lines, and some electrical components, there was virtually no synthetic material involved in the thing's construction. I stared till a Mexican man (wearing a cowboy hat; smoking a cigar) drove it away. The man's name was Felipe Jesus Santisteban. He went by Jesse, or Chuy. He wore sunglasses, a brush mustache, absolutely no expression. Then I chased him down, made an offer, and it was mine. We went to the courthouse and made the deal immediately.

A few days after buying the truck Daphne and I were on the way to get some fuel at Amigos, Marfa's westernmost gas station, listening to Steve Earle on the Kraco "Auto-Stop" cassette deck Jesse/Chuy'd installed, doing a mellow twenty-five, having a rural-lifestyle moment, when a small, calico border collie ran out in front of us. Daphne screamed, I stamped on the brakes, the wheels locked, and the dog disappeared beneath us as we slid to a diagonal stop.

Daphne jumped out and said, "Oh my God we've killed it!"

Steve Earle said, "Her hair was black and her eyes were blue."

I backed up, pulled into the parking lot of a Dollar General, and saw the dog in a quivering ball with blood and asphalt mixed in its fur. The expression on the dog's face said all it wanted to do before it died was apologize. I started crying. The dog looked *even more* apologetic, tried to get up, as if to relieve us of any responsibility, and failed. I looked away and saw that the woman behind the register of the Dollar General was crying. Unable to look either at her or the dog my gaze fell on the truck's big white grill and rebar-reinforced bumper. *Killing machine* went through my head. *What did I buy this thing for?*

Then the dog started wagging its tail.

A thirtyish, fleshy-faced man in a cowboy hat was walking across the highway from the feed store. The man picked up the dog and said, "I think Shiner's learned his lesson." Noticing the tears in our eyes he added, "I've run over lots of dogs. He'll be all right. If he's hurt bad—like internal injuries—he'll throw up blood and die. If he lives he's learned his lesson."

Though fall had brought cold weather an ice cream truck continued trolling the streets. Once, in a dust storm, I heard its little jingle blare extra loud and then fade away completely, due to the ever-changing direction of the wind. A bunch of kids and parents were huddled together buying cones.

I visited the Marfa and Presidio County Museum, a small, white house on highway 90, a couple hundred feet east of where I'd hit Shiner (who lived). A woman in her sixties, with gray hair and olive skin, greeted me as follows when I entered the building: "You're one of those writer people."

"Yes."

"You're the one who bought Whosehisname's truck."

"Jesse. Chuy."

"You ought to be ashamed of yourself—taking that truck out of Marfa! From that *old man*." Pause. "His sister used to work for me." She said this as though it gave her a claim on his property.

"What makes you think I'm taking it out of Marfa?"

She replied, primly, "One of my colleagues that I work with here wanted to buy it. *He* thought you were taking it."

Having established the dispensability of politeness in this exchange I said, "Too bad."

"Well," she said. "Lots of people *liked* it, but you were just the one who had the nerve to ask him for it."

I walked through the museum. Marfa once had the highest per capita airplane ownership in the United States. It still has the highest-elevation golf course in Texas. It is in the wrong time zone—Central balloons inexplicably out around the town and its surrounding emptiness, leaving El Paso to the west and Ojinaga to the south in Mountain Time. The topsoil is said to go down thirty feet.

As I was leaving I again bumped into the woman who'd greeted me. She was answering a visitor's question about the town motto.

I inquired, "Does Marfa have a motto?"

"Yeah," she said. "'Get out of here.'"

I replied, "*With the truck.*"

In the center of the dash was a sign, punched out on a label maker, that read, VAYA CON DIO. It must once have said, VAYA CON DIOS; but the *s* was gone, a ragged edge in its place. I imagined that this had happened in a moment of savage, God-forsaking frenzy. Savage-yet-lazy God-forsaking frenzy, as Jesse/Chuy, or whoever'd done it, abandoned the whole enterprise, eventually painting the sign and the whole vehicle over, inside and out, with that same sky blue. I imagined that as Jesse/Chuy had started tearing it off he had had a change of heart.

He now lived, and shared a bedroom with, his sister, Beda. I'd drive over to his house and talk with him in front of his garage on hot afternoons, when Wallace, wherever he was, was surely writing (even if it was only a postcard to Michael Meredith: "Beware of dandelions, the scourge of all art-grass (horizontally, anyway) Yrs., Dave Wallace").

Jesse's voice was a deep mumble, not unlike the truck's engine at the low end of a gear, just after shifting. All his utterances were steeped in uncertainty and unintelligibility. He always sounded like his mouth was full. At first it was: with a cigar. But then he quit and the sound persisted. One day he asked me what sounded like, "Bone aches today?" I finally puzzled this out as, "Brakes OK?" Another time he said with a disjunctive mildness and unusual clarity, "*Goddamn* Border Patrol." But mostly ours were one-sided conversations.

Me: "I can see how Al Gore could just kind of be unlikeable to some people."

Jesse: "Yrp."

"But he's the most qualified to be president."

Jesse: "Yrp."

At Ray's Bar, watching the second presidential debate between Bush and Gore, a Latino man on my right leaned over and whispered in my ear, using an exaggerated Mexican accent, "Who jew gonnato voté for? Nay-dair? Nay-dair? Nay-dair? Nay-dair? Nay-dair? Nay-dair? Nay-dair? Nay-dair? Nay-dair?"

"No," I said.

Ray, the owner/bartender, asked, "Are you a Republican?"

"No."

Daphne, on my left, looked at the TV and said, "We need a woman up there."

Ray said, "Yeah, an Indian woman, so she can go: 'Wah wah wah!'" He covered and uncovered his mouth while making toma-hawk-thwacking gestures.

My right-side neighbor leaned in close and whispered in my ear, "*Are jew Repooblican?*"

"Who are you gonna vote for?" I asked.

"I can't vote!" he said, with great pleasure.

The menu at Ray's consisted of one item: flash-frozen pizza. Ray was proud of it because "In regular frozen pizza every single cell is broken." I ordered one. He microwaved it, placed it on the bar, and, after I ate a few bites, wiped the corner of my mouth with his damp bar rag.

My wheedling neighbor left and was replaced by Paul, an American Indian who ran a rock/gem shop in town. He invited Daphne and me over for a stew that contained "pork chops and nothing canned."

The debate ended. Daphne left. Ray said, "She looks like a blue blood." He turned to Paul and added, "Her people killed your people."

Two young women entered the bar: a British art critic with heavy glasses, comically stooped posture, mousy-before-it-was-cool-to-be-mousy brown hair, and a tall, erect, blond, Austrian artist (both doing residencies at Chinati).

Ray proclaimed: "Europe has come!"

They ordered beers. Ray told the Austrian, "Katherina, you make my heart burn."

She replied, awkwardly, "Well, good."

Ray said, "It's OK, I can take some Tums."

The phone rang. Ray answered and announced: "I am a grand-father to twins!"

Everyone cheered.

James Cheney and Teresita, the parents of Lineaus's new litter of puppies, begat: Primo Levi (completely black, inclined to staring; Auschwitz survivor, memoirist, and antifascist), Jane Addams (blue-eyed, fuzzy-gray-furred, with more a of rabbit's than a dog's physicality; antipoverty crusader), Emma Goldman (golden coat, proud demeanor; anarchist), Billie Holiday (one long, white glove on an otherwise black coat; revolutionary vocalist), Charlie Chaplin (black-and-white-and-gray, with soulful eyes; communist), and two nondescript others that, so far as I can recall, never got named.

Lineaus briefly had thirty-seven dogs. Most of these puppies met bad ends worthy of their namesakes. Emma got kidnapped and, Lineaus believed, taken to Mexico. "They love Marfa dogs down in OJ." Jane Addams was shot and killed. One of the nameless ones met an unknown end. The other got taken by a coyote. I helped dress Primo Levi's wound after he got bit through the bottom of his eye socket by a neighbor's guard dog, holding him still as Lineaus injected a syringe full of hydrogen peroxide into the wound. Pink foam geysered out of his face. That should have taught him a lesson. But it happened again. And I saw it. Primo nipped at the neighbor's dog and the dog struck, fast, like a snake, jaw clamping down in the same spot as before. Lineaus and I got out the hydrogen peroxide again. Primo later got shot by ranchers (he was running the meat off their cattle), lived, and was shot again. But he survived. An architect and cabinetmaker adopted Billie Holiday and renamed her Nadine—saving her from a life of hardship. Charlie came back to New York with us.

Leaving Marfa I gave the truck back to Jesse and asked him to look after it for me. He agreed, almost without seeming to agree, which is how Jesse did everything in my presence—without seeming to.

A sign on one of the roads out of town read: "Will the last one moving out of Marfa please turn of [*sic*] the lights."

* * *

D aphne and I didn't come back to West Texas for years. But we kept up via our *Big Bend Sentinel* subscription.

> MARFA – The mystery deepens regarding the skeleton found in the closet of the Marfa and Presidio County Museum.
>
> First discovered in 2001 by museum volunteers going through old boxes, the human remains have been autopsied and the skeleton has spent months being examined by forensic anthropologists at Texas Tech University and the University of North Texas. Now, the remains have returned to Presidio County.
>
> "The cause of death appears to be blunt force injury," Chief Deputy Rusty Taylor said.
>
> The skeleton is nearly complete and relatively few bones are missing: the patellas, some ribs, facial bones, part of the pubic bone, her teeth, a couple toes, and a few bones of the spine.
>
> Who was she? How did her bones end up inside a black trash bag in a box in the closet? Who gave her to the museum and why? No one seems to know...

When I briefly returned, in 2002, it was to meet Michael Meredith and drive the truck back to New York.

Then Daphne and I came back together, in 2008, and found the town transformed. (We were, too: by a young son and infant daughter.) Marfa was now a place of restaurants, cocktail bars, theater, lectures, concerts, a film festival, a gourmet store (no more trips to *Furrs*). But perhaps the biggest change: where once so little seemed likely to happen that I'd walk around open to everything, now, with the town in a constant state of *happeningness*, I felt a need to shut it all out.

I realized this in stages. Initially I pretty much reveled in the fact that it was possible to routinely go out to a concert, drink a bottle of

Barolo, eat well, and have a substantive conversation that didn't seem certain to veer off into insanity. I liked this Marfa. Then, late in the evening, I found myself in the company of a handful of attractive, educated, new settlers in the town. People who had moved here to, as one friend put it, "chill and do their cool thing." One cannonballed a joint/Cabernet combo, pulled out a Dairy Queen uniform, and declared, "I'm doing shifts."

General exclamation: "No way!"

"Yeah, it's a great place to work. Love the crew. We all want to be on the soft-serve machine."

I thought, *That's crossing the divide here in a real way.* Then he shouted, "No! I just found this uniform out on the highway. I've been tricking people with it all week!"

I pictured a local quitting. Not knowing that a discarded uniform— *Take this job and shove it!*—would become an ironic party trick.

And then in the summer of 2012, Daphne and I published a coauthored article about the town in *Vanity Fair*. The piece, titled "Lone Star Bohemia" (Daphne: "two beers"), was bifurcated. Part one outlined Donald Judd's arrival, the founding of the Chinati Foundation, the history of the town, and contained some service journalism on all the new amenities: Maiya's, "an Italian trattoria whose owner-chef was just nominated for a James Beard award." Cochineal, whose owners used to run an "Upper East Side restaurant Ruth Reichl described, in her two-star review, as 'astonishingly exuberant, accepting no limits and recognizing no boundaries.'" And the Food Shark, "a silver-and-orange truck with a constantly changing menu—Veracruz-style shrimp, pork banh mi, brisket braised in Guinness." It parked most afternoons under a massive corrugated-steel canopy in the middle of town known as "the Shade Structure"—a gathering place for the constantly arriving tourists and the ever-more-numerous new residents, who had chosen Marfa as their place to build furniture, restore adobes, make prints, light concerts, design clothing, start a Montessori school, DJ rare country songs a couple of hours a week for the local NPR station (smallest listenership in the lower forty-eight), or operate a pirate radio station from a "jailbroken" iPhone (recently shut down by the FCC).

The rest of the piece circled around a former Chinati artist in residence, the painter Jeff Elrod. Rob Weiner had invited him to Marfa in 1998. (Elrod: "None of us would be here without Rob: there should be a statue of him on the courthouse lawn.") He returned in the late '00s and, to the detriment of his work ethic, became the center of a scene that obviated any need to travel down to OJ for thrills. To him Marfa was like "a badass international airport bar. I'm in a first-class lounge of American Airlines. I'm talking with really interesting people from all over the world who I won't ever see again."

One evening, reporting for *Vanity Fair*, I found a live hollow-point handgun round marked "S&W .40" in the gravel outside the El Cheapo liquor store. When I pulled it out over drinks in the court-yard of the El Paisano hotel an acquaintance whistled and said, "Law enforcement carries that." A lawyer drinking a margarita immedi-ately disparaged the prosecutors in Presidio County as "weaklings" who wouldn't even go after murderers. I thought of the female skeleton in the closet of the Marfa and Presidio County Museum. "Nothing gets prosecuted here but drugs."

Then I went to the Masonic Lodge and found a note explaining that the '70s Marguerite Duras movie, *India Song*, would be shown later in the evening, signed, "Love, Nicolas." So I went across the street to Maiya's for a drink. An older, bald, grizzled man with a patch over his left eye sat in the window. Jeff Elrod was at the bar with a slender, dark-haired woman in a tight teal dress.

I pulled out the bullet. Teal Dress grabbed it and slammed it down on the concrete bar.

"Whoa! That could go off!" I shouted. Manic laughter. Elrod clamped it between his teeth and bit down hard.

I asked if they'd be attending the French movie and lecture.

"What kind of *French* movie?" Teal Dress wanted to know.

Hard to say. A frustrated iPhone search—AT&T was still useless in Marfa—led to the conclusion that it was about leprosy.

"*Leprosy?!*" Teal Dress hollered. "I'm going to go rub myself on a leper and come to this lecture and say"—she pressed her dress tight against her body and pointed at her chest—"This is leprosy!"

"How do you rub yourself on a leper so it *takes*?" Elrod asked.

His friend began pistoning on the barstool, feigning intimacy with a leper. I headed out.

In front of the bookstore, dressed in black, Marianne Stockebrand seemed, by virtue of her impeccable posture, to tower above the Texan Francophiles gathered around her.

"Ben Schonzeit, the painter, is in town visiting his son," she told me.

I surmised that he'd just been eating in Maiya's window and said so.

"Oh," she said. "You know, he does paintings that look like photographs. Still."

"Photo-realism?"

"Yes. He still does it."

"Hmm."

"He's very attractive."

"With the eye patch?"

"Yes."

The film contained no leprosy. The subject was, nominally, ennui. Staged tableaux of various languid diplomats in a subcontinental French consulate were overlaid with passages of poetry. Stockebrand began to loudly sigh. Next she began to laugh. After an hour she said, "I'm leaving." When the screen said "Fin" I went to Elrod's studio, a cinder-block-and-steel building two doors down from the only stoplight in town—about as urban as Presidio County gets.

The studio was, as one local put it, "the center of some scene that defines Marfa for this moment that I think is self-destructive, not sustainable." But ideas came out of it. In 2008, the New York installation artist Justin Lowe co-created, with Jonah Freeman and Alexandre Singh, a multiroom piece called *Hello Meth Lab in the Sun*, described by an awestruck Roberta Smith, the lead art critic for the *New York Times* (and, like Marianne Stockebrand, a former partner of Donald Judd, or so rumor had it), as "an immense, labor-intensive, maniacally contrived walk-through." The creative and financial support for the piece came from a gallerist with an outrageous name—Fairfax Dorn—that contrasted with a subtle-cum-self-effacing, always-behind-the-scenes style. But when I asked Lowe if he had hung out at Elrod's studio while making the piece his reply was, "Hell yeah, I did. Like every day." Smith was so into the piece that she wrote, "Like Alice's rabbit hole, [it] will take you as deep as you want to go." The artists re-created a burned-out methamphetamine lab, a red-carpeted Upper East Side mansion, and a hippie Valhalla. Lowe told us, "By the end it felt like the whole town had contributed in one way or another."

The whole town that had sprung up through the demographic artistry of Rob Weiner.

Now cars at odd angles filled the lot. A sign that read GALLERY, advertising the space next door, had been defaced with the addition LAME. Elrod—"a Puck for the ages," per Rob Weiner—later told me he hoped someone would add an accent to the E and make it LAMÉ GALLERY.

A dozen people were inside, among them the New York artist Christopher Wool (short-cropped hair and concentrated features), best known for stenciling black text on white canvas:

SELLTHE

HOUSE S

ELL THEC

AR SELL

THEKIDS

A canvas that, following a 2013–14 solo Guggenheim show, would sell for $26.5 million.

Wool played pool. When Elrod caught sight of me he proffered a whiskey bottle and a cue, while, at the same moment, a tall, tattooed woman sauntered up, plucked off my hat, and placed it on her own head.

Wool teamed up with Tavahn Ghazi, a perhaps-too-handsome (if not the town's handsomest) young musician who'd moved to Marfa from the Bay Area to complete an album, and who told me, "I wake up in San Francisco, life's too easy—I'm the captain of my neighborhood. What it's like in Marfa, in comparison, is that every single person I'm around is absolutely one hundred percent better than me." He gestured around Elrod's studio. "I want to fight to become this incredible person—that is the exact goal and point of all of this mess."

Everyone's attention coalesced around our game. Watching were: a sound artist who had collaborated the week before on a piece with Elrod (at Chinati), using audio tracks from the *Terminator* movies broadcast from aged boom boxes and scavenged MP3 players; a wiry and stoned performance artist who, during the Chinati Foundation Open House Weekend in 2010, incinerated hot dogs over a flaming grill in Elrod's parking lot and threw them at a crowd that had gathered for an impromptu concert; a handful of teenage-looking girls working the Jodie Foster-in-*Taxi Driver* vibe; a visiting MFA candidate from the University of Michigan; and a young curator who had publicly stated her opinion that Daphne and I were "provincial" (owing, we guessed, to our early departure from a lecture she'd organized... which led us to further surmise that she'd intended to denounce us as philistines but got confused—a description that appeared verbatim in *Vanity Fair*).

In an upset Wool and Ghazi were defeated. A dark-haired young woman began to holler, repeatedly, "*Ma che cazzo?!*" (Italian for "What the fuck?!")

Wool gave a gracious nod.

I asked the "*Ma che cazzo?!*" woman, "Do you speak Italian?"

She said, "That's the only Italian I know."

Shortly thereafter Daphne found herself in Elrod's studio with the photographer and filmmaker Larry Clark (*Tulsa*; *Kids*) and David Hollander, an LA transplant (and child star—in *Airplane!* he mock-suavely brings a girl some coffee to be told, "I take it black, like my men"). Hollander, with his wife, Jennifer Lane, cofounded CineMarfa, the town's current film festival (a previous one self-destructed). They'd just featured '70s and early-'80s No Wave films alongside banned and sexually explicit work by Clark. Before one screening, a local punk band called Solid Waste played a set. Clark was smitten and shot a film in Marfa, featuring the lead singer. It won the 2012 award for best picture at the Rome Film Festival.

Videos were projected on a wall, and visitors drifted in and out. At midnight a group, ranging in age from ten to fifty, decided to go on a full-moon bike ride out on Ranch Road 2810, site of Daphne's long-ago rattlesnake encounter. After a couple miles the riders stopped, and an illuminated Frisbee was thrown between two rock outcroppings, above the spot where, more recently, the actor Javier Bardem killed the Marfa National Bank president, Chip Love, in the film *No Country for Old Men*. Two border-patrol SUVs idled down the road, observing. When it was proposed that the group head out and visit the border-patrol checkpoint, five miles south of town—naked—Daphne went back to Elrod's.

Red Tecate cans mingled with cans of spray paint. Solid Waste discussed their first album with great solemnity. Clark took in the scene with a slightly detached air. Hollander (actor!) adopted a British accent to impersonate Doris Lessing upon winning the Nobel Prize. ("Oh Christ"—waving a hand in dismissal of it all—"I'm sure you'd like some uplifting remarks.")

As the evening wound down there was an attempt to appoint Daphne as Clark's designated driver, a job she did not want, and managed to evade by noting that she had come by (non-tandem) bike. He helped by declaring that he wasn't leaving.

Are you getting the idea here? A circus. But a *studied* one.

I was kind of pleased by the fact that the young curator had decided to dismiss Daphne and me as "provincial." Being the subject of gossip affirms one's existence. And it gave me the opportunity to try out that one-liner about provinciality getting confused with philistinism. Which, of course, like all glib and petty acts, I soon regretted. I wrote the young curator: "Making explicit things that usually go unstated and simmer, significantly, beneath daily life, is something I like to do. What you said about us colored last summer in Marfa. So I'm the one who put that line in the piece. Also, of course, I'm the one who made a farcical scene out of your India Song screening. If you're mad or embarrassed about any of this, please know that I am the rightful target for such feelings." But somehow it wasn't in me to be 100 percent gracious. Viz.:

> I, too, was a pretentious person in my 20s. I think there's an element of courage and daring to opining beyond one's years. Pretension is even a form of HOPE at times. So *I* hope we can maybe take this awkward introduction to each other as a jumping off point to something other than strained smiles at the Food Shark.
>
> Here's hoping.
>
> ⸱ Sean

Shortly thereafter I was seated in the garden of my favorite airport bar, when a woman screamed, "*You!*"

I looked up. Yep—she meant me.

"That thing you wrote!" Pause. "What kind of person would write that? And that *letter* you wrote. I *read* that letter. You're a"— pause— "*bad person.*"

The woman yelling all this was attractive, strawberry blonde, around twenty-five. She was the young curator's sister. I had been talking with some acquaintances, and just been introduced to a young poet in town on a Lannan residency: long-haired, strapping, almost Byronic. I was looking at the poet when the screaming started. As it became clear that I was the target, and that something I'd written was the catalyst, his face registered a combination of revulsion and desire—would his poetry incite someone to make a scene in a restaurant's courtyard? He seemed to hope for and against this with equal force.

Not wanting to shout back, I moved across the courtyard and asked if I could sit and talk with her for a moment.

"I guess so," she said.

I often wonder about the devaluation of true virtue that is inherent in the desire to be *seen* as a good person, a desire I possess with force equal to that of my desire to indulge my cravings for money, top-shelf alcohol, exclusive real estate, high-end appliances. It sometimes seems that the two fight each other to a constant stalemate, leaving me to live my life on the blasted battlefield; my persona created through a standoff between opposing compulsions.

The woman said, "When I read it on the airplane I cried and cried."

I imagined her tears beading on the glossy pages of *Vanity Fair*; a mystified seatmate.

"It was anonymous," I replied. "Nobody even knows it was her."

"Everybody in *town* knows."

"So *what?!*"

With this three other eavesdroppers at separate tables exploded: "That's everything!"

I replied, "But it was *common knowledge here already*! She'd *publicly denounced us*!"

Everybody in town knew everybody's secrets. (There were only skeletons in the museum closets.) But holding Marfa up to scrutiny in the wider world broke a spell (or code) among the tiny group of people, almost a family, of new settlers in Marfa, most of whom (DQ ironists aside) wished, honorably, and accurately, to be depicted as incredible people.

I said, sincerely, "It's really great that you love your sister this much."

"She's really brilliant, and you just have no idea."

"I can tell that she must be special."

"You have *no idea*." She rolled her eyes at me. "You're probably going to write about *this* now."

I said, because I suddenly, unexpectedly, respected and liked this woman, that I wasn't planning to. Jabo's utopian lyrics came to mind: "You respect me/and I respect you." Somehow…

Shortly after my dressing-down in the courtyard of the airport bar I gave a ride across town (in the blue truck) to a Mexican man in his fifties who pointed at two young women in sundresses, and, with a commingled look of sadness and lust, asked, "What are they all *doing* here?"

He looked like he was going to cry, and *his* tears wouldn't be falling through pressurized cabin air onto the pages of a magazine.

It was like a prank was being played on his libido.

Was Marfa too cool, or too harsh, to be a utopia? Certainly I wouldn't be accosted—at least not verbally—for breaking *omertà* in the twin cities of Presidio and Ojinaga. There is now even a "Restaurant" attached to Presidio's Three Palms hotel, site of the "'Pancho Villa' type" casting call back in 2000. From the menu:

> Foie gras!
> Nice and tasty!
> Made from French ingredients!
> Cooked by Italian chef!
> Awarded by world's assosiation [*sic*] of chef!
> Proved to be good for your health!
> AS LOW AS €19!

Here was the old Marfa. And, cuisine aside, some serious people have now drifted down there. Lineaus sleeps outside with his dogs on some land he bought. And a landscape painter called Rackstraw

SEAN WILSEY

Downes—former Chinati artist in residence and recent MacArthur genius-grant recipient (Weiner: "He's our Corot") works there, alone, chronicling the land, for half the year. They both occasionally appear in Marfa for a meal or a lecture. As Downes told Daphne and me, he ventured into town "to play."

Considering all this Marianne Stockebrand said to us, "This is the golden age of Marfa. Right now."

Whatever the truth (golden age or decadent decline), we're all just a skein upon the land. Ice storms freeze the fountain at the El Paisano, knock out the power, encase everything in glass—cacti, spiderwebs, rental cars. Icicles hang off the wires of ranch fences. And when the storms pass clouds dome the entirety of the sky, forming a gray lid with a burning orange rim and a fierce band of blue running 360 degrees around the whole horizon.

As I write this I'm living in Marfa. Happily. Looking up the other day I saw a cave. It was dusk, and the cave was hollowed out of some low, cottony cumulus and lit like a room—the only point holding sunlight in the dark sky, as though someone had got home from work and switched on the lights. Later I saw a gleaming white ∧, like a letter from an alphabet, embossed in some high, pale-gray/white clouds.

The weather takes me back to the town as I first knew it, and the people who were here then and gone now.

When I finally did publish a book (not on Marfa), David Foster Wallace wrote an e-mail to Dave Eggers and asked him to pass on "congratulations from the guy he drove through sewage with."

Margrét Blöndal, Sölvi's mom, just wrote me about Wallace:

Once he remarked that it was obvious that Sölvi was raised by
a woman by the way he left the toilet seat closed. We did in fact
not talk much but we were comfortingly curious in each other
company and the three of us could sing together. I ordered
some books by his recommendation amongst them Trickster
Makes This World and Assessing Schizophrenic Thinking which
titles stick to my mind. Once he read a prose of mine where
I had misspelled the word fond and it became found. Instead
of correcting me he respectfully asked if it was intentional. He
sent me a postcard or two with photographs of his dogs. I sent
him an English translation of a story by the Icelandic writer
Thorbergur Thordarson. In search of my beloved. I always
assumed that I would see him again. His unexpected death made
me profoundly sad.

And Michael Meredith gave me a copy of the theme song Wallace
had picked for himself. I called Jabo at his home in Austin and asked
him if he could write it out as sheet music:

"OUTRO"

Since there's an intro to this book I thought there should be an "outro." That way we can have one last moment together. And I can restate what brought all these pieces together; what made me write them. The push-pull between escape and engagement.

Marfa: the escapist's final destination.

9/11: inescapable.

Skateboarding: escape at any second.

Rats: escape from formless, failure-convinced, fear-of-fatherhood.

Soccer: the world's escape!

Etc.

And here are a few late-breaking facts:

Google, Inc. decided my take on Updike could get them out of trouble:

> Dear Sean,
> I am a lawyer with the Electronic Frontier Foundation, a public
> interest group dedicated to, among other things, promoting

fair and balanced copyright laws. More information about us is available here: www.eff.org.

We are working on a friend of the court brief in support of Google in the Authors Guild v. Google case. As you may have heard, the Author' Guild believe the Google Book Search (GBS) project violates copyright law. We believe Google's activities are protected and legal fair uses, and we'd like to help explain to the court some of the public benefits of GBS. We noticed that [a] Google web site has a (somewhat dated) testimonial from you. We'd like to include that testimonial in our brief, but we'd also like to update it. Would you be available to chat with me briefly regarding your experiences with GBS? If so, when might be a good time? I am in San Francisco, but we can do this by phone and I will do my best to accomodate your schedule.

Thanks for considering it,

Corynne

The updated version was a chapter in this book. And I am a member of the Author's Guild.

I made it back to San Antonio and visited Geri's grave. And I've been corresponding with her youngest son, La Verne, who writes: "I have talked about you many, many times and it's important that you understand that I've always said that I have a little brother… You were never simply my friend, but always my brother. Because I was my mother's youngest and often times your babysitter… I have felt sad many times when I thought about you and then had to remember that space and time between us. But, I have never ever once referred to you as my 'White' brother, only my 'Lil Brother.'"

Verne said he trusted me "with my mother's aura and our family history. So, come at me like a family member, don't fly in and back out, be prepared to stay."

Mike Gernhardt, the astronaut I met in Houston, has occasionally kept me up to date on his life:

> Hey Sean...
> I just got back from a submarine expedition in Pavilion Lake in Canada, where we have discovered these life forms called microbiolites, which used to dominate the earth 2.5 billion years ago... they look like huge prehistoric coral formations. It was almost like finding life on another planet as it was the first time human eyes have seen most of these (as they are too deep for scuba... we flew these small one person submersibles... kind of like a mini lunar rover). I am heading out to the desert next week to do a simulated 2 week lunar mission living in the rover... should be fun.

As for the kitchens of the present, my kids are taking over. Two days ago they cleaned the whole thing. While I lay down and read *My Pilgrim's Progress*, George W.S. Trow's final book, their talk drifted my way.

Owen: "This is actually fun."

Mira: "Yeah!"

Owen: "And pretty easy!"

After I submitted my expenses for the Danny Meyer profile I got a panicked message from the managing editor of the *New York Times Magazine*: "Sean! *This BILL!*" Accelerated breathing. "From Eleven Madison Park!" Exhale. "*Call me.*"

But they paid it.

Michael Meredith's work was featured in a group show at the Museum of Modern Art. He took me to see it and, in the café, we bumped into Danny Meyer and his kids. Soon a procession of cheerful people bore Michael and me multiple plates of ridiculously good food.

As we all talked together (tables are communal) I thought, *Danny runs his whole business on intuition*. (If only NASA could do this.)

I just stumbled on a 1977 *Texas Monthly* article that states as a fact that Marfa's name is actually taken from an obscure Russian novella called *Marfa Posadnitsa* ("*Marfa the Governor's Wife*"), by Nikolay Karamzin. I can find no trace of it in the English language.

But I recently discovered what George W.S. Trow did when he gave up on New York: he lit out in a Chevy truck, bought on a whim, bound for Marfa.

ABOUT THE AUTHOR

Sean Wilsey was born in San Francisco, in 1970, and lives in Marfa, Texas. He is the author of a memoir, *Oh the Glory of It All*, and the coeditor, with Matt Weiland, of two collections of original writing: *State by State: A Panoramic Portrait of America* and *The Thinking Fan's Guide to the World Cup*. He has an ill-maintained website, *ohtheglory.com*, and at least owns the domain name *seanwilsey.com*. He is at work on another memoir, *I Am in Love*, about, among other things, his experiences as an apprentice gondolier in Venice, Italy. For many years he was the editor-at-large for *McSweeney's Quarterly Concern*, and on the staff of the *New Yorker* magazine.

ACKNOWLEDGMENTS

The author is grateful to the editors who first assigned and helped shape these pieces:

Dave Eggers, Robert Halpern, Mary-Kay Wilmers, Thomas Jones, Matt Weiland, David Shipley, Barbara Paulsen, Daniel Eisenberg, Mark Kirby, John J. Donohue, Frank Flaherty, Ilena Silverman, David Lidsky, Aimee Bell, and Andi Winnette.